Voyage of the Harrier

Around the World in
the Track of HMS Beagle

Julian Mustoe

Produced by Resolution Press 2015
www.julian-mustoe.com

ISBN 978-15151203063

Copyright © Julian Mustoe 2010   All rights reserved.

This text is registered. It may not be copied, reproduced or transmitted by any method without the written permission of the author.

In memory of my stepmother Anne
A wise woman and an intrepid traveller

Foreword

  There is one activity so clearly meant for Ancients, so perfectly tailored to their physical capabilities, so cleverly designed to preserve and enhance their vitality that it is bewildering that few, so very few, ever discover it.
  It is an activity that has as its prime precondition the slow and unconscious absorption of experience. It is an activity that enlivens the muscles as it oils the joints. It lengthens, preserves and justifies life. It throws the practitioner among the beautiful and adoring young. It confers an inviolable mantle of authority and allows you to wear a cute hat.
  It takes you to faraway places, unreachable by jet by your richer and more moribund contemporaries. It tempts your taste buds with exotic offerings and disallows constipation by scaring the shit out of you. It fills your ancient eyes with new wonder. It contradicts the cynics and negates the naysayers. It is the way a man, especially an old guy, should live. And perhaps best of all, you may, if you choose (and why not?) use it to wallow luxuriously in the soothing mud hole of the world's envy.
  When the alarms and excursions of your life are over, when your kids are doctors and your wives have found better things to do, when your enemies have had their comeuppances and your friends all bore you, when obituaries prove interesting and when the prospect of earning even one more dollar appals, then the moment has come to look about for a boat in which to sail around the world. There simply ain't nothing else worth doing.

          author unknown

Table of Contents

1.	To the Canary Islands	1
2.	Robert FitzRoy, Charles Darwin & Me	11
3.	Atlantic Ocean	19
4.	Salvador	29
5.	Winter Journey	37
6.	Rio de la Plata	42
7.	The Pampas	50
8.	Shipwreck	62
9.	Argentina	70
10.	In the South	88
11.	Chile and Peru	107
12.	Pacific Ocean	128
13.	Australia	144
14.	South about Africa	159
15.	Homeward Bound	175
16.	After the Voyage	185

Appendices

A. Map of the Voyage of the Beagle	199
B. Map of the Voyage of the Harrier	200
C. HMS Beagle	201
D. Whaleboat	204
E. Harrier of Down (first)	205
F. Harrier of Down (second)	210
G. Table of Distances	214
H. Ship and Boat Rigs	218
I. Parts of a Sail	221
J. Beaufort Wind Scale	222
K. Glossary of Sailing and Yachting Terms	223
L. Spanish Terms used in the Text	230
References	231
Picture Credits	236
Bibliography	242
Acknowledgements	252
Index	253

Chapter 1
To the Canary Islands

Desire has trimmed the sails, and Circumstance brings but the breeze to fill them.
     George Eliot, *Daniel Deronda*, 1876

In his *Narrative* of 1839 Robert FitzRoy, the commander of HMS *Beagle*, wrote that;

> a few mottled, hard-edged clouds appearing in the east; streaks (mare's tails) across the sky, spreading from the same quarter; a high barometer (30.3); and the smoke from chimneys rising high into the air, and then going westward; were the signs which assured us of a favourable wind. A light "cat's paw" rippled the water, we made all sail, the breeze increased, and at noon our little vessel was outside the Breakwater, with a fresh easterly wind.[1]

The date was 27th December 1831 and the place where the *Beagle* raised her anchor was Barn Pool, under the lee of Mount Edgecombe, in Plymouth Sound. On their third attempt at departing Robert FitzRoy, Charles Darwin and the crew of HMS B*eagle* were at last off on a voyage around the world.

The tidal streams are strong and turbulent in the half-mile stretch of water that lies between Barn Pool and Drake's Island. It is a part of Plymouth Sound where it is easy to make a mistake.

FitzRoy's *Narrative* does not mention what had happened six days earlier at the start of their second, unsuccessful, attempt to set sail. Darwin's diary records that;

> From weighing to letting down our anchor everything was unfortunate. - We started at 11 o'clock with a light breeze from NW & while tacking round Drakes Island, our ill luck first commenced. It was spring tide & at the same time lowest ebb; this was forgotten, & we steered right upon a rock that lies off the corner. - There was very little wind or swell on the sea so that, although the vessel stuck fast for about half an hour, she was not injured. Every maeneuvre was tried to get her off; one that succeeded best was making every person on board run to different parts of the deck, by this means giving to the vessel a swinging motion. - At last we got clear.[2]

The famous voyage of the *Beagle* very nearly did not happen at all.

Drake's Island. Mount Edgecombe, Barn Pool distant at the right

Twenty eight years after the *Beagle's* successful departure, Darwin published a book, *On the Origin of Species by Natural Selection*, which changed forever the way in which mankind regards itself and views the natural world. No longer a being apart, after Darwin man has taken his place as a part of the evolving pattern of life on earth. Like everyone else I am an heir of Darwin's world view, but his book has also had a more particular influence upon the later part of my life.

Ever since I was a schoolboy I had wanted to sail a yacht around the world. As a young man I had not sufficient money to go voyaging and in middle life I was restricted largely to weekend sailing by jobs, wife and children. In my late fifties I re-read Darwin's *Origin of Species* and also his book about his circumnavigation, the *Voyage of the Beagle*. The interest of the *Origin* and the charm of the *Voyage* pushed some parts of my life into alignment. I decided not just to sail around the world, but to do so with a purpose. Following the track of the *Beagle's* voyage would give direction to my long-held ambition and convert a generalised plan into a proper project.

Harrier of Down in Barn Pool, Plymouth. July 2001

An entry in my log aboard *Harrier of Down* reads:

> Is this really the OFF? A gentle breeze in the anchorage in the early morning is presumably caused by the pattern of the weather rather than just being another sea breeze. At 1300 I get my anchor and sail gently out of the bay. Outside force 2 from the southwest, so it is a slow sail towards the Eddystone. I look astern to Plymouth Sound flanked by the green hills of Devon and Cornwall. When shall I see this land again? Who of my friends will still be alive when I return? Time, time, hurrying time.

My circumnavigation began gently. A light zephyr drifted me out of Cawsand Bay on the western side of Plymouth Sound on 30th July 2001, a day after my 68th birthday. It settled into a southwest breeze force 2 or 3 in the afternoon. I worked *Harrier* steadily to windward until, on the evening of 2nd August, I fixed my position 80 miles west of the Ile d'Ouessant, the most westerly point of Brittany. Ouessant (anglicized to *Ushant*), should never be sighted by the ocean navigator, for fear of heavy weather coming in from the Atlantic. I now had enough sea room to head south across the Bay of Biscay. This is an anglicization of the Spanish Golfo de Viscaya, referred to in French as the Golfe de Gascogne. After I had turned the first corner, my voyage was marked by the disappearance of all seabirds except manx shearwaters, fulmars, storm petrels and gannets. Two whales, also headed south, swam alongside *Harrier* for half an hour in the late evening darkness.

Harrier and I crossed the Bay of Biscay in fine summer weather and with moderate southwesterly winds. The *Beagle*, sailing in winter also had gentle weather. Aside from one short gale near Madeira, the wind for the *Beagle's* passage did not exceed force 5. There are few people who are blessed with such an iron constitution that they are never seasick. I find that I need the first two days at sea to be fairly calm in order to acquire my sea legs. Bad weather encountered early in a passage has me joining the sufferers on the lee rail. However, once I am adjusted to life afloat, I am able to eat and drink with a gale of wind blowing over the deck. Darwin never became immune to sea sickness. An early entry in his diary records;

> I often said before starting that I had no doubt I should frequently repent of the whole undertaking. Little did I think with what fervour I should do so. I can scarcely conceive any more miserable state, as when such dark and gloomy thoughts are haunting the mind as have today pursued me.[3]

Many famous navigators, including England's greatest fighting admiral Lord Nelson, have suffered from seasickness throughout their seagoing careers. For Darwin, as for Nelson, *mal de mer* was a constant trial. Darwin's refuge was his hammock. 'I found the only relief to be in a horizontal position'.[4] Obtaining that position was not so easy at first.

> I intended sleeping in my hammock – I did so last night & experienced a most ludicrous difficulty in getting into it: my great fault of jockeyship was in trying to put my legs in first. The hammock being suspended, I thus only succeeded in pushing it away without making any progress in inserting my own body.[5]

FitzRoy had himself to show Darwin how to do it. Darwin then grasped that;

> the correct method is to sit accurately in the centre of the bed, then give yourself a dextrous twist & your head and feet come into their respective places.[6]

Despite Darwin's susceptibility to sea sickness and his troubles with a hammock, FitzRoy was complimentary about the expedition naturalist. 'Darwin is a very sensible, hard-working man and a very pleasant messmate'. He said, 'I never saw a "shore-going fellow" come into the ways of a ship so soon and so thoroughly as Darwin.'[7] In addition to help with 'the ways of a ship' FitzRoy gave Darwin a copy of Charles Lyell's recently published *Principles of Geology* as a welcome-aboard present.

On 11th August, 40 miles off the coast of Galicia, *Harrier* and I reached the brisk northerly summer winds known as the Portuguese trades. The sun shone, the wind was force 4 over the stern and we bowled along on course at a pace of more than 100 miles a day. Just two days later I was some 50 miles west of Cabo Trafalgar and not far from the site of the battle. The Battle of Trafalgar itself was a turning point in the history of naval warfare. Besides being the occasion of the death of Lord Nelson, Trafalgar was the last major sea battle to be fought entirely under sail.

Later, at the end of the Napoleonic wars, the Royal Navy no longer needed a fleet of large line-of-battle ships which spread acres of canvas, carried 120 muzzle-loaded guns and were manned by crews of 700 men. The smaller naval ships dating from the time of the Napoleonic wars were, however, still useful for duties such as the suppression of piracy, combating the transatlantic traffic in slaves and protecting maritime trade routes. Some of these small naval vessels were converted for survey duties. The *Beagle* was such a vessel.

The turmoil of the Napoleonic era turned the monolithic Spanish South American empire into a number of independent states, ready and able to trade with the world on their own terms. Argentina and Chile were two of the countries that emerged from this revolution as promising new markets for British manufactures. Seaborne trade requires good navigational information and, in particular, correct charts. In the 1820s and 30s the coasts of South America needed to be described, surveyed and charted accurately for the purposes of peace rather than war. The Admiralty sent the *Beagle* to South America to make these charts.

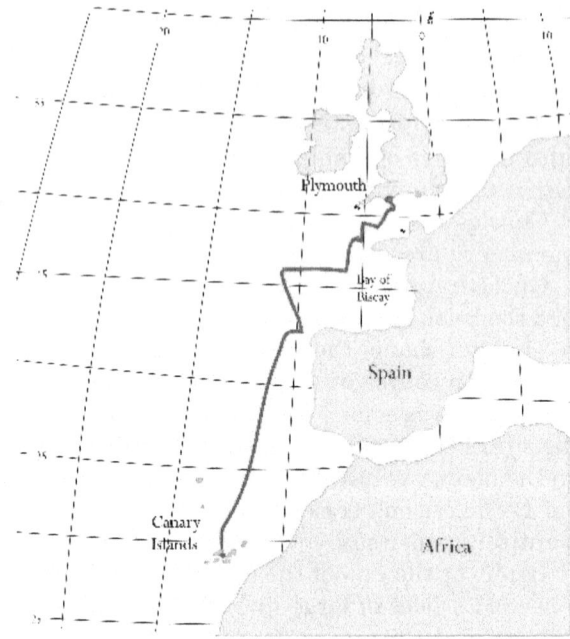

From time immemorial, mariners have found their way about the oceans of the world by observing the sun, the planets and the stars. During the last two hundred years, since the invention of the chronometer, they have been able to do this accurately. One of the purposes of the voyage of the *Beagle* was to report on the performance and accuracy of the various types of chronometer available in the early nineteenth century. On her voyage she had aboard 22 chronometers together with a technician, George Stebbing, to maintain them.

When I twice sailed a small yacht across the Atlantic in the 1960s, the only way to find the position of a ship in the open ocean was by celestial observation. Forty years later we are in the age of the Global Positioning by Satellite (GPS) system and finding your position at sea is just another automatic operation. However, celestial navigation remains for me a satisfying technique. I began my circumnavigation with a modern chronometer and using my beautiful, traditional sextant. The resulting position fixes were more accurate than many a modern push-button navigator can credit.

HMS *Beagle*

At the latitude of Gibraltar, the Portuguese trades merged seamlessly into the Atlantic northeast trade winds. We continued to sail south in sunshine with easy sailing conditions towards the Islas Canarias (derived from the Latin *canis*, meaning *dog*). On the evening of 17th August, the top of Pico del Teide (***Mount Teide***) on Tenerife, the highest mountain in Spain, appeared over the southern horizon exactly on cue. Next day I sailed into the Puerto Desportivo Radazul, six kilometres south of Santa Cruz de Tenerife and tied up at the quay in front of the harbourmaster's office.

'Welcome to Tenerife", he said in good English. "Where are you from?'
'Plymouth.'
'Plymouth! How long did it take you?'
'Twenty one days.'
'Twenty one days! Can you cook on that little boat?'
'Yes', I replied, bridling slightly.
'And do you have a refrigerator on board?'
'No. She is a bit small for that.'
A pause for thought. 'Well, I congratulate you!" he said.
"Twenty one days ..... without refrigeration!' 'Would you like a cold beer?'
Yes please!'

Puerto Desportivo Radazul

In winter the Portuguese trades are unreliable and sometimes the winter wind on the coast of Portugal comes from the south or west rather than the north. The *Beagle* therefore took a more westerly course than mine. She passed within sight of Porto Santo and Madeira on 4th January and next morning she was off the southern point of the Ilhas Salvagens. On 6th January 1832 she anchored at Santa Cruz de Tenerife, ten days out from Plymouth. Here she had bad luck.

    The Spanish authorities refused to let her people land because news had arrived of an epidemic of cholera that was affecting England and parts of northern Europe. The *Beagle* could not afford to wait for 12 days at anchor in quarantine. FitzRoy gave the order 'Up jib!' and they immediately set sail for the Ilhas Cabo Verde (anglicised to *Cape Verdes*) with nobody having set foot on Tenerife. 'This was', as FitzRoy recorded, 'a great disappointment to Mr Darwin'.[8] He had to watch the mighty peak of his dreams, the Monarch of the Atlantic, disappear astern untrodden. For my part I decided that my visit was a chance to try to fulfil Darwin's ambition and to walk to the top of Mount Teide.

    In June 1799 Alexander von Humboldt and Aimé Bonpland had walked from Santa Cruz de Tenerife via the town of La Laguna and the villages of Matanza and Victoria to the town of La Orotava. Here, at an altitude of 400 metres, they hired guides and mules for the ascent of el Teide, of 3718 metres. Two days later they were on the summit, and a few days after that they were back aboard the frigate

Pizarro in which they then sailed for South America. It was Humboldt's account of the ascent of El Teide, in his *Personal Narrative of Travels to the Equinoctial Regions of the New Continent* that fired Darwin with a desire to travel and which later led him to accept the invitation in 1831 to sail as expedition naturalist aboard the *Beagle*.

On 28th August 2001 I took the bus from Santa Cruz to La Orotava where I arrived at mid-afternoon. La Orotava is still, as in Humboldt's time, surrounded by banana plantations. I then set out on foot for the peak carrying a 15 kilogram rucsac. By dark, at half past eight, I had reached the village of Benijos, at 900 metres. It was delightfully cool in the mist after the sweltering heat of Santa Cruz. I spent the night in a small hotel and at nine o'clock next morning I set off again up the mountain.

The chestnut forest which so delighted Humboldt has now disappeared, to be replaced by vineyards and terraced fields of maize. Small brown birds with a slight flash of yellow on their wings flitted across the fields. The country cousin of the domestic canary is a rather dowdy affair.

By mid-day I was clear of the cultivated land and found myself walking through a beautiful forest of pine with an understory of juniper. It was lovely country, but there is an awful lot of it. Up and up I trudged through the scented air observing butterflies and huge bright blue dragonflies go past and watching kestrels hovering overhead. I did not get to the col of 2000 metres at el Portillo, from which el Teide is usually approached, until well after dark. Here there was no hotel and the only restaurant was closed.

I camped down on one of the terraces of the restaurant. The owner's dog sensed my presence and it barked and whined in its kennel all night. I awoke somewhat jaded to find that the restaurant would not open until mid-day. After a snack of chocolate and some biscuits I shouldered my rucsac again. As the morning sun gathered its strength I put my feet onto the track leading up the mountain. By half past twelve, after walking in the baking heat across a volcanic landscape resembling the surface of the moon, I reached a height of 2600 metres. Here the effects of the heat, my age, the size of the mountain, the weight of my rucsack and hunger together induced my legs to refuse to carry me upwards any further. I was still 1100 metres from the summit.

By good luck at this height, I encountered a party of goat hunters crossing a high col in an enormous four-wheel-drive vehicle. I had no scruples about asking them for a lift and I was extremely glad when they said yes. They took me back down to el Portillo where

I found that the restaurant was at last open. That meal tasted pretty good - hunger is the best sauce. From el Portillo a bus took me down the mountain and back to *Harrier* at Radazul

Mount Teide.   The path from el Portillo

So, one way and another, I failed to get up the mountain, but I did have a good walk over memorable country. Failure to reach the summit of Humboldt's mountain was 'a great disappointment' to Mr Mustoe, too. I shall want to return to Mount Teide one day, approach the mountain properly and perhaps have more success.

Chapter 2
Robert FitzRoy, Charles Darwin and Me
There is properly no history: only biography.
Ralph Waldo Emerson, *History*, 1841

Robert FitzRoy, the commander of the *Beagle* was born at Ampton Hall in Suffolk on 5th July 1805, three and a half months before the battle of Trafalgar. As a younger son of an aristocrat he was born into the traditional recruiting ground of the officer class of the Royal Navy. His great-great-great grandfather, Henry FitzRoy the first Duke of Grafton, was the illegitimate son of King Charles II and Barbara Villiers. The surname FitzRoy means "son of a king".

Barbara Villiers with Robert FitzRoy's great-great-great grandfather

Duke Henry was killed aboard his own ship' fighting the French at Cork in 1690. Robert's father, Lord Charles FitzRoy, fought in Flanders and became a general while his uncle William FitzRoy joined the Navy and became an admiral. Robert FitzRoy inherited from his father's family an aristocrat's confidence, a devotion to patriotic duty, the traditions of the Navy and strong sense of *noblesse oblige*.

During the Napoleonic Wars it became evident to the Admiralty that the time-honoured methods of officer recruitment, purchase and patronage, were no longer adequate for a post-Nelsonian navy. In 1808 the Royal Naval College was created at Portsmouth in order to provide the Navy with a corps of professional and technically trained officers. FitzRoy entered the college in 1818 at the age of twelve. He was an outstanding pupil. The principal of the college, the Reverend George Inman, said of him; 'There was a collegian passing yesterday who won the first medal – his name is FitzRoy; and he did what has never been done before; in passing for a lieutenant he got full numbers'.[1]

In 1826, while the young FitzRoy was serving as a midshipman on the frigate *Thetis*, the Admiralty sent the *Beagle* to South America together with a supply ship, the *Adventure*. The two ships sailed under the command of Captain Philip Parker King, the son of a former governor of New South Wales in Australia. On her voyage south in the 1820s the *Beagle* made the first accurate charts of the Atlantic coast of Argentina and she investigated some of the little-known waters around the large southern island of Tierra del Fuego (*Land of Fire*).

The human cost of the *Beagle's* first voyage was high. Nine sailors and two officers were lost from accidents and disease. In addition, she returned without her captain. The bleak landscapes of the south, the weight of his responsibilities and the loneliness of command turned the mind of her captain, Pringle Stokes, to despair. On 31st May 1828 in the harbour of Puerto Hambre (*Port Famine*), on the western shore of the Estrecho Magellanes (*Strait of Magellan*), Stokes went to his cabin, loaded his pistol and shot himself in the head. He died in delirium 12 days later.

The commander of the South American station, Admiral Sir Robert Otway, passed over the *Beagle's* second officer, Lieutenant William Skyring, as Stokes's successor. The large saltwater lake of Seno Otway (*Otway Water*) on the north side of the Strait of Magellan commemorates the admiral and the adjacent Seno Skyring (*Skyring*

Water) is named after his disappointed subordinate. Otway transferred the 23 year old Lieutenant Robert FitzRoy from his flagship *Ganges* and appointed him the new captain. FitzRoy joined the *Beagle* in December 1828.

In his first command FitzRoy was very successful. He quickly gained the confidence of the demoralized crew of the *Beagle*. During the next 18 months they made useful contributions to the charting of the stormy waters off the southern end of South America. Among their discoveries was what is now known in English as the Beagle Channel on the south side of the island of Tierra del Fuego. This time in FitzRoy's life is commemorated by the naming of Canal FitzRoy. located between Otway and Skyring waters.

FitzRoy returned the *Beagle* to Devonport in October 1830. He arrived with a high reputation. His commander Captain King wrote to the Admiralty;

> I trust that their lordships will permit me once again to express how much I feel that Commander FitzRoy, not only from the important service he has rendered, but from the zealous and perfect manner in which he has effected it, merits their distinction and patronage; and I beg leave, as his senior officer, to recommend him in the strongest manner to their favourable consideration.[2]

Robert FitzRoy aged about 30

FitzRoy's mother, Frances Anne Stewart, was the younger half-sister of Robert Stewart, better known by his courtesy title of Lord Castlereagh. Castlereagh was Foreign Secretary in Lord Liverpool's administration and the chief British representative at the Congress of Vienna in 1814. In addition to a second helping of the standard aristocratic attitudes, FitzRoy inherited from his mother's family a disposition towards melancholia. During his time aboard the *Beagle* he was subject to prolonged bouts of suppressed anger and black depression. His hereditary affliction coloured much of his behaviour during his command of the *Beagle's* second voyage. Nevertheless, in 1831 at the age of 25 FitzRoy was clearly the best officer in the navy to lead another surveying voyage to South America.

Charles Darwin's grandfather Erasmus Darwin had been a prominent doctor in Lichfield and was the author of the famous narrative poem *Zoonomia*. He was also a noted amateur scientist. In 1783 he published an English version of Carl Linnaeus's *Systema Vegetabilium*. One of his sons, Robert Waring Darwin, was Charles's father. Robert Darwin was a successful doctor in Shrewsbury and an even more successful money lender. On his mother's side Charles was related to the Wedgwoods, one of the leading families of the British industrial revolution. Thus Charles Robert Darwin, together with his brother and sisters, entered into comfortable private incomes and secure positions among the gentry of Regency society.

Charles Darwin was born on 12th February 1809 in his father's house, The Mount, in Shrewsbury. By coincidence, this was also the exact birthday of Abraham Lincoln. The blood flowing in Darwin's veins was red rather than blue. Nevertheless, Darwin too lived under the shadow of a family ghost. Grandfather Erasmus had been a formidable domestic tyrant. One of his sons, Charles's uncle Erasmus, had committed suicide in 1799 and another uncle, who was also named Charles, died at the age of twenty in a medical school accident.

Charles Darwin's father Robert, his grandfather Erasmus's eldest surviving son by his first marriage, was a large, powerful man of whom it was said that when he entered a room it was like the tide coming in. However, Robert Darwin had learned from his experience of a domineering father. He was careful to give his own children the emotional room they needed to grow up and develop. Robert Darwin was not an easy, affable man but he was thoughtful and he was just. His son Charles loved him, but he remained in awe of his father and of his paternal inheritance until the end of his life.

The young Charles' educational career was erratic and only moderately successful. During his early school days he was bored by the classical curriculum at Dr Butler's school at Shrewsbury. At the age of sixteen he was sent to Edinburgh University to study medicine. He found lectures there tedious and operations, in the days before chloroform, horrified him. He left Edinburgh in 1827 at the age of eighteen without qualifying.

This wayward adolescent behaviour, like that of many men who later become eminent, drew down paternal gunfire. He was told that: 'You care for nothing but shooting, dogs, and rat catching, and you will be a disgrace to yourself and all your family.'[3] His father, almost as a last resort, decided at the end of 1827 to send his feckless younger son to Christ's College, Cambridge, to read for the church.

Since childhood, Darwin's real interests had been field sports and natural history. At Christ's he did as little work as possible on his formal studies but his interest in the natural world brought him the friendship and help of Adam Sedgwick, professor of geology, and the professor of biology, John Henslow. These two men helped Darwin to engage seriously with the things of the mind that interested him the most. In early 1831 it seemed that Charles Darwin was fated to become just another country parson with a lively interest in natural history.

During that summer FitzRoy was busy at Devonport preparing the *Beagle* for another surveying voyage in southern waters. Nevertheless, he was not so busy with his ship as to forget his personal needs. FitzRoy knew that he had an unruly temper and at the back of his mind there lurked the spectre of his family affliction.

The crew-list of the *Beagle* was short of a naturalist and he knew that he himself needed a congenial shipmate as an antidote to depression and as a fence against despair. FitzRoy wrote to Francis Beaufort, the hydrographer of the navy, to ask for the appointment of 'some well-educated and scientific person who would willingly share such accommodation as I had to offer, in order to profit by the opportunity of visiting distant countries as yet little known'.[4] The old-boy network sprang into action with the result that on the 29th of August at Shrewsbury Darwin opened a letter the contents of which were to change the course of his life. In it John Henslow wrote that:

> I have been asked .... to recommend a naturalist as companion to FitzRoy employed by Government to survey the S. extremity of America. I have stated that I consider you to be the best qualified person I know of who is likely to undertake such a

situation – I state this not on the supposition of yr. being a finished Naturalist, but as amply qualified for collecting, observing, & noting anything new to be noted in Natural History.[5]

At first Darwin's father opposed the plan. He viewed the project as wild, unsettling, uncomfortable, useless and unbecoming to a clergyman. No doubt he also, in the way of fathers, thought that it would be expensive. However, influenced by the arguments of his brother-in-law Josiah Wedgwood, Robert Darwin changed his mind just in time for his son to accept the job. In an attempt to mollify his father, Charles offered that he would have to be 'deuced clever to spend more than my allowance whilst on board the Beagle'. 'But they tell me that you are very clever'[6], Dr Darwin answered with a smile.

Charles Darwin aged about 30

Nevertheless, his mind made up, the doctor wrote to his bank with instructions that all of his son Charles's bills should be paid in full without question. With his father's approval secured, Darwin hurried to London. On 4th September Beaufort introduced Darwin to FitzRoy. The two young men liked each other immediately. For Darwin FitzRoy was: 'my beau ideal of a Captain'[7] while in Darwin FitzRoy recognised the kind of inner tranquility of character that he himself lacked but knew he needed.

Turning to my own project, it took place more than a century and a half after this historic meeting. Like Darwin I went up to Cambridge as a young man. At Magdalene College I, like Darwin, frittered away a lot of time and obtained an adequate but not outstanding degree. After Cambridge Darwin's father paid for him to go voyaging for five years while mine paid for me to train for five years to become an architect. We were both lucky to have fathers who were generous and indulgent towards their wayward sons.

One of the few things with which I may reproach my father is that while I was growing up he would not buy a yacht and take my brothers and me sailing. No argument of mine could affect the outcome. My father, a successful London lawyer, was never prepared to venture onto the water in anything smaller than an ocean liner. I had to wait until my early twenties before I could begin to sail on the sea, and I have been involved with yachts ever since. I must be a genetic sport in my family, for my son James takes after my father. James has told me that his idea of travel is on land in an air-conditioned limousine. It is sometimes asserted that interests and aptitudes may skip the generations.

In my professional career, and away from yachting, I have been occupied with work as an architect, with teaching architecture and with research into the use of computers in architecture. An unhappy marriage and a catastrophic divorce in my middle years left with me a profound dread of another matrimonial entanglement, and I have remained single ever since. FitzRoy and Darwin inherited their ghosts. My own spectre is of a social character, and it takes the form of a divorce court full of smug, vengeful lawyers.

I embarked on my own voyage aboard *Harrier of Down* with much less personal baggage than FitzRoy or Darwin. I had no great reputation to support, no unknown waters to explore, no family to found, no career to build and no human cargo to transport anywhere. In my 25 foot sailing boat I had only the wish to go sailing, to recreate the famous second voyage of HMS *Beagle* and to satisfy my curiosity about the world. What else is there to say about my character, history and personality? I hope, gentle reader, that you will learn more about these matters as you read the rest of my account of the voyage of the *Harrier*.

The author aged 68

Chapter 3
Atlantic Ocean

> *I n the steep Atlantic stream.*
> John Milton, *Comus*, 1637.

Harrier and I departed Radazul, Tenerife, on 8th September 2001. In the evening light I, like Darwin, watched Mount Teide slowly sink beneath the northern horizon. Next morning I was alone, sailing quietly across a sunlit sea. I could look forward to a peaceful ten-day or two week passage while sailing before the northeast trades.

An ocean passage in a yacht is a heaven-sent opportunity to read. I settled down in *Harrier's* cabin with a paperback edition of John Locke's *An Essay Concerning Human Understanding*. Locke wrote his revolutionary *Essay* during the most formative years of the seventeenth century scientific revolution and it was published in 1690. He rejects medieval rationalism. 'What have been the effect,' he wrote, 'of those multiplied curious distinctions, and acute niceties, but obscurity and uncertainty, leaving the words more unintelligible, and the reader more at a loss?'[1]. In Book II of the *Essay* he sets out a version of empiricism that has influenced thinking, particularly scientific thinking, ever since. Charles Darwin, more than a century later, was heir to a modified version of Locke's empirical principles. We are today equally indebted to the movement of thought that was first clearly articulated by John Locke.

A yacht equipped with a junk rig is an easy boat to sail in trade wind conditions. The modern version of the junk rig, whose design is derived from the ancient Chinese model, has many advantages particularly for the short-handed cruising yachtsman. There is no standing rigging because the mast is self-supporting, the sail is fully battened and therefore very robust, and all control lines can conveniently be brought to the cockpit. Reefing the sail is quick and easy. Deckwork, which can be dangerous in heavy weather, is much reduced when sailing with a junk rig. The rig has a low-tech character and it minimises stresses on hull or sails. *Harrier's* junk rig was well adapted to an ocean voyage. However, even when refined and tweaked, the rig is not as aerodynamically efficient as a Bermuda sloop and a 'junkie' cannot expect to win races in competitive sailing.

Harrier's hull was built to the Folksong design, which is close copy of the better known Folkboat. The disadvantage of the Folksong, and indeed the Folkboat, as a live-aboard boat, is that her cabin is small and the headroom very restricted. The cabin was suitable only for a midget. I bought her with the intention of adapting her along the lines of the modified junk-rigged Folkboat *Jester*. This famous boat abounds in original concepts and ingenious features created by her first owner, the great yachtsman and navigator Blondie Hasler. Apart from her junk rig her most conspicuous feature is the raised turtle deck over the middle third of her hull. *Jester* was built with a circular conning hatch amidships.

    I removed the original fibreglass deck from the Folksong hull, built a raised deck over her full length and moved the conning hatch from amidships to aft. This gave full sitting headroom to *Harrier* below, or standing headroom for people no taller than 1.60 metres, together with an additional extra cabin aft in the space once occupied by her cockpit. In order to improve the accommodation during her refit at Devonport Dockyard, FitzRoy had the deck of the *Beagle* raised and I, for similar reasons, raised the deck of *Harrier*.

    Why have I named my boat *Harrier of Down*? In field sports hares are pursued by a breed of dog called a beagle. To my purpose, beagles are in their turn followed by human riders known as harriers. In my yacht *Harrier* I follow the *Beagle*. The qualifier 'Down' refers to the fact that after his return to England in 1836 Darwin married and moved to Down House in Kent, where he lived for the rest of his life. By an irony of fate, human harriers are nowadays themselves being hunted down by politically-correct zealots who call themselves animal rights activists.

    Most large cruising yachts nowadays are equipped with a refrigerator and freezer and many have a diesel generating set to power them. Some yachts of medium size have a refrigerator but *Harrier* was too small to carry a refrigerator, let alone a freezer. She must, therefore, be victualled using tins, or dried or salted provisions. Aboard *Harrier* I rely on a mixture of durable, tinned and dried ingredients. Flour, rice, dried peas, dried beans and dried chick peas are cheap, available everywhere and last for many months if kept dry. A pressure cooker is needed to cook dried pulses within a reasonable time.

    Potatoes will keep well for a month, while uncooked eggs will last a similar time if coated with Vaseline. Citrus fruits, cabbage, onions, dried ham and most types of salami are good for at least two weeks, even in hot weather. Cooking with these materials a healthy, if a slightly monotonous diet, varied somewhat by tinned goods can be maintained for many weeks at sea. A diet that consisted exclusively of tinned food would be excessively boring.

At sea I am a vegetarian from necessity but not from conviction. As soon as possible after my arrival in a new port I like to sit down to a steak and a bottle of wine. FitzRoy's and Darwin's diet afloat was more frugal than mine;

> We have never yet (nor shall we) dined off salt meat. Rice and peas and calavances [chick peas] are excellent vegetables, and, with good bread, who could want more? ... nothing but water comes on the table.[1]

I, at least, allowed myself wine at a meal and a whisky in the evening while at sea.

Aboard a yacht even as small as *Harrier* it is possible to carry food sufficient to last for many months. Fresh water, however, is more of a problem. Water is heavy and it is difficult to carry more than 100 litres on a boat the size of *Harrier*. By using fresh water only for cooking and drinking, and by utilizing liquid saved from tinned supplies, a ration of two and a half litres a day per person of fresh water is adequate. A minimum of one litre a day is needed to maintain health over a period of time.

My passage from Radazul to Porto Praia (*Port Beach*) in the Cape Verdes was uneventful so far as the navigation and sailing went. The belt of calm winds known as the horse latitudes are absent from the eastern part of the Atlantic in summer. However, the world news that reached me by short wave radio was sensational. It was an eerie experience to be sailing across a blue sea under the white clouds, with no worries and miles from anywhere, while hearing about suicidal maniacs attacking the World Trade Center in New York and the Pentagon in Washington, and killing thousands of people. What, I wondered, are we going to do when some of these people get their hands on an atomic bomb?

World Trade Centre, New York, on 9/11

The principle factor determining the speed of a sailing boat through the water is her length. Other things being equal, a longer boat sails faster. The *Beagle* was 27.5 metres overall while *Harrier* was a mere 7.6 metres long. During the circumnavigation, I rarely made a passage in a shorter time than the *Beagle*. I reached Praia on the south coast of the island of Santiago on 19th September, after sailing a distance of 850 miles. In January 1832 the *Beagle* took nine days to make the same passage. For both vessels, the winds on passage to Praia were favourable but light.

In January 1832 the *Beagle* spent three weeks in Praia, mainly because a subsidiary part of her commission from the Admiralty was to make measurements of magnetic variation and dip wherever she went. For his part Darwin, as ship's naturalist, spent the time ashore collecting plant specimens and geologising.

At the time of the voyage of the *Beagle,* the accepted scientific theory about the geological history of our planet was what was known as catastrophism. On this view the present state of the earth is the result of at least one worldwide flood and one or more episodes of cataclysmic volcanism. The oceans are the residue of the floods and the mountain chains were created by giant earthquakes and volcanoes. According to a subsidiary defensive theory, the forces producing these upheavals are no longer active in the world.

Charles Lyell was the most influential exponent in English of the alternative theory of geological uniformitarianism. According to Lyell, the earth has evolved by means of processes that are seen to be at work today. Continents and islands rise and fall, the atmosphere erodes the land and volcanoes play their part by emitting ash and lava. Lyell's book, *Principles of Geology*, was a precursor of the modern theory of plate tectonics. Darwin read it and its two further volumes aboard the *Beagle*. He came to see the history of the earth through Lyellian eyes.

What was then known as Quail Island, in Praia harbour, is a complicated sandwich of volcanic and sedimentary deposits. The exercise of disentangling the island's geological history set Darwin thinking, under the influence of Lyell's book, about the processes by which the scenery of the world has come into being. His mind began to stir with ideas about geological evolution and the transformations undergone by the solid earth. One forgets nowadays that in the early nineteenth century geology was the lead science, as physics is for us.

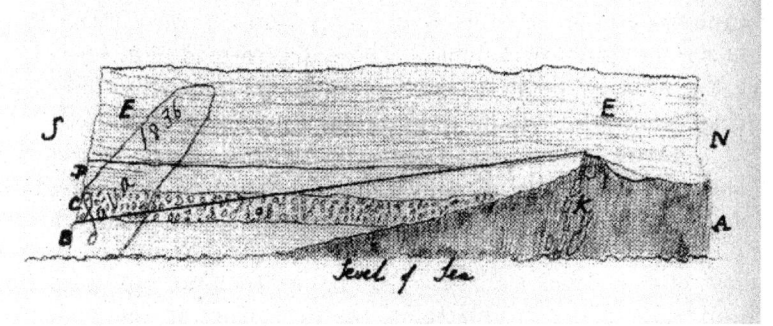

Section of Quail Island, Santiago.   Sketched by Charles Darwin

In 2001 I found the Cape Verdes very different from the Canaries. The Canaries are a part of Europe and nearly all the facilities of the mainland are available there. Tourism is the big industry and it clearly brings in a lot of people and money. The Cape Verdes, on the other hand, is a small impecunious republic moored off the coast of Africa and trying to earn a living mainly from subsistence farming. This they might be able to do successfully were it not for their rapidly increasing population. The result for the islands is a claustrophobic picture of too little work, too many people, too few skills and a somewhat bleak national future.

Furthermore, the sight of dangerous-looking foreigners with staring eyes paying in large sums of money at the bank added the rancid odour of the drugs trade to the sultry atmosphere. The Cape Verdians are a friendly and helpful people, and many work hard for the good of their country; but there is a melancholy about the islands that communicated itself and which lowered my morale. Perhaps the tourist industry will one day do for the Cape Verdes what it has done for the Canaries.

On the afternoon of 1st October I sailed out of Praia harbour and once again headed south on the cool breath of the northeast trade winds. My destination was the city of Salvador, the ancient capital city of Brazil, situated on another continent and in another hemisphere.

The voyage of the *Harrier* was my retirement project. However, when the *Beagle* sailed from Plymouth in 1831 the oldest officer on board was the purser, George Rowlett, at thirty six. FitzRoy was twenty six and Darwin was a mere twenty two years old. The voyage of the *Beagle* was a young man's expedition. All the crew were volunteers and many officers and men were veterans of the *Beagle's* first voyage to South America. 'Those determined admirers of Tierra del Fuego'[2] as FitzRoy described them. Many of the officers and ratings were selected and recruited by FitzRoy personally.

Five of them, FitzRoy himself, Bartholomew Sulivan, John Stokes, Arthur Mellersh and Charles Johnson became admirals. Robert McClintock, the ship's surgeon, later became well known as a polar explorer. Benjamin Bynoe, the assistant surgeon, became a fellow of the Royal College of Surgeons. In later life, midshipman Philip Gidley King was elected to the legislature of New South Wales and the *Beagle's* first lieutenant John Wickham became a magistrate in the state of Queensland in Australia. Finally, Darwin's later work made him one of the most famous men in history. The *Beagle's* quarterdeck were a very clever bunch.

As recently as the 1950 edition, the Admiralty publication *Ocean Passages for the World* contains detailed instructions for navigating the world in a sailing vessel as well as recommended tracks across the oceans for steamers. My copy of *Ocean Passages* suggested crossing the Equator under sail at 25 degrees west. This point lies 950 miles south of Praia. With the assistance of the steady northeast trade winds I reached 25 degrees west on 10th October where, in 5 degrees north, I encountered the northern edge of the Doldrums.

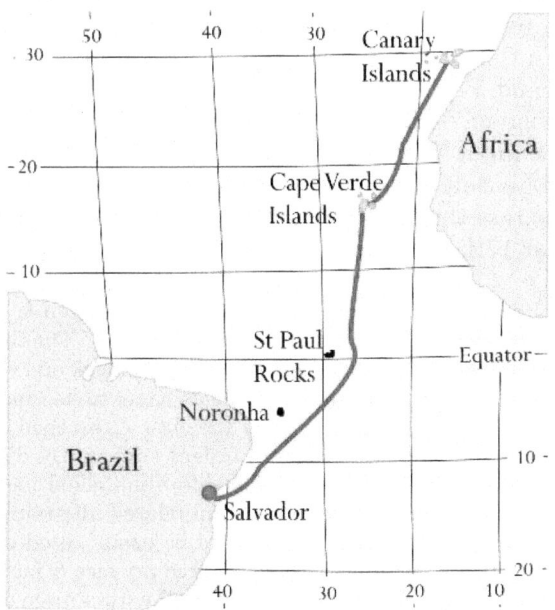

This zone of low atmospheric pressure, which is turbulent and of varying width, migrates slightly north and south with the seasons of the year. For the next eight days I worked my way slowly south through light contrary winds, overcast skies and, for two days together, continuous torrential rain. Struggling through the doldrums under sail gave me plenty of opportunity to practice the sailor's virtue of patience. In 2 degrees north I emerged from the Doldrums into the beginning of the southeast trade winds. From that point until I arrived in Salvador I had reasonable, if not ideal, sailing conditions.

In 1832 the *Beagle* took a more westerly course than *Harrier* to visit St Paul Rock at 29 degrees west. Darwin and FitzRoy landed on the top of this enormous underwater mountain whose summit projects only 15 metres above the surface of the sea. Apart from clouds of brown boobies and noddies which darkened the sky, Darwin found only one inhabitant of the rocks, a small black spider. The *Beagle* then sailed southwest towards the Equator, 50 miles away.

The plane of the Equator, which divides the figure of the earth at its greatest diameter, possesses, like every Euclidean plane, area but no volume. When he is exactly on the Equator the European navigator passes instantaneously into another world. Lines of longitude converge towards the south rather than the north, the seasons of the year are reversed, climate becomes colder further to the south rather than the north, cyclonic atmospheric pressure systems rotate clockwise and Pole Star lies on or below the north horizon. The constellations of Andromeda, Ursa Major and Orion appear upside down in the night sky. I saw that Orion's sword, rather than hanging down from his belt, was sticking up, proudly.

To cross the Equator calls for ceremony. Darwin recorded in his diary for 17th February 1832;

> About 9 oclock this morning we poor 'griffins', two & thirty in number, were put altogether on the lower deck.- The the hatchways were battened down, so we were in the dark and very hot.- Presently four of neptunes constables came to us, and one by one lead us up on deck.- I was the first & escaped easily: I nevertheless found this watery ordeal sufficiently disagreeable.- Before coming up, the constable blindfolded me & thus lead along, buckets of water were thundered all around; I was then placed on a plank, which could be easily tilted up into a large bath of water.- They then lathered my face & mouth with pitch and paint, & scraped some of it off with a piece of roughened iron hoop.- a signal being given I was tilted head over heels into the water, where two men received me & ducked me.- at last, glad enough, I escaped.[3]

My own crossing of the line was more sedate and more technical. I stood in *Harrier's* conning hatch and watched the sea slide by as we sailed gently onward to the south. In my hand, an instrument little bigger than a Mars Bar displayed my position on the earth in increments of one hundredth of a minute of latitude, a distance that is less than two metres. At the exact moment when the display was all zeros, I sipped a glass of malt whisky. Like Alice, I passed in a moment through the looking glass into a new world.

During the whole five years of the *Beagle's* voyage, Darwin never became immune to seasickness. However, the warm weather and favourable breezes of the tropical South Atlantic helped him to cope. He found that life aboard ship was conducive to work. He constructed a plankton net. 'it is a bag four feet deep, made of bunting, & attached to a semicircular bow. This by lines is kept upright, & dragged behind the vessel.'[4]

I am quite tired having worked all day at the produce of my net. - The number of animals that the net collects is very great & fully explains the manner so many animals of a large size live so far from the land. - in their forms & rich colours. - It creates a feeling of wonder that so much beauty should apparently be created for such little purpose.[5]

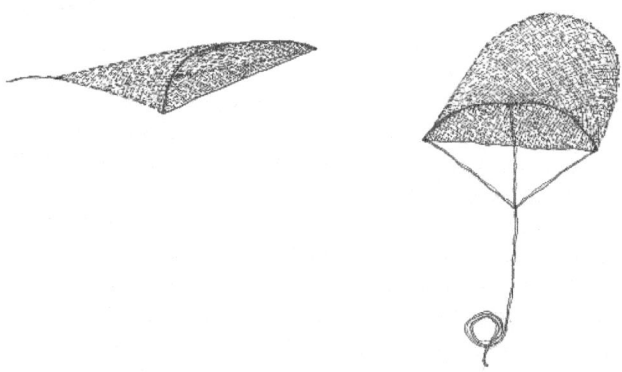

Darwin's plamkton net

At the age of 22 Darwin was one of the first naturalists to appreciate the importance of plankton in the oceanic food chain.

Darwin's microscope

Aboard *Harrier* I made a mistake over the first decision that I took in my new hemisphere. In 1832 the *Beagle* sailed to the west to visit the Brazilian island of Fernando da Noronha before heading southwest for Salvador, or Bahia as the city was then known. I misread a yachtsman's pilot book and understood from it that Fernando da Noronha is not a port of entry for Brazil. I therefore set sail from the point of my crossing of the Equator directly for the port of Salvador de Bahia on the Brazilian mainland. On the last day of October I had the white sand beaches of Bahia in sight to starboard. Shortly after dark I sailed round the Banco de Santo Antonio situated off the entrance to the great Bahia de Todos os Santos on which Salvador lies. The bay was discovered on All Saints Day, 1st November, 1501 by Amerigo Vespucci - he after whom the Americas take their name - and so he named it Bahia de Todos os Santos (*All Saint's Bay*). It is a huge inland sea, many time the size of Poole Harbour.

I anchored in the lee of the north shore below the cliff-top church of Santa Maria. For the first time in 29 days my bunk in *Harrier's* cabin was still. I had arrived 169 years and eight months after the *Beagle* dropped her anchor in the bay. Early the next day, feeling pleased with myself, I pumped up my rubber dinghy and rowed ashore to the ultra-modern building of the Yacht Clube da Bahia. The date was 1st November 2001. I had stepped ashore in the bay 500 years after Vespucci to the day.

Chapter 4
Salvador

The intense luminosity of the day, the varied colours and forms of the vegetation, the variegated plumage of the birds, all bore the grand seal of tropical nature.
       Alexander von Humboldt, *Personal Narrative*, 1814-25

It is difficult for us to appreciate nowadays the sense of wonder and discovery Darwin felt on his arrival in Brazil, some 331 years after Vespucci, at a land of tropical fruitfulness. We are used to sitting on our sofas and watching natural history films and television programmes about the tropics and to seeing full colour book illustrations of tropical plants, animals and birds. But for Darwin the sight of coconut palms, mango trees, banana plants, monstera vines and bamboo groves was at once novel and revealed the the exotic splendour and fecundity of nature. He travelled about Salvador and its neighbourhood in a kind of botanical trance.

Brazilian forest at the time of the *Beagle*

Salvador was founded by the Portuguese in 1549. A rocky, defensible site was chosen for the city by the first governor-general, Tome de Souza. It survived the Dutch wars of the seventeenth century and remained the capital city of Brazil for more than 200 years. The national government was transferred to Rio de Janeiro in 1763. Salvador (*Saviour*) remains an important commercial port today but it no longer displays a metropolitan glamour.

The colonial core of the city is nowadays undergoing a renewal. Churches and monasteries, built of dark stone, are being restored and new uses are found for streets of large stuccoed terrace houses. These houses are being repainted in traditional ice-cream colours with white cornices, window surrounds, door openings and balconies. In its heyday in the eighteenth century the Cidade de Sao Salvador da Bahia de Todos os Santos must have been very pretty.

Pelorinho, Salvador city

In North America, the United States gained her political independence from Britain in 1776. Brazil, however, left the worldwide Portuguese empire in 1815. As an independent nation Brazil remained more oriented towards Europe than did the United States. In the nineteenth century the great cities of Brazil were all located on the sea coast. They were in communication with one another by ship while Europe, on the other side of the Atlantic Ocean, was more readily accessible to the traveller than was the interior of this vast country.

The centre of gravity of Brazil remained on the Atlantic coast until the middle of the twentieth century. In 1960 the new capital city of Brasilia, planned by Lucio Costa with many buildings designed by Oscar Niemeyer, was inaugurated during the presidency of Jucelino Kubitschek. Brasilia is sited in the interior of the country on the South American savanna, the c*errado*, at an altitude of 1000 metres above sea level. Brasilia is intended to open up the hinterland of the country. It bears the same relationship to Rio de Janeiro as Washington does to New York, Ankara to Istanbul or Canberra to Sydney. One of the foundation institutions of Brasilia was a new university. The buildings of the university came from the Niemeyer design studio.

National Congress of the Federal Republic of Brazil. Designed by Oscar Niemeyer

The *Beagle* was in Salvador for only three weeks during her first visit in 1832, but I spent five months aboard *Harrier* in the bay. I had been offered a contract at the Universidade de Brasilia and it took a long time for the research grant to come through. Much of the delay was the result of a prolonged strike at all the federal universities of Brazil. During the strike no teaching was done and very little attention was paid to things like academic administration.

While I was waiting for a decision from Brasilia, I did some cruising in the Baia de Todos os Santos. The ocean swell rarely penetrates and stormy weather is rare. I visited the charming little holiday town of Itaparica and sailed up the Paraguaçu river. The Paraguaçu is rather like a larger version of the River Dart. I also sailed round the Ilha dos Frades (*Isle of Monks*) and visited a small island that has no motor cars, the Ilha Bom Jesus.

The Baia de Todos os Santos is one of the last places in South America where some trade is still carried on in boats under sail. Fruit and vegetables are brought from the surrounding countryside to market in Salvador in shallow-draught sailing boats about 15 metres long known as *saveiros*.

A Saveiro under way in Bahia de Todos os Santos

They set a large gaff mainsail on an unhewn wooden mast with a small jib forward. They are faster over the water than they look. A *saveiro* has no engine. From my anchorage on the Rio Paraguaçu I watched three working *saveiros* sailing downriver towards the bay. A noble sight.

The famous Carnaval at Rio de Janeiro, which is held just before Easter each year, is an immense display that is put on to please the spectator. The Salvador Carnaval is more domestic, and people are supposed to participate in it rather than just watch.

And so on 12th February I took the bus to Campo Grande, a large square in the nineteenth-century part of Salvador. All round the square grandstands had been put up, and these and the streets themselves were packed with thousands of people. At intervals of about 200 metres an the immense articulated lorry moving forward at a slow crawl punctuated the crowd. The trailer was made up of batteries of loudspeakers some three metres high, forming a platform overlooking the sea of people. On the platform were rows of pretty girls, a rock band and a singer. The songs came out of the loudspeakers at a volume sufficient to cause an earthquake. For 100 metres in front of and behind the lorry, on the street and in the grandstands, the entire audience from school children to grandparents bopped up and down in a high state of glee in unison to the deafening beat of the music. Pop music is not my favourite kind of din, but it was touching to see so huge and so spontaneous a display of Brazilian *joie de vivre*.

After Carnaval, the city was occupied for two days in clearing up, while I went back to my routine of reading, working on *Harrier* and waiting, while moored at the Aratu Iate Clube. But waiting can sometimes turn into plain loafing as the entry in my diary for the 25th of February suggests.

A Day at the Club

At mid-morning I go ashore and drink a cold guarana under the shade of the waterside pavilion of the club. Soon the regulars arrive. Antonio, Pascal, Otavio, Jean-Pierre, Bandeira, Cleber. Two tables are pulled together. They converse and I listen, trying to improve my Portuguese.

Presently lunch arrives. Excellent Bahian food and delicious Brazilian sucos. The waiter clears away, we sip our coffees and the gentle afternoon breeze begins to blow in under the roof of the pavilion and across the tables.

'I'm going to burn down this pavilion', announces Jean-Pierre.
'What! But you can't do that! Where would we meet to talk?'
'That is exactly why I must burn it down'.
'Oh?'
'Yes. Every day that I come to the club I sit here in this pavilion and talk. It is very nice. My friends are very clever and I learn many things. But the day goes by and I get nothing done. So, the pavilion has to go'.

We finish our coffees thoughtfully. Then, '.... it sounds as if you have water in your fuel tank - have you drained the sump? .... the harbour at Itaparica was uncomfortable in the north wind, so I moved to a place inside the marina pier .... I don't know why the Magellan will not register with the NMEA protocol - do you know, Jean-Pierre? .... a good anchorage on the way to Maragogipe is at the west end of Ilha do Monte Cristo, in three metres off the house on the islct .... yes, Volvo spares are ridiculously expensive .... your genoa might set better if you moved the sheet block outboard' ..... And so the whole of another afternoon passed by in pleasant, varied and interesting ..... conversation.

My social life continued on board *Harrier* as well as ashore at the club. Otavio and José climbed down the conning hatch, moved at a crouch into the cabin and sat down on the bunk.

> 'Welcome to the yellow submarine', I said.
> 'You have an amazing amount of room below for such a small boat', said Otavio. Both he and Jose spoke excellent English.
> 'Yes, I have full sitting headroom everywhere. Standing headroom would be of little advantage aboard Harrier since there is nowhere to walk about.'

After a while the conversation turned to the *Beagle* and her times. I said that;

> 'I have the original account of her voyage, written in 1837 and 1838. It is the most expensive book on board. I had to have the original 1839 edition microfilmed at the Cambridge University Library and all 700 frames of the microfilm photocopied. The whole thing cost more than £300. But it is the essential document for my voyage'.

Jose turned to the page in the *Narrative* describing Bahia in 1832. He read FitzRoy's words aloud.

> Bahia has declined ever since its separation from Portugal: Unsettled weak governments, occupied too constantly by party strife to be able to attend to the real improvement of their country, have successively misruled.... that rich and beautiful country....[1]

'That sounds familiar', said José, looking at Otavio.
'Things have not changed very much', said Otavio, looking into the middle distance.

Darwin, for his part, could not see that Brazil was, at least potentially, a rich and beautiful country. Both sides of his family had been involved for generations in the movement to abolish slavery. In 1772 it was finally made illegal in Britain, and the Slavery Abolition Act of 1833 ended slavery in the British Empire. The Darwins were instrumental in the movement of opinion that resulted in Britain being the first imperial power to take this step. Charles Darwin admired the natural environment of Brazil but his hatred of slavery, which he described as 'that scandal to Christian nations'[2], blinded him to much of the life of the country. He commented that;

> If to what Nature has granted the Brazils, man added his just & proper efforts, of what a country might the inhabitants boast. But when the greater parts of it are in a state of slavery, & where this system is maintained by an entire stop to education, the mainspring of human actions; what can be expected; but that the whole would be polluted by its part.[3]

Slavery in Brazil was not abolished until 1888, five years after Darwin's death.

Some 169 years after Darwin wrote those words, the news arrived in Aratu that I had been awarded the contract at the school of architecture in the Universidade de Brasilia. The rapid increase in the speed and capacity of computation has resulted in a worldwide concern with the possibilities and roles for the computer in social and human life. A sub-section of this concern is a topic known, for want of a better title, as artificial intelligence. My doctoral thesis had been on the use of artificial intelligence in architectural design. I was invited to Brasilia to continue with this line of investigation.

The point of intersection between architectural design and artificial intelligence is an area of vigorous controversy. It is one of the points at which an understanding of computation engages with the study of the capacity of the human mind.

A computer is simply a very powerful machine for carrying out logical procedures, while the human mind is an entity whose method of operation is not illogical but rather it is non-logical. It is possible to understand the operation of a computer in full detail, right down to the metal, as the phrase has it. The brain, like a computer, can in principle be described accurately and scientifically. On the other hand the mind, while it is dependant upon the functioning of the brain, is a non-material entity different from the brain and it defies scientific analysis.

The mind is the seat of the human capacity for intellectual and artistic invention. A great deal of confusion in the study of artificial intelligence is the result of a failure to distinguish between the different natures and capacities of the biological brain and the non-material mind.

Some investigators have assumed that, given sufficient power, a computer can function precisely in the manner of the human mind. Optimism about automatic architectural design springs from this conviction. At Brasilia I was able to publish a paper showing that this is impossible, and will remain so, because the working of a computational machine and the functioning of a non-material mind are different in kind and are incompatible with one another. A role remains, however, for the computer in the production of architectural, and indeed of all, design projects.

A modern computer far exceeds the human mind in the capacity of its factual memory and in its ability to carry out complicated logical operations repeatedly, rapidly and without fatigue or error. These functions make the computer well adapted to the processing of verbal, textual, numerical and graphical information. I left behind me at Brasilia the framework of a computer program for organising and facilitating the handling of information in design and construction projects.

Harrier remained afloat at the Aratu club marina for more than a year during the time that I lived and worked in Brasilia. On 27th February 2003, I returned to Salvador, the club, *Harrier* and to the sea.

Chapter 5
Winter Journey

The heart's thought that I on high streams
The salt-wavy tumult traverse alone.
Ezra Pound, *The Seafarer*, 1912

At the marina of the Aratu Iate Clube, I hauled *Harrier* out for a refit. I painted her, scrubbed the bottom and made a few small improvements to her arrangements on deck. Is there no end to the enhancements one can think of making to a yacht? I owe a great deal of thanks to the members and staff of the club for looking after *Harrier* so well during the time that I was away in Brasilia.

On 2nd April 2003, looking our best, *Harrier* and I sailed out of the Baia de Todos os Santos, leaving to port the old city of Salvador high on its cliff overlooking the bay. We turned south for Uruguay and the Rio de la Plata, nearly 2000 miles away. Winds were light and variable for the first four days. On 6th May the breeze stood into the northeast, and I convinced myself that this was the arrival of the northeast trade wind. For two days I sailed along contentedly in expectation of a prosperous passage. But someone up there was monitoring my thoughts. Early on 8th May, sitting in the main hatch having my morning stare, I looked aloft and was horrified to see that the upper section of *Harrier's* mast had rotated through 180 degrees on the lower part. Her mast is a two-part aluminium extrusion, and as with every junk rig the mast is unstayed. It could only be a short time before the top of the mast fell.

That afternoon the Cyclops radar reflector at the masthead fell with a crash onto the port side toerail forward, leaving the other end of the upper mast section aloft, held there by the cable to the masthead tri-colour navigation light. I tied a sharp knife onto the end of a boathook and with this extension I could reach and cut the cable. I then lashed the five metre long mast section securely on deck and, as the evening drew in, I paused to consider my position.

I was 200 miles from the coast of Brazil. *Harrier* had no engine and no radio. I had plenty of food and water on board but it was not reasonable to continue to Uruguay with a crippled boat. However, I had stowed away forward a foresail of a Soling and it was now time to see if this really would serve as part of a jury rig. I fixed the clew of the Soling sail as far up the lower section of the mast, which was still standing, as I could reach. The tack I tied to my stemhead fitting and the head was brought aft and sheeted to a cleat. I now had a squat triangular sail to work with. It turned out that we could sail slowly across or downwind, but no progress could be made to windward. So began a weary nine-day drift towards the coast.

I had to come to terms with the fact that my predicament was neither a dream nor an episode in a novel. I really was marooned far from help. *Harrier's* familiar cabin now took on the aspect of a floating prison cell. As any lonely prisoner must discover, the hardest thing to do is to discipline one's mind to work properly in the new situation. It is far from an easy thing. To maintain a functional mentality despite the realisation that one is helpless and at the mercy of events calls for deliberate effort.

Day after day we crawled towards the Brazilian port of Vitória in light southerly winds. Each day I made a conscious mental resolution to think positively and to forbid the situation to overcome me. On the 18th of April I could see ahead the Morro Mestre Álvares to the north of the Bahia de Vitória, 20 miles away. After lunch I was lying on my bunk and trying to be patient. A yacht under way makes a continuous sequence of small sounds - a rope rendering through a block, something moving in a locker, the water lapping against the hull. Presently I became conscious that a new and unfamiliar sound had entered the acoustical background. I got up and looked on deck to investigate. Close alongside was a small fishing boat with four men on board.

'Boa Tarde.'
'Boa Tarde. Voce vai para Vitória?'
'Si. Voce quer ser rebocardo?'
'*Yes, please!*'

I gave them the end of a towline and we set off at seven knots towards the land. Four hours later they put me alongside the Dutch yacht *Colinsplaat*, just in front of the marina of the Iate Clube do Espiritu Santo. The fishermen came aboard *Harrier* out of curiosity about her accommodation and I gave them all the cash that I had in my wallet. I hope that I was the most profitable fish that they caught that day. They returned aboard their boat and disappeared into the night. I never saw them again. Those four fishermen were true mariners and perfect gentlemen.

In Vitória I made arrangements to have the mast repaired. A nearby boat yard turned a metre long hardwood plug on a lathe to fit tightly inside the two mast sections. A set of 24 stainless steel screws held the plug in position, making the mast at least as strong as it was originally. This work could not have been done without the generous help of the members and staff of the Iate Club do Espirito Santo. All this took a month to complete and on 16th May I sailed from Vitória, again bound for Punta del Este in Uruguay.

The month of May is too late in the year to be going south along the coast of Brazil. The northeast trade winds are rare or absent in early winter. However, the Brazilian customs service had ordered me to take *Harrier* out of the country immediately or pay them a hefty fee in customs duty. They were so anxious to see the last of *Harrier* that they would only give me clearance for a non-stop passage to Uruguay. With my new status as an unwanted immigrant, I could not follow the course of the *Beagle* in proper detail and make a visit to Rio de Janeiro.

When Darwin received his mail at Rio in 1832 he learnt that the girl he left behind, Fanny Owen, had forsaken him and married another. Fanny was a shallow, sparky girl, and had Darwin married her she would have lead him a merry dance. Rio was also an eventful place for the rest of the crew of the *Beagle*. Four members of a shore party contracted malaria there and three of them died of the disease.

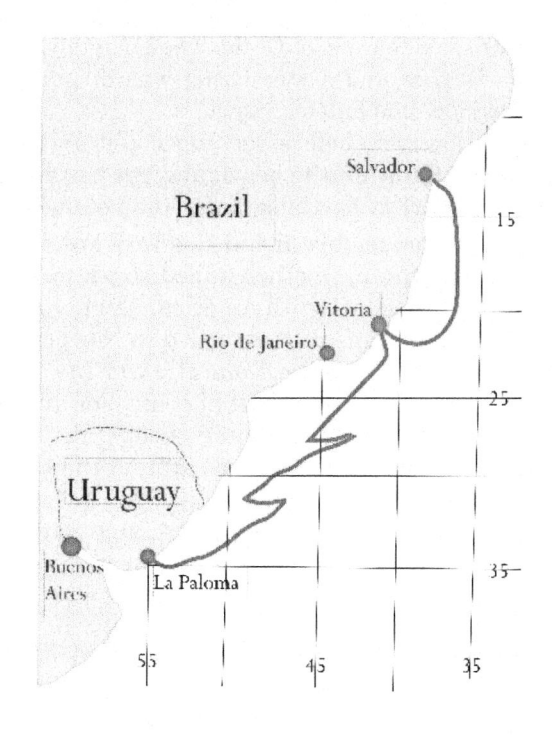

The distance from Vitória to Punta del Este in Uruguay is about 1500 miles. During this passage I had contrary winds, several episodes of calm and two southwest gales. *Harrier* is too small to make progress against gale force winds, and each gale blew me back on my course by some 80 miles. *Harrier* proved herself to be a stout boat during these rough episodes. I could only be patient during the setbacks, and help her to make the best speed possible to the south when the weather permitted. It was slow, weary work and it gave me plenty of time to reflect that, with so many delays, I was absent from my job in Brasilia for too long.

The winter weather moderated after the passing of the second gale. The wind settled into north of west as a sailing breeze. I put *Harrier* onto a close reach and we steered a southwesterly course towards the entrance to the Río de la Plata (*River of the Silver*). The name is often anglicized to River Plate. By 8th June I had reached the latitude of the border between Brazil and Uruguay, where the language spoken changes from Portuguese to Spanish.

A few miles to the south of the border the voyage of the first solo circumnavigator, that of Captain Joshua Slocum aboard the gaff yawl *Spray*, nearly came to an end. At daybreak on 11th December 1895 the *Spray* went aground on a remote Atlantic beach near the present seaside town of Chuy. The Uruguayan coast guard sprang to his assistance and a steam tug was dispatched to the *Spray* from Montevideo, 250 miles away.

However, before the tug could arrive, Slocum was able to kedge the *Spray* off the beach and get her afloat again. She 'lost her shoe and part of her false keel, and received other damage, which, however, was readily mended afterward in dock'[1] in Maldonado. Slocum and the *Spray* then sailed south to Tierra del Fuego and on to the west coast of South America. After crossing the Pacific, Indian and Atlantic oceans they returned to Newport, Rhode Island in June 1898. His book, *Sailing Alone Around the World*, was published in 1900 and has never been out of print. For almost as far back as I can remember a favourite winter occupation has been to sit by the fireside with his book and sail around the world again with Slocum and the *Spray*.

People on other yachts are able to catch fish with ease, but when I put a line over the side, the fish just fall about laughing. During the interval between the two gales at sea I had again tried my luck with hook and line. I caught no fish, but I did hook a black-browed albatross, or mollymauk. It made desperate efforts to get free while being towed along the surface of the water by my line. When I hauled the bird close alongside I saw that the hook had lodged inside the tip of the bird's beak. Grasping the shaft of the hook in one hand and the beak of the bird in the other I was able to disengage the unfortunate creature. The bird flopped back into the water, swam for a few strokes, took off and disappeared over the waves. Had the roles been reversed I would not have been so lucky. A man floating in the sea will be attacked by a flock of albatross. They will kill him by stripping the flesh from his head.

At last on the 12th of June I was some 40 miles off the small fishing port of La Paloma, on the Atlantic coast of Uruguay. From this point on her passage south from Rio de Janeiro in 1832 the *Beagle* turned west into the Río de la Plata and anchored in Montevideo harbour on 26th July, seven months out from England. For myself, I did not want to risk another winter southwest gale on a lee shore. Rather than follow the course of the *Beagle* I decided to divert to La Paloma.

I was three miles from the harbour breakwater when the weather demonstrated that it had not finished with me yet. Fog came down and the shore marks disappeared in the murk. I anchored off in 20 metres for a day at almost exactly the spot in the lee of Cabo Santa Maria where the *Beagle* had dropped her anchor 171 years before. On the morning of Saturday 14th June the visibility cleared. I got my anchor, sailed round the end of the breakwater and picked up a mooring near the fishing fleet inside the harbour of La Paloma. The passage from Vitória had taken me one day longer than it took me to cross the South Atlantic Ocean from the Cape Verde islands to Salvador in the northern autumn of 2001.

Chapter 6
Río de la Plata

There is no more abominable roadstead than that of Monte Video in a pampero
          Sir Horace Rumbold, *The Great Silver River*, 1882

At the Río de la Plata the *Beagle* had reached the northern limit of her work area. The instructions that FitzRoy received from the Admiralty in 1831 said that;

> To the southward of the Rio de la Plata the real work of the survey will begin. Of the great extent of coast which reaches from Cape San Antonio to St George's Bay, we only know that it is inaccurately placed, and that it contains some large rivers, which rise on the other side of the continent, and some good harbours, which are undoubtedly worth a minute examination. .... It should .... be born in mind there, and in other places, the more hopeless and forbidding any long line of coast may be, the more precious becomes the discovery of a port which affords safe anchorage and wholesome refreshments.[1]

Early in August 1832 the *Beagle* made an abortive visit to Buenos Aires (*Good Air*) from Montevideo during which she was fired on by a guardship and was refused permission to land because of "a vexatious regulation with respect to quarantine"[2]. FitzRoy would have little difficulty in recognising the present-day bureaucratic situation.

On her return to Montevideo FitzRoy was asked by the captain of the port and the chief of police to help to suppress a revolt by a troop of black soldiers who had seized the Citadel. The Citadel occupied the site of the present-day Plaza Independencia. Doubtless the trouble was that the soldiers had not been paid. FitzRoy landed a party of 50 armed marines and sailors and camped in another fort by the harbourside. He and his men were glad when the rebellion expired without their involvement and that they were able to return on board the next day.

Life in Montevideo soon calmed down. Three months after the *Beagle's* constabulary episode Darwin was able to go to the Montevideo opera and hear a performance of Rossini's *La Cenerentola*.

On 19th August 1832 the *Beagle* sailed south to begin her survey of the coast of Patagonia at Bahía Blanca (*White Bay*). She made the first accurate survey of this great bay and harbour. Here FitzRoy chartered two small vessels, the Paz (*Peace*) of 15 tons and the Liebre (*Hare*) of 9 tons, to survey the shallow and complex coast south of Bahía Blanco as far as the Río Negro. Leaving these two yacht-sized boats to their work, the *Beagle* returned to the Río de la Plata. Subsequently she made two more visits to Río de la Plata in order to consult the Argentine authorities and to obtain supplies of 'wholesome refreshments'.

The *Beagle* lost no crew from disease or accident during her time in the Río de la Plata. However, an important change took place among the supernumeraries. The health of the expedition draftsman, Augustus Earle, was failing. He invalided at Montevideo in August 1832 and returned to England. FitzRoy and the *Beagle* were without an illustrator for a year and a half . Then 'The disappointment caused by losing his services was diminished by meeting Mr Martens at Monte Video, and engaging him to embark with me as my draftsman.'[3] FitzRoy wrote to Darwin, 'I am sure you will like him, and like him much .... He is a gentlemanlike well informed man - his landscapes are really good .... Though perhaps in figures he cannot equal Earle'.[4] Most of the well-known images of the voyage of the *Beagle* are by Conrad Martens, much of whose work is now held by the Mitchell Library in Sydney.

On her last visit in 1833, the *Beagle* remained at Montevideo during the second half of November, while the officers prepared charts from their survey data and provisioned the ship for her forthcoming voyage to Tierra del Fuego and Chile. While they worked on board the ship, Darwin stepped ashore and went exploring in western Uruguay.

I spent the months of the southern winter of 2003 in Uruguay aboard *Harrier* moored in La Paloma. The time passed quickly. I had some special metal fittings made, obtained items of equipment from England and tidied up the last of the pieces of work that remained from my contract at the University of Brasilia. Also, I was visited by my girlfriend.

Karen stepped off a plane from England at Montevideo airport on 24th September. Together we set off exploring western Uruguay in the footsteps of Darwin. He travelled from Montevideo to Colonia del Sacramento, Carmelo and Mercedes on horseback. I am terrified of horses, and we travelled in the relative comfort and safety of local buses. Colonia, the most picturesque town in Uruguay, was established by the Portuguese in 1680 as a base for smuggling goods across the Río de la Plata into the Spanish colonies. It still serves this purpose. We loafed for two days in Colonia before travelling on to Mercedes.

About 30 kilometres to the northeast of Mercedes, up the Río Negro (*Black River*), lies the village of Villa Darwin. At the Mercedes bus station Karen and I were discussing how we could visit the village that bore such a distinguished name. A fair-haired young man standing nearby overheard our talk and he offered in good English to drive us there in his pickup truck. Carlos was an agronomist and as we drove through well stocked, pastoral country he explained that the Uruguayan people were the greatest beef eaters in the world, greater even than the Argentines. Furthermore, Uruguayan cattle are fed exclusively on grass and the process is entirely natural. Carlos took us to Villa Darwin and then a short distance on to the bend in the Río Negro that is described by Darwin in his diary entry of 24th November 1833.

> The view of the R Negro from the sierra is decidedly the most picturesque that I have seen in this country. The river is rapid and tortuous; it is about twice as large as the Severn (when banks full) at Shrewsbury; the cliffs precipitous and rocky; & there is a belt of wood following the course of the river; beyond which an horizon of grass fills up the view.[5]

Here, atop the cliff at Cerro de los Claveles, we found a large grey granite obelisk bearing the name DARWIN in bold Trajan letters. We picnicked in the shade of the monument. I congratulated myself on a gratifying discovery and we both enjoyed the majesty of Darwin's view. 'This is one of your best escapades, Julian', she said.

The small intensely purple epiphytic flower, the clavele, after which the spot is named, was growing on the surrounding trees. In Darwin's day the landscape of Uruguay consisted entirely of grassland, with some willow-like shrubs along the watercourses. Since that time extensive woodlands of eucalyptus, maritime pine and a kind of birch have been planted for fuel and building material. Many parts of Uruguay are now as well-wooded as the English Midlands.

Karen flew from Montevideo on 5th October. I returned to *Harrier* at La Paloma and sailed westward on 23rd October. In a fresh northeast wind I sailed along the southeast Atlantic coast of Uruguay. During the night I took the passage inside Isla de Lobos, (*Isle of Seals*), off Punta del Este. Next day brought an introduction to the turbulent weather of the Río de la Plata. Stormy grey clouds heralded a spectacular thunderstorm, with three hours of calm succeeding some strong gusts of westerly wind. During the following night, in gentler weather, I stood off and on south of the lighthouse on Isla de Flores (*Isle of Flowers*) and the following morning the 25th of October I finally sailed into Buceo, the yacht harbour of Montevideo and the home port of the Yacht Club Uruguayo.

At Buceo I experienced once again the wonderful hospitality of the yachtsmen of South America. I was given full use of the facilities of the Yacht Club Uruguayo including a space in the club's repair yard. Here I carried out some further strengthening of *Harrier's* mast in preparation for the rougher waters of the south. Three and a half weeks after entering Buceo I set off, at midnight, westward for Buenos Aires in the track of the *Beagle*.

The Río de la Plata and its surrounding lands enjoy a benign Mediterranean climate except for one powerful and frequent meteorological event. Cold high-altitude air falling down the sides of the Andes mountain chain to the west will displace the warmer and lighter air of the plains. While the moving cold air races eastward across the Pampas it forms a characteristic dark, turbulent, cigar-shaped cloud across its line of advance. The pampero arrives, heralded by its cloud, at the Río de la Plata as a storm in which winds of as much as 100 knots can occur.

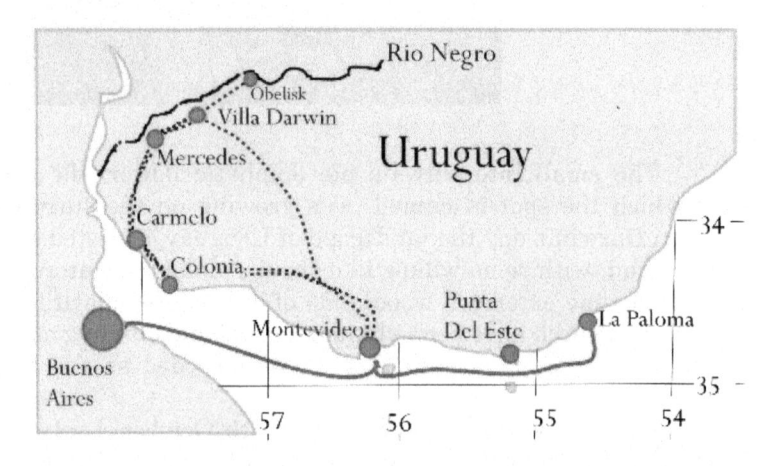

I was only one hour out from Buceo when I saw a dark wall of cloud approaching across the river from the southwest. The cloud stretched from one horizon to the other and by the glow of the lights of Montevideo I could see above me the vapour of the cloud writhing in its winds. As I sailed under the cloud I seemed to be passing beneath a gigantic bridge. At sea level the gentle breeze continued to blow me on towards Buenos Aires, unaffected by the turmoil above. Soon after, the easterly breeze strengthened to a brisk sailing wind and we flew across the muddy waters of the Río de la Plata under short canvas. We completed the 135 mile passage in what is for *Harrier* the very fast time of 25 hours. At no time were we in water deeper than seven metres. I anchored in the shelter of the Ante Puerto Norte for the night, and in the morning sailed into the marina of the Yacht Club Argentino. Here *Harrier* floated low on her marks, for at Buenos Aires the water, as well as the air, is fresh.

Presently I was sitting at a table with a cold beer under the Ceibo tree on the harbourside terrace of the Yacht Club Argentino, getting to know some of the members. Could there be a more pleasant and welcoming place for a chat?

> 'Are you a biologist? Is that why you are interested in Darwin and the *Beagle*?', asked Niceto.
> 'No. In fact I am an architect by training. The idea of following the track of the Beagle interests me as a way of turning a circumnavigation by yacht into a proper project. I am a very project-oriented person. I don't think that I could just sail westward from one island to the next for three years without having some purpose in view. It would drive me potty.'
> 'Hmm. I work at my business here and I make some money but I don't feel as if I have a purpose in life. Everything seems a bit aimless, really.', he replied.
> 'I think that I may have an answer for you. So far as I know very few of the voyages of the great Spanish explorers have been re-done in a yacht. Why not get into your boat and follow the track of de Solis, Orellana or Mendoza? Then write a book about it. Nothing like a good project to give one energy and direction.'
> 'A nice idea, and I may do it.' he replied. 'But let me first speak to my wife. She may have an opinion about this!'

I spent two weeks in Buenos Aires making arrangements to have a new aluminium mast made in case the repairs to my existing spar turn out to be inadequate. My visit was a short one but I was able to visit the Plaza de Mayo, the Parliament Square of Buenos Aires and the Museo Histórico Nacional. Not all of my time, however, was taken up with the higher tourism. Carlos and I were sitting in a pavement cafe on the Plaza Roma having breakfast and watching the pretty girls go by.

'There is a good-looking girl, the one in white shorts. Nice legs', he said.
'Yes, a fine pair of understandings I should say'.
'Do you know that there is a unit of measure for pretty women?' he asked.
'Do you mean the millehelen?'
'Yes. And do you know its definition?'
'A millehelen", I answered, "is that quantity of feminine pulchritude that is sufficient to launch one ship'.
'Quite right', he said.

Carlos´s knowledge of English playwrights was much more extensive than my rather patchy readings in Spanish literature.

Darwin, too, had an eye for the girls. He wrote to his sister Caroline that;

> Our chief amusement was riding about & admiring the Spanish Ladies, - After watching one of these angels gliding along the streets: involuntarily we groaned out. "how foolish English women are, they can neither walk nor dress", - And how ugly Miss sounds after Signorita: I am sorry for you all, it would do the whole tribe of you a great deal of good to come to Buenos Aires.[6]

After so short a visit. I did not feel that I was ready to leave such an interesting country as Argentina. But the summer season was running on and it was time to be moving again. I returned to Montevideo more slowly than I had come. By following the coast of Uruguay all the way back to Montevideo, I could use the sea breeze during the afternoon and evening and the brisk land breeze at night and in the morning. Some 40 hours out from Buenos Aires *Harrier* was back on her mooring at Buceo.

The Yacht Club Uruguayo has a flourishing fleet of Optimist sailing dinghies. In these tiny craft the cadet members of the club learn how to handle a boat and how take part in a sailing race. Boys and girls are retired from the Optimist class at the age of 15 on account of old age. Late one sunny afternoon, when I was on deck splicing some lines and watching a party of white-winged coots patrolling the anchorage, a group of five Optimists sailed close by my mooring. They were returning from sailing in the bay outside the harbour. Each dinghy contained a budding helmsman and a young trainee crew, and they were all singing together. Uruguay is a country in which the children are happy.

At last, a month after my arrival, I managed to extract from the customs service a vital spare part sent to me from Germany. In Uruguay, a yacht on passage may import spares free of customs duty, but there is a sting in the tail of the arrangements. It takes a long time to deal with the red tape, and in order to get possession of the item one must employ the services of a customs agent. The fee that the agent charges is more than the duty on any but a large and expensive import. They get you coming and they get you going.

I departed from Montevideo for Patagonia and the south on Wednesday, the last day of 2003. My first destination was Bahía Blanca and I expected the passage to take about a week. Until reaching the Río de la Plata I had been yachting. From now on I would be voyaging. As with the *Beagle*, the real work of the voyage of the *Harrier* now began.

Chapter 7
The Pampas

The pampas are, in most places, as level as a billiard table.
　　　William (WH) Hudson. *Long Ago and Far Away.* 1918

On her first cruise south from the Río de la Plata in September 1832 the *Beagle* made a running survey of the coast of what is now the Argentine province of Buenos Aires. She sailed 'within surveying distance of the coast'[1], which was five miles or less, so as to be able to take surveying azimuths and elevations. At frequent intervals she was obliged to anchor and fix the position of the ship from which the measurements were taken. Because of the nature of her duties, she often brought up at places where the modern yachtsman would not dream of dropping his anchor. From a spot just outside the surf of Cabo Corrientes, close north of what is now the modern artificial port of Mar del Plata, she had to clear out in the middle of the night because the wind suddenly came onshore. She was only able to lift her anchor and get clear in time because a rise in the barometer, which was closely watched, gave warning of an imminent change in the weather.

At the time of the *Beagle's* voyage, the industrial process of casting large objects in steel had not been developed. Her anchors were made by the traditional technique of forging together slabs of wrought iron. Wrought iron is satisfactorily resistant to corrosion by seawater but anchors made in this way are not strong. The *Beagle* broke three anchors while weighing them on her passage to Bahía Blanca. During the five years of her circumnavigation she broke and lost a total of at least six anchors.

For *Harrier* and me, the 400 mile coastline of Buenos Aires was a thing to avoid going aground on rather than something to be investigated. I therefore kept 50 miles offshore all the way to Bahía Blanca. The passage took me five days in fine summer weather with a following breeze. I sailed into the great bay on 7th January 2004.

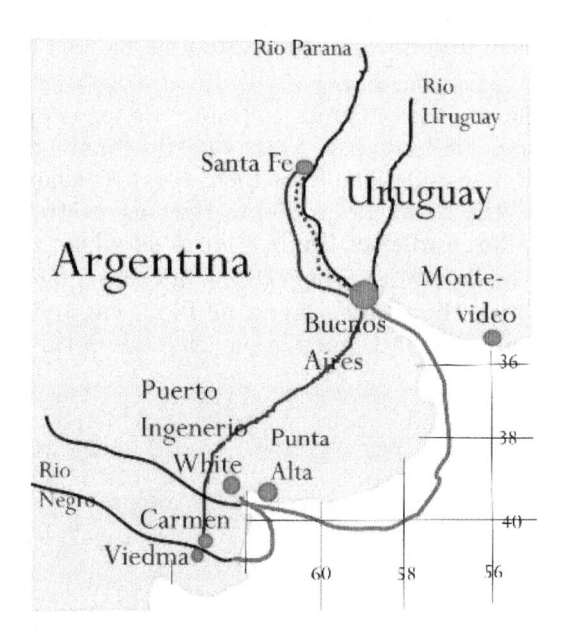

When the *Beagle* arrived off Bahía Blanca she was baffled as to how to get across the Banco del Norte that guards the eastern side of the bay. She dropped her anchor just outside in Rada de Monte Hermoso (*Bay of the Beautiful Mountain*). Here FitzRoy had a piece of good luck. The sail of an unknown small boat was seen to be approaching. She turned out to belong to a fellow countryman, James Harris. Harris piloted the *Beagle* over the bank and into the large bay that forms the centre of Bahía Blanca and which was and is known as Puerto Belgrano.

Harris was a Welshman who lived with his Spanish wife at Carmen de Patagones on the Río Negro, 280 kilometres to the south. He was a sealer and because of his work he was familiar with the coastline of the district in great detail. FitzRoy came to an agreement with Harris to employ him as pilot together with Mr Roberts, another sealer also living at Carmen. It was from Harris that FitzRoy hired the two small boats, the *Paz* (*Peace*) and *Liebre* (*Hare*).

John Wickham and Philip King went aboard the *Paz* with Harris while John Lort Stokes and Arthur Mellersh squeezed into the *Liebre* with Roberts. Roberts was a very tall and strong man. When the *Liebre* went aground, Roberts would simply jump over the side and push her off into deeper water. FitzRoy referred to his new fleet fondly as 'the little schooners'.[2]

Nowadays, the entrance to Bahía Blanca is easy to find and its navigation is well marked. This is partly thanks to the efforts of the *Beagle*. Her instructions from the Admiralty asked for attention to be given to the coast 'From Monte Hermoso to the Río Colorado, including the large inlet of Bahía Blanca, of which there are three manuscripts in this office which differ in everything but in name'[3] The chart which the *Beagle* made in 1832 was the first accurate representation of Bahía Blanca, a bay the size of the Thames Estuary.

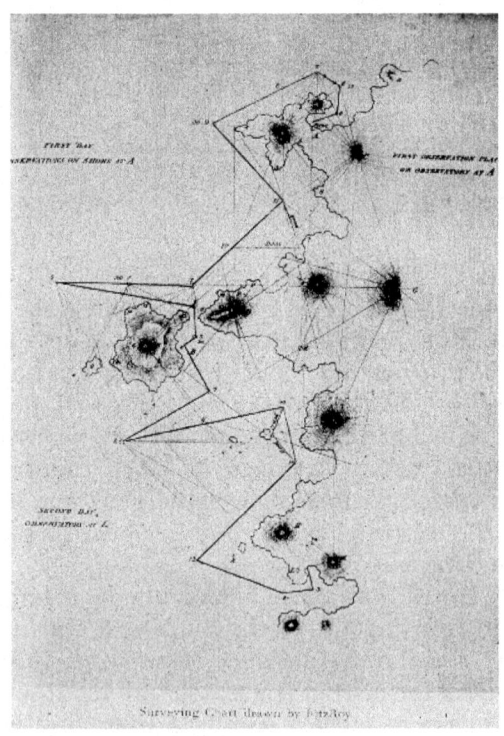

Working up a chart

It shows that Puerto Belgrano is sufficiently large and deep that, in FitzRoy's words, 'any number of line-of-battle ships might enter the port'.[4] He had a good eye for topography and geographical possibilities. Puerto Belgrano now accommodates the Argentine naval base of Punta Alta (*High Headland*), the largest naval base in South America.

The bay may be spacious enough for a fleet of men-of-war but it suffers, from the point of view of the yachtsman, from a shortage of well-sheltered small boat anchorages. The yachts of the Club Náutico Bahía Blanca at the top of the bay at Puerto Ingeniero White are sailed dry. After a day's sailing you crane out and spend the evening spinning yarns high and dry in the club boat park. I was one of six people who climbed up a ladder and crammed themselves into the cockpit of Antón's tiny yacht, an Alba 19 built in Argentina.

"Welcome to Bahia Blanca. Where have you come from?'
'Montevideo. I had a good passage and anchored last night off the beach just east of Punta Alta. Harrier is now in the shelter of the fishing harbour over there.'
'Why do you come to Bahia Blanca?'
I gave my usual explanation about the voyage of the Beagle and handed out the description of my project that I had had translated into Spanish for just such an occasion.
'Are you alone? Where is your wife?'
'Yes, I am solo. I am divorced, retired and my children are grown up. I am a free man.'
'Well, welcome again to Bahia Blanca. We think that you are really the brother of David Niven'.

If so, then it was my brother who got the good looks.

Punta Alta itself, which is only high in relation to a very low and featureless coastline, is now separated from the water of Puerto Belgrano by the reclaimed land on which the naval base is built. I was taken to see this famous little hill by Teresa, the curator of the Museo Municipal de Ciencias Naturales Carlos Darwin in Punta Alta. The hill, some 15 metres high, has been kept open and undeveloped because of its historical importance. Here in 1832 Darwin excavated a number of fossilised bones of the extinct giant mammals of South America. He brought his finds back to the *Beagle* 'notwithstanding', in FitzRoy's words, 'our smiles at the cargoes of apparent rubbish which he frequently brought on board'.[5]

The fossils included remains of the Toxodon, a kind of hairy hippopotamus, a Mastodon or giant elephant, the Glyptodon which was an armoured creature least unlike a modern armadillo but much larger, the Macruchenia which looked like a compromise between a llama and a camel, and the Megatherium. This animal must be one of Nature's most bizarre creations. The Megatherium was a ground sloth with long curved claws on all four feet, like the modern tree sloth. It stood four metres high and weighed three tons. No tree could support it.

Megatherium americanum
Afinidad: Perezosos
6m de largo, 5,000 Kg

He also found the skull of what he believed to be a rat or a hare of enormous size. He later wrote to his sister Caroline to say, 'There is another head as large as a Rinoceros ....Conceive a Rat or a Hare of such a size - What famous cats they ought to have had in those days!'.[6]

Darwin's personal evolution from feckless undergraduate to respected scientist began at Punta Alta. His fossils were crated and sent to John Henslow, Darwin's old tutor in natural history, at Cambridge. Henslow distributed them to expert paleontologists. They were immediately recognised as an important contribution to science. The reception of his discoveries at Punta Alta by experts in Britain marked the beginning of Darwin's scientific reputation. John Henslow was one of the godfathers of the modern theory of evolution in the natural world.

Darwin's work at Punta Alta earned him the respect of the crew of the *Beagle*. FitzRoy coined for him the nickname 'Philos'[7], standing for "expedition natural philosopher". During the rest of the voyage Darwin was known by everybody on board the *Beagle* as 'Philosopher', simply as 'Philos' or occasionally as 'Flycatcher'.

One of the most common archaeological artefacts in the Pampas is a carefully fashioned piece of stone about the size of a tennis ball, made with a shallow groove around its circumference.

When two or three such balls are connected together by leather thongs the bolas provided the Indians with a formidable weapon for use in the chase and for war. When whirled above the head and then released the bolas would strike and truss the legs of an animal or an enemy, and bring them to the ground. Darwin tried his hand at throwing the bolas but he only entangled the thongs around the legs of his own horse. As he recorded in the *Voyage of the Beagle*, 'The gauchos roared with laughter; they cried that they had seen every sort of animal caught, but had never before seen a man caught by himself'[7] Charles Darwin was dreadfully clumsy.

From Bahía Blanca the *Beagle* returned to the Río de la Plata, leaving the schooners to their survey work. *Harrier* and I, however, continued on southward. I had been warned off my next port of call, Viedma on the Río Negro, by Marcos of the Yacht Club Sudeste in Buenos Aires. He recommended 'NOT ENTERING Viedma. It is not buoyed and is surrounded by shifting sandbanks'.

I remembered, too, the experience of William Hudson in these waters. The first chapter of his best-known book, *Idle Days in Patagonia,* describes an adventure that was far from idle. One stormy night in 1905 he was on passage from Buenos Aires to the Río Negro aboard 'a very curious boat, reported ancient and much damaged; long and narrow in shape like a Viking's ship, with passenger's cabins ranged like a row of small wooden cottages on the deck: it was ugly to look at and it was said to be unsafe to voyage in.'[8]

Carmen de Patagones

To judge from his account, the ship struck a shoal at night in Bahía San Blas, about thirty miles north of the entrance to the Río Negro. The crew became paralysed by panic but the Atlantic swell lifted the unmanaged ship over the bank and into calmer sheltered water. Here, when she drifted onto a beach in the middle of nowhere, Hudson and three other passengers were able to wade ashore.

It took them three days to walk across dry, uninhabited savanna country to the town of Carmen de Patagones on the north bank of the river. Carmen, now the twin town of the provincial capital Viedma which lies on the south bank, was important in Darwin's travels and I particularly wanted to pay it a visit. In the 1830s Carmen was the most southerly Spanish settlement in Argentina.

Without the advice of a local pilot and the assistance of the American GPS system I would not have dared to ignore Marcos's advice, nor to forget the experience of Hudson, by taking *Harrier* into the Río Negro. However, weather and tidal conditions were perfect when I arrived off the river on 18th January and my entrance went smoothly. Once inside I found myself in a sheltered shallow river about the width of the Thames at Westminster.

There were wide reed beds on the south while the north bank was lined with willows, banks of pampas grass and clumps of alder and Lombardy poplar. Behind the trees were low hills covered with brown Patagonian scrub. Barely a house was in sight. Flocks of burrowing parrots and roadside hawks flew overhead while *Harrier* and I were inspected by a party of five black-necked swans. These ornamental creatures look like the products of a high-art porcelain workshop. I remained at anchor in this piece of paradise for a day before sailing 15 kilometres up the river to Carmen and Viedma.

At the end of her second cruise from the Río de la Plata, to Tierra del Fuego and the Falkland Islands, the *Beagle* returned to Maldonado. There, in April 1833, the beagle caught the hare and she took back aboard the weather-beaten men from the *Leibre*. She then sailed back to the Río Negro to recover the men aboard the *Paz*.

The casualties on the voyage of the *Beagle* were few for such a high-risk undertaking. However, her crew suffered two losses during this time in the south. At East Falkland the ship's clerk, Edward Hellyer, had drowned while swimming in kelp encumbered water in an effort to recover a duck he had shot. One of the marines, Corporal Williams had fallen overboard from the *Paz* during the night while she was at anchor in the Río Negro. His body was found the next day three miles downstream.

At the Río Negro FitzRoy settled, at his own expense, the large sum which was due to Harris and Roberts for the use of the schooners. He had assumed, without confirmation, that because of the success of the surveying work of the schooners, the Admiralty would re-imburse his costs. It turned out that the Lords of the Admiralty refused to pay, and FitzRoy was left to pick up the bill himself.

Darwin was amazed that boats as small as the schooners could survive the winter weather at sea and still conduct an accurate survey:

> To survey an unknown coast in a vessel of 11 tuns, & with one inch plank to live out in the open sea the same gale in which we lost our whale-boat, was no ordinary service. It seems wonderful that they should last one hour in a heavy gale, but it appears the very insignificance of small vessels is their protection, for the sea instead of striking them sends them before it.[9]

I know the feeling.

At the mouth of the Río Negro Darwin left the *Beagle* and sailed with Harris up the river to Carmen de Patagones. From Carmen he set out on a ride of geological exploration to Buenos Aires and on to Santa Fe. The ride would, in FitzRoy´s words, 'satisfy even his love of adventure.'[10] Perhaps FitzRoy was a little envious of Darwin's freedom to roam. He wrote to his sister Frances that Darwin was;

> a good pedestrian, as well as a good horseman; he is a sensible, shrewd, and sterling good fellow. While I am pottering about the water, measuring depths and fixing positions, he wanders over the land - and frequently makes long excursions where I cannot go, because my duty is Hydro- not Geo-graphy.[11]

Both FitzRoy and Darwin considered themselves to be philosophical, or as we would say nowadays scientific, men. They were members of the last generation of English gentlemen who could unselfconsciously be occupied with serious scientific pursuits. After them the dead hand of Thomas Arnold and the English public school settled onto the neck of the British establishment. Thus began our long national decline under the control of the British amateur.

When Darwin arrived at Carmen he learned that the settlers had recently had all their cattle rustled by raiding parties of Araucanian Indians. This bellicose people had occupied, since ancient times, the southwestern part of the Andes mountains. They had repulsed in war the Incas and subsequently the Spanish conquistadors. They thought nothing of attacking places hundreds of kilometres from their home territory. The Araucanians drove the cattle stolen from the Río Negro across the Andes and sold them to other Spanish settlers in central Chile.

At the time of the *Beagle's* visit to South America a ferocious territorial war was in progress in Patagonia. Detachments of the Argentine army had been sent south from Buenos Aires for the purpose of breaking the power of the Indian tribes. Every adult Indian captured in battle was shot or sabred while children were sold into slavery. The Indians responded by cutting the throat of any European who fell into their hands. Darwin's route to Buenos Aires took him for 1000 kilometres through this bloodstained battlefield. He admired the plains Indians of Argentina, if not necessarily the ferocious Araucanians, as 'a tall exceedingly fine race' [12]. He was horrified at the war. 'Who would believe in this age in a Christian, civilized country that such atrocities were committed?'[13] Were Darwin to return to Earth today what, I wonder, he would think of our sanguinary modern world?

Darwin's journey would have been suicidal or impossible had he not received the help and protection of General Rosas, the commander of the Argentine army in the south. This larger-than-life individual was the leader of what Darwin thought was 'such a villainous, banditti-like army [as] was never before collected together'[14]. Rosas gave Darwin and his gaucho travelling companions the use of army horses and permission to shelter at army encampments along the way to Buenos Aires. With this safe-conduct in his pocket Darwin declared himself 'altogether pleased with my interview with the terrible general'.[15]

General Juan Manuel de Rosas
with his wife Encarnación

Darwin started for the north on 11th August 1833. He rode for three days from Carmen to reach the camp of General Rosas on the Río Colorado. Then for two more days to the fort at Bahía Blanca and for a further 13 days across the Pampas before reaching the city of Buenos Aires. A pampa is an extensive grassland devoid of trees – a prairie. Despite alarms about marauding Indians, he paused to climb most of the way up the Sierra de la Ventana, some 20 kilometres north of Bahía Blanca.

From his account, it seems that he and his party camped on the south side of the main Ventana massif. Next morning he walked up a secondary ridge, from which he could look down onto the Valle Intersierra separating him from the summit. Today Ruta Provincial 76 goes through the Intersierra. After searching the valley below for Indians with his telescope he descended and then climbed nearly to the summit of what are now known as the Tres Picos, of 1070 metres. He must have ascended about 1500 metres that day as well as walking some 15 kilometres in winter over very rough ground. Darwin was a fit young man in 1833.

With an undiminished appetite for adventure and geology he rode for a further seven days north from Buenos Aires, through country that was also threatened by Indian raids, to Santa Fe. He returned in greater safety as a passenger aboard a river boat down the Río Paraná. When he reached Buenos Aires he found that he was involved in a revolutionary war. Buenos Aires was surrounded by units of the Argentine army loyal to General Rosas. With much difficulty he and his assistant Symes Covington entered the city and obtained passage on a ship to take them to Uruguay. They rejoined the *Beagle* in Montevideo harbour on 4th November. By the end of 1833 Darwin was a hardened and experienced traveller.

One of the principles upon which I designed my voyage of the *Harrier* is that it should be conducted in as authentic a manner as possible. I followed the track of the *Beagle* as closely as I could and as far as possible I navigated under sail alone, as did the *Beagle*. In this way I hoped to be able to understand the thoughts and actions of a Royal Navy survey ship of the 1830s. Travel by a modern ship or in a yacht that is propelled by a motor would cloud the issue. However, I am unwilling and unable to follow my principle in connection with most of Darwin's journeys ashore. This was because on land he travelled on horseback.

If I ever mount a horse the animal will lower its head, one ear will fold forward and the other turn inward. A thought bubble appears above its tiny brain that reads 'I have got a complete idiot on my back this time. Lets see who is boss around here'. Just as Karen and I travelled by bus from Montevideo to Mercedes in Uruguay, so I decided that I would follow Darwin's route to Buenos Aires and Santa Fe sitting in a genuine bus seat rather than on an authentic saddle.

I travelled from Carmen de Patagones to Bahía Blanca, a five day ride for Darwin, in five hours on 22nd January. He described the country as far as the Río Colorado as a desert. Now the undulating landscape is a pattern of wheatfields, short dry pasture and some remaining patches of Patagonian scrubland. I passed through the small town of Pedro Luro, built on the site of General Rosas's camp of 1833. The delta of the Colorado, which extends for 90 kilometres at its frontage onto the sea, is nowadays intersected by a system of irrigation canals and ditches. All is grain fields, patches of horticulture and cattle grazing in grass up to their shoulders. The Río Colorado is usually taken to be the northern border of Patagonia.

Drier country then re-appeared all the way to Bahía Blanca. Here I was met again by my local contact, Antón. He looked after me most hospitably for three days, including driving me at first light to the foot of the Sierra de la Ventana (*Window Peak*). I walked up the mountain in the cool of the early morning. Wild flowers, of which I could identify only dandelions, carpeted the moorland. Higher up dwarf blackberries in fruit nestled amongst the rocks. Rufous-collared sparrows were everywhere and high-altitude white-rumped swallows swooped overhead. A herd of five guanaco paused from their grazing to look at me with weary expressions. Just another camera-toting tourist.

From the window through the summit ridge, from which the mountain takes its name, it was a short scramble to the top of the cerro at 1025 metres. I sat there for an hour feeling pleased with myself and admiring the view. Darwin thought that the view from the Ventana 'was nothing: the plain was like the ocean without its beautiful colour or defined horizon'[16] From the summit I looked out onto a vast level plain of pasture land, wheat fields and clumps of trees extending in all directions as far as the eye could see. Darwin, a native of the lush county of Shropshire, underestimated the ability of dry country to be brought under productive cultivation.

During my journey on to Buenos Aires and Santa Fe in the height of the southern summer I travelled through 1200 kilometres of what are known as the Humid Pampas. These flat well-watered lands are the breadbasket of Argentina. They contain the country's capital city and several large towns. For hour after hour huge fields of grain, vast fields of potatoes, sunflower and soya, together with rich pastures, forests and orchards passed by the windows of the coach. The productivity of the land was almost palpable. It seemed to me that Argentina could feed the world if she were given the chance.

At Santa Fe I discovered to my disappointment that passenger boats no longer ply the Río Paraná. No restful river journey nor fresh riverine scenery for me. So after three days in Santa Fe I retraced my journey by travelling the whole 1500 kilometres via Buenos Aires and Bahía Blanca by road in a coach. On 3rd February, the day before I reached Viedma, I received an e-mail from my stepmother Anne saying that she had arrived in Viedma, travelling north from Puerto Madryn in Patagonia.

In the Mustoe family some of the generations are out of synchronisation. Anne was my age. She had bicycled around the world twice, and her journeys were genuine journeys. No Land Rover full of support personnel or camera crew followed her. She travelled alone with what she could carry on the pannier of her bicycle. Anne had written five books about her adventures and was now in South America to reconnoitre her next trip.

I like to think of Anne as having stepped into the shoes of Freya Stark or as being the thinking man's Dervla Murphy. We spent two days in a comfortable Viedma hotel swapping stories and travel plans before she boarded her coach to Bahía Blanca and then over the Andes to Santiago in Chile. I returned to *Harrier's* cabin.

It was wonderful to meet again my long-time best friend and fellow restless traveller. Neither of us knew that it would be our penultimate farewell.

Chapter 8
Shipwreck

For a seaman, to scrape the bottom of the thing that's supposed to float all the time under his care is the unpardonable sin.....A blow on the very heart.
     Joseph Conrad *Heart of Darkness*, 1899

Every country in South America has a Río Negro. The Argentine Río Negro rises in the Cordillera Andes and after crossing the plains of Patagonia it flows between the twin cities of Viedma and Carmen de Patagones before discharging into the South Atlantic Ocean at 40°50' south. The water of the Patagonian Río Negro is in fact remarkably clean and is no more black than that of any other river. Viedma and Carmen both have well-patronised bathing beaches fronting their river. For a week I lay *Harrier of Down* off the jetty of the Club Náutico la Ribera, in an eastern suburb of Viedma, while awaiting the arrival of a parcel of mail from England.

At the end of February 2004, in the height of the southern summer, I got my anchor and dropped down on the ebb tide beneath the old railway bridge and under a long span of electricity cables hanging not very far above my masthead. The mouth of the river, where I brought up to await high tide over the bar, is 15 kilometres downstream from Viedma. At my anchorage no building was to be seen.

The seaward end of the Río Negro is encumbered with shifting, unmarked sandbanks. It is possible, however, to keep to the channel provided shore marks were observed and a close watch was kept on the echo-sounder. All went well for my exit in the morning. On a sunny day, I emerged into deep ocean water, turned to starboard and headed for Tierra del Fuego more than 900 miles to the south. Intermediate stops were planned for Puerto Deseado, Puerto San Julián and the Río Santa Cruz. Although I had been sailing on the sea for more than 40 years this departure towards the extreme south induced in me a certain foreboding and a mild fluttering of the heart.

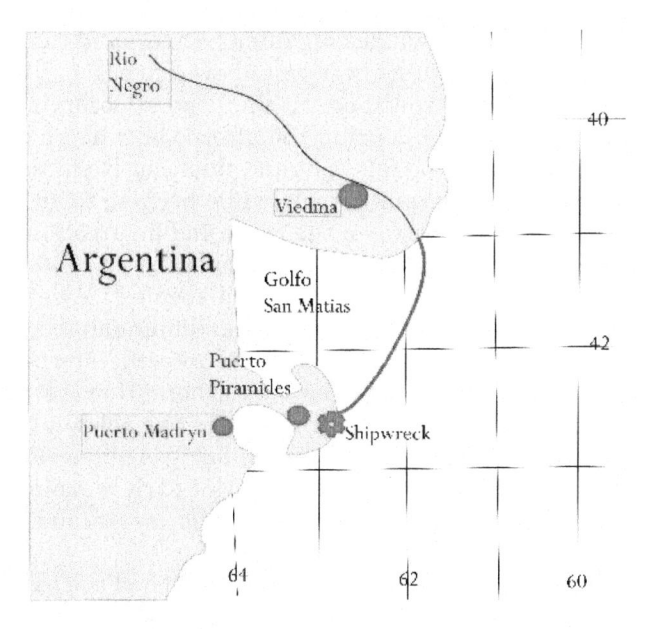

A north-easterly breeze carried me comfortably on towards the Peninsula Valdés. *Harrier* was a Folksong hull, a close copy of the Folkboat design, that I had modified under the influence of Blondie Hasler's famous *Jester*. Her single junk sail was a very efficient rig when the wind was coming over the quarter. By dawn I had the lighthouse on Punta Norte in sight.

The Peninsula Valdés is a piece of arid plain that projects from the trend of the Patagonian coastline for about 110 kilometres out into the Atlantic Ocean. The whole peninsula is nowadays a huge nature reserve containing only some widely scattered sheep farms and the village of Puerto Pirámides.

Two large gulfs, the Nuevo and the San José, cut into its south and north coasts. Aerial photographs seem to show that the peninsula was once struck by a large two-part meteorite. The two gulfs look like the principle impact craters while the broken landscape around them was formed by the fall of smaller fragments. During the *Beagle's* voyage Darwin came up with a number of novel and quite speculative geological theories, many of them confirmed later on. Perhaps my speculation too will be proven to be correct one day.

The warmer waters of the two gulfs provide a sheltered breeding ground for the southern right whale. Sea elephants, fur seals, sea lions and killer whales are often seen around the coast and flocks of Magellanic Penguins nest just above the beach. I decided to sail southwards close to the shore in the hope of observing some of these creatures of the sea. During the afternoon, when I was about ten miles offshore, the wind fell light and then slowly shifted into the south. In the evening I began to tack, while keeping to an avenue of relatively smooth water between the coast and an area of tidal overfalls further out to sea. This was my first mistake.

By midnight I was on port tack and keeping a careful lookout ahead. The seaward coast of Valdés is low and uninhabited, and I was well aware that I must shortly go about onto the starboard tack. There were no lights or marks to be seen ashore. However, I seemed to be safely in 35 metres of water when I went below to put fresh batteries into the ship's torch. I possess a fairly well-developed sense of impending danger but on this night my early-warning instinct deserted me. The excursion below deck was my second and fatal mistake.

I rummaged in a forward locker in search of the batteries. As I was inserting the batteries into the torch I heard a sudden noise from the bows that I shall never forget. A loud crunch was followed by a sweeping, hissing noise. I dashed for the hatch. Had I collided with a floating tree, or a fishing boat? I looked out and saw that we were in surf and that the waves were heeling *Harrier* onto on a steep shingle beach. 'Good God, what have I done? What have I done?'.

I threw the rubber dinghy out of the hatch and pumped it up on the beach. It was just possible to launch the dinghy through the surf and take a kedge anchor out into deeper water. Back on board it became clear that the tide was falling rapidly. It was impossible to pull *Harrier* off with the kedge line. I fired four red parachute flares and I called for help on my VHF radio. There was no response. I learned later that I had run aground at the very top of the highest spring tide of the month on the most remote part of the coast of Patagonia.

Daylight returned at 0600. I found that we were ashore on a straight featureless beach which stretched north and south as far as the eye could see. *Harrier* was heeled onto her starboard side with her bow pointing to the south. Her keel was now embedded half a metre into the shingle but she seemed to be undamaged. I spent the morning digging something like a ton of shingle away from her keel so as to form a channel leading back into the water. At the mid-day high tide

I tried to pull her off with the line to the kedge anchor. It was again impossible to move her.

In late afternoon, I went ashore and set off on foot to search for help. The Peninsula Valdés measures about 80 kilometres north to south and more than 100 kilometres east to west. The land is dry and covered with stones, pebbles and low thorny shrubs. It is a nature reserve of international significance. I did not then know that, apart from a few widely separated estancias, or sheep farms, the peninsula is uninhabited. I walked until dusk when I lay down beside a gravel track to recover my strength for another kilometre or two of walking. It began to look as if I should have to spend the night out in the wilds, an object of interest to the vultures circling overhead.

I looked up when I heard the crunching sound of a car approaching along the track. It was a four-wheel drive Isuzu pick-up truck. As it drew alongside I hailed the blue-eyed girl who was behind the steering wheel. 'Stop! Stop!'. She drove past, looking me straight in the eye. 'Stop! Stop! Please, please!'. The car halted a few metres further along the track. Without leaving the wheel she said in English, 'This is a nature reserve. You are not supposed to be here'. 'I know', I replied, 'I am here because of an emergency. My sailing boat is stranded on the beach over there': I did not notice that her companion, another girl, had got out of the other side of the car and that she was holding a large hunting knife behind her back. They consulted one another in Spanish and evidently concluded that I was honest and not dangerous. They took me into the car and gave me some water. I was so thirsty that drinking the water made a burning sensation at the back of my mouth.

Maria and Victoria were sisters who own one of the Valdés estancias, La Irma. They were out in their pick-up to check the condition of the wind pumps that supply drinking water for their sheep. It is a journey that they make no more frequently than every week or ten days, and no other people ever come to such a remote spot. We drove about 12 kilometers back to their estancia, a distance that I was too exhausted to walk even had I known of its existence. Maria and Victoria saved my life. Peninsula Valdés is large, dry and stony, and there are few people around. You could die in the wilderness without anyone knowing. My bones might still be there.

I spent the night at La Irma but I could not sleep for feelings of remorse and anxiety. Next morning Victoria and Maria drove me for an hour and a half in their pick-up truck to the nearest town. Puerto Pirámides is sited on a small protected cove on the northeast side of the Golfo Nuevo. There are a number of boats here which could have been used to refloat *Harrier* but the owners all refused to help. They said that it was a matter for the government coastguard service, the Prefectura Naval Argentina, and it was not for them to get involved. Victoria tried to persuade the Prefectura to send a party to the beach, but they would do nothing until they had obtained written permission to proceed from Buenos Aires. That would not be available until the next day.

With the help of Victoria and Maria I gathered together a band of helpers from the Pirámides volunteer fire brigade, or bomberos, and some helpful local men. One man from the Prefectura accompanied us out to the beach. *Harrier* was lying on the shingle as before and was still undamaged despite an appreciable surf. We dug a large trench under her keel towards the sea and awaited high tide and the Prefectura launch. This boat did come into sight but, but despite an adequate depth of water, she would not come near the beach. At six o'clock everybody left and the launch disappeared from the horizon.

I decided to spend the night in *Harrier* and I went aboard my stricken boat. I closed all the hatches and waited. High tide in the middle of the night reached us but did not float *Harrier*. At the highest water she was rocked from side to side for about three hours by the surf while her keel remained stuck in the shingle. The motion was most violent as she crashed onto the beach first on one side and then on the other. In the morning I went on deck and found that the mast had snapped off a metre above the deck. Feeling rather battered mentally and physically I stepped onto the beach and sat on the shingle in the grey early light. I looked at my beautiful crippled boat lying on her side. The mast and sail were half buried in shingle and a crack had appeared on her port topside. 'No, no, no, no!', but it was clear that *Harrier* was doomed.

At midday, as I was trying to free the mast and sail from the accumulating shingle, a party of five Prefectura arrived with Victoria and Maria. The men surveyed the situation, conferred in Spanish, and departed. The girls then took me in their pick-up to a small hotel in Pirámides. Late that afternoon we went to the office building of the Pirámides Prefectura. An officer had arrived from the main office in Puerto Madryn 50 kilometres away. With the help of Stephen, a Spanish speaking American scuba diver living locally, we arranged that the Prefectura would send a strong party of men to the beach the next day. They said that their launch would be in attendance and would pass a long line ashore with which to pull *Harrier* off.

When I got to the beach with Victoria and Maria it was clear that the Prefectura were making a complete mess of the job. No trench had been dug under *Harrier's* keel. At high water the men began a futile effort to shove *Harrier* into deeper water against the resistance of her embedded keel. The result was as I had warned. The surf breaking against Harrier's hull pushed her back up the beach with a force that no human strength could oppose. Just outside the surf a small RIB from the Prefectura was trying to assist with a line to *Harrier's* bow. They might just as well not have bothered, for one of its two small outboard motors was not working.

While this farce was going on the Prefectura launch stayed on the horizon more than a mile away. With a rise of the four metre tide there was in fact plenty of water to take their boat right up to the beach. Her engines had the power to pull *Harrier* into the water against the force of the surf but her captain would not come near to help.

The stricken *Harrier* with the author

During the next two days Harrier's hull began to give way. Two large cracks appeared in her sides below the waterline where she struck the shingle as she was pounded by the surf. By now she might well have sunk even had the Prefecture succeeded in refloating her. I removed as many things as possible from her cabin and stacked them on the beach above the reach of the waves. The men of the Prefectura departed and Victoria and Maria went to their pick-up truck 500 metres away to wait for me. I stood in the surf alongside *Harrier* and put my hand onto her deck. 'Goodbye Harrier. I loved you and I have let you down'. I climbed the slope to the top of the lonely beach, looked back at my stricken boat, and wept.

I had made a stupid mistake and put *Harrier* onto the beach. The Prefectura, from incompetence and cowardice, had failed to rescue her. A few days later *Harrier's* hull was reduced to fragments by the waves of an Atlantic storm beating onto the Valdés beach. I returned to Buenos Aires dogged by guilt and remorse and convinced that my voyage around the world had been cut short.

The wreckage of *Harrier*

The loss of *Harrier* was like a bereavement. Death, of a boat or of a person, is final. However, some of her equipment could be salvaged and it was stored in a barn at La Irma. I travelled back to Buenos Aires where I stayed for a few days in a troubled and distressed state of mind. My voyage was over, my plans for the future gone and the ambition of a lifetime set at nought. And it was all my fault.

When my step-mother Anne learnt of the disaster she at once offered to help me to buy another boat. My immediate response was to ask her to take time to think carefully about committing herself to such an expensive step. She came back a few days later with a renewed offer of help. My life took another, and more hopeful, turn.

After a prolonged search I found a small yacht moored in the marina of the Yacht Club Argentino at San Fernando, in the northern part of the city. She was affordable and she could be readily adapted to ocean voyaging.

In the same way as putting up or converting a building, so constructing or converting a yacht always takes twice as long and costs twice as much as was planned. My new boat was no exception to this rule. For 18 months I lived in the suburb of San Isidro while working on my new boat. I found the manual work therapeutic. As the conversion of the new *Harrier* progressed my feelings of regret and remorse slowly abated. The hand can help to heal the heart. At last, on 15th October 2005, I launched her at the marina of the riverside Club Nautico Sudeste in San Isidro. In the evening I organized a small party of my most faithful helpers. My lovely landlady Adriana agreed to perform the launching ceremony. She poured a bottle of champagne over *Harrier's* bow. With the new boat afloat my project was re-launched and the future opened up.

The new *Harrier* was slightly larger than the old. She was a quarter-tonner designed to the International Offshore Rule by Doug Peterson of San Diego and built in 1981. I converted her from racing to cruising by taking a metre off the length of the mast and re-rigging her as a cutter. She was equipped with a wind vane steering gear, a solar panel and wind generator on a stern gantry and a heavy anchor and chain on her bows. Her hull was a classic modern fin keel design, and despite the extra weight that I added, much of it on the ends of the boat, she continued to sail very beautifully. I painted her yellow and she became the very image of a strong, dainty ocean cruising yacht.

Chapter 9
Argentina

Probably the most impressive characteristic of Patagonia is the sense of limitless space and freedom:
Sophie Blacksell, *Patagonia*, 2005

At 0900 on 6th December 2005 I said goodbye to my friend and helper Carlos at the Yacht Club Argentino marina at Darsena Norte in Buenos Aires. I sailed the new *Harrier of Down* the 20 miles across the Río de la Plata to Colonia del Sacramento in Uruguay. There we spent eight days alongside the quay at the Puerto Deportivo.

On the night of the first time that I tried to leave Colonia for the Atlantic ocean, I ran into a gale from the southeast. As the wind rose I was floating in a mere four metres of water and the rocky shore of Uruguay was only eight miles to leeward. Forty knots of wind came out of a clear sky as I coped with matters on the heaving deck in bright moonlight. On my second attempt to leave, I was greeted by the well-known cigar shaped cloud coming up high in the sky from the west. Soon the pampero was upon me. The sky darkened with thunder and lightning were all around, rain poured down and powerful gusts of wind arrived from every direction. All was over in an hour and a half. The weather seemed to be tempting me out from shelter only to give me a pasting. I began to understand why the Río de la Plata was known to the old Spanish navigators as *El infierno de los marineros*.

I tried to get out of the Río de la Plata for the third time on 16th December. I worked *Harrier* slowly east against moderate contrary winds and reached Buceo, the yacht harbour of Montevideo, at 2300 on the 17th of December. Here I found that a strong wind, now from the west, made it difficult to enter the harbour. I therefore sailed a mile further on and anchored in sheltered water off the holiday beach of the suburb of Trouville. It was as well that I lay down in my bunk without taking off my oilskins. An hour later I woke to hear the wind generator screaming. I rushed on deck to find that the wind had suddenly swung through 180 degrees and was now blowing strongly towards the beach. I got under way before the seas had time to build and motored between the harbour entrance lights into the security of Buceo. Here a boatman of the Yacht Club Uruguayo showed me to a good mooring. I sat in the cockpit for half an hour with a glass of wine in my hand watching the waves sending clouds of spray over the breakwater, while a flock of gulls wheeled and soared overhead in the wind.

In 1832 and 1833 the *Beagle* made her second and third voyages south to Tierra del Fuego from the Río de la Plata. Her course during these trips was complicated. In these years she called at the Falkland Islands twice and retraced her track several times because of the needs of the survey. My plan was to take *Harrier* to all the places in the south, except the Falkland Islands, Cabo de Hornos and the eastern half of the Estrecho de Magellanes, that were visited by the *Beagle* but in geographical sequence, and without following all her backtracking and diversions.

During the first and second voyages to the south FitzRoy had found that the *Beagle* was too small to carry sufficient stores for a cruise of more than a few months duration. While his ship was at the Falklands during her second trip south he therefore decided to buy out of the sealing trade, on his own recognizance, a 170-ton schooner. She was taken back to Maldonado in Uruguay where she was refitted to serve as a tender to the expedition. For her third, and longest, trip to the south the *Beagle* had a consort. She was renamed *Adventure* in memory of one of the ships that had taken part in the *Beagle's* earlier survey of the late 1820s.

After ten days meeting old friends in the charming land of Uruguay I departed from Buceo and headed for the south in full earnest. At first all went well. The breeze was favourable, the colour of the water changed from brown to blue, and mollymawks and white-chinned petrels skimmed the waves. A sealion thrust his round snout into the air on my port side and looked at me with watery brown eyes. Or was this a specimen of Bill Tilman's Giant South Atlantic Sea Frog? Early on New Year's Day 2006 *Harrier's* wind vane steering gear lost control of the rudder. Inspection showed that part of the control linkage had failed and was now on its way to the bottom of the ocean. I diverted to Mar del Plata 100 miles away and arrived at the marina belonging to the Yacht Club Argentino at 1000 on 2nd January.

By good fortune, my friend Marcos Gallagher was on holiday at his family estancia of San Cornelio, only an hour's drive outside the town. With his help I was able to obtain spares and repair the steering gear. Nothing went wrong on the next leg of the journey to Puerto Deseado 760 miles to the south. With the aid of an Argentine large-scale harbour plan I entered the river on 2nd February. Here I picked up a mooring opposite the Club Nautico Capitan Oneto. I was escorted to my mooring by two pretty little black-and-white Commerson's dolphins. *Harrier* lay there for two weeks, not half a mile from the spot where the *Beagle* and the *Adventure* had anchored for 27 days in December 1833 on their third and final voyage south from the Río de la Plata.

At Deseado *Harrier* was joined by crew. Stephen is an American wildlife photographer who lived in Argentina. I had met him in Puerto Pirámides at the time of the wreck of the first *Harrier*. He spoke fluent Spanish and was familiar with the ways of boats. His experience of sailing yachts was limited but he was very keen to make an ocean passage under sail. He arrived on board an awesome collection of underwater cameras and flash guns. He at once set about photographing *Harrier* and her adventures with great energy and enthusiasm. He also brought a wet suit and diving gear, and showed himself to be fully aquatic.

Stephen

During her stay at Puerto Deseado, the *Beagle* made the first accurate charts of the river and its estuary. Darwin explored ashore as much as he could. In company with Edward Chafers, the master of the *Beagle*, he made a boat trip as far up the Río Deseado as the shallowness of the water would allow. The spot where they camped is known today as el Mirador Darwin. My local contact, Marcos Olivia

Day, arranged for us to visit the Mirador by land. We travelled in a four-wheel-drive pick-up truck 45 kilometres to an estanacia, Paso Cerro, built at the head of a small green valley leading down to the main river. We walked for an hour downstream beside the river before reaching the site of Darwin and Chafers' camp. The place was clearly identifiable from the painting made at the time by the ship's artist, Conrad Martens.

El mirador Darwin

When we returned to the pick-up I read aloud to the group an extract from Darwin's diary.

> The plain, as is universally the case, is formed of sandy chalk, & gravel, from the softness of these materials it is worn & cut up by very many vallies. – There is not a tree, &, excepting the Guanaco, who stands on some hill top a watchful sentinel over his herd, scarcely an animal or a bird. – All is stillness and desolation. One reflects how many centuries it has thus been & how many it will thus remain.[1]

As I read his words, I pointed to the crest of a hill on the other side of the river. There, silhouetted against the sky, stood a lone guanaco watching over his herd.

A guanaco. The animal is about the size of a deer. It is related to the lama, and distantly related to the Old World camels.

    Marcos, who is a lawyer and retired judge, returned us to the town at the end of a day full of fascinating history. Marcos, I should say, has navigated the coast of Patagonia not in the comfort of a yacht but by kayak. Furthermore, he has rounded Cabo de Hornos (*Cape Horn*) in his kayak. Some people make one feel by comparison a bit of a wimp.

    When leaving Puerto Deseado on 4th January 1834 the *Beagle* struck heavily on a rock 'which is not far from mid-channel, just without the entrance'.[2] FitzRoy and Chafers dived under the vessel to assess the damage. Part of her false keel and some of the copper sheathing had been torn away. They both emerged from the cold water with cuts from the jagged copper plates. Since the *Beagle* had sprung no leak she continued out to sea.

    The rock the *Beagle* struck was afterwards named Roca Beagle. It remained an acute danger to navigation until it was blown up by the Armada Argentina in 1963. After surveying the coast to the south of Puerto Deseado the *Beagle* arrived at Puerto San Julián, in 48 degrees south. *Harrier* followed in her track and sailed into the river on 20th February 2006.

In the year 1520 Fernando de Magallanes (anglicized to *Magellan*) nearly lost his life in a mutiny, while his fleet wintered at San Julián. He executed two of the ringleaders, Juan de Cartegena and Pedro Sancho de Reina, on what is now called Punta Gallows, across the river from the modern town. The grisly reputation of the place was enhanced when, in 1582, Francis Drake had Thomas Doughty beheaded for theft. Nobody mutinied on the *Beagle*, nor did Stephen mutiny aboard *Harrier*. Indeed, Stephen loved small remote places and he spent many happy hours exploring the town and meeting the members of the Club Nautico el Delfin.

In the days of Magellan the country was sparsely inhabited by nomadic Indians. They were large men with loud voices and a fearsome reputation as fighters. They reminded the Spaniards, who were small men, of the giant Patagón, a character in a popular romance of the time, *Primaleón de Grecia*. The *Primaleón* was the *Harry Potter* tales of its time. Patagón has given his name to nearly the whole of southern part of South America.

The giant Patagón with his bolas

In January 1834 the *Beagle* sailed from Puerto San Julián to Tierra del Fuego (*Land of Fire*) and the Falkland Islands before returning to Patagonia at the Río Santa Cruz, arriving on 13th March.

Harrier sailed directly down the coast and anchored in the river off the little town of Santa Cruz on 25th February.

'It's a pity that we don't have the time to visit the Falklands. I would like to see them and you could get some good pictures of the islands, the fauna and the war sites', I said to Stephen.

'Did you know that the UN calls them the Falklands/Malvinas?', he replied. Stephen sympathised with the feelings of many people in his adopted country.

'Yes. And while I am in Argentina I refer to them in the same way. I am a guest here and I wish to be a good guest. But aboard Harrier and elsewhere they are the Falkland Islands.'

'Every Argentine is taught at school, by direction of the government, that the islands are theirs and that the British are invaders', he answered.

'I know. But Spain abandoned her claim to the islands in the 1770s, before there was an Argentina. France evacuated her settlement at Port Louis in 1767. Our claim is sound in law and the Falklands are secure in our possession. Furthermore the people like it that way.'

'Well maybe, but I can see how the Argentines think that islands close to their country must belong to them.', Stephen said.

'Perhaps. But on that argument the Channel Islands belong to France, St. Pierre and Miquelon belong to Canada and Australia belongs to Indonesia. History, as well as geography, has its claims.'

Stephen and I tacitly agreed to leave it at that.

At Santa Cruz we were most cordially and generously welcomed by the people and by the captain, officers and ratings of the Prefectura. Few yachts enter the river in any year and none of these were much concerned with the history of the place. We found that people were as interested in the voyage of the *Harrier* as we were in the part that the town played in the voyage of the *Beagle*.

The Río Santa Cruz is the largest river in Argentine Patagonia south of the Río Chubut, some 610 miles to the north. In April and early May 1834 FitzRoy and Darwin together with 23 officers and sailors embarked in three whaleboats on a trip intended to reach the headwaters of the river. The river current was too fast for the boats to sail against it. Shoulder harnesses were made and everyone, including FitzRoy himself, took his turn to march along the bank of the river, hauling the heavy boats upstream. They made their way slowly westward until, after 17 days of work, their provisions began to run low. They were about 150 miles from the Atlantic and within sight of the Andes but they were obliged to turn back. Had they continued upstream for a few days more they would have been the discoverers of Lago Argentino, the largest freshwater lake in Argentina.

While the river party was away inland, the *Beagle* was laid ashore on a wide beach near what is now known as Punta Quilla (*Keel Point*), on the port hand near the entrance to the Santa Cruz estuary. Here she was hove down and the damage sustained at Puerto Deseado was repaired. Jonathan May, the ship's carpenter, and his team completed the work within a single tide. He is one of the unsung heroes of the voyage of the *Beagle*. Conrad Martens' most famous image of the voyage illustrates the repair of the *Beagle's* hull at Punta Quilla.

Beagle at Punta Quilla

The Río Santa Cruz was wide and fast running, the town was small and clings to its position on the south shore, the land on either bank was flat, featureless and unbounded while the large sky over all seemed to extend in every direction to infinity. The place appeared to be set apart from the rest of the earth and contemplating it induced long thoughts in the mind of the beholder. Darwin observed of the Patagonian landscape at Puerto Deseado that 'in this scene without one bright object there is a high pleasure, which I can neither explain or comprehend.'[3]

The distance from the mouth of Río Santa Cruz to Estrecho de le Maire, separating Isla de los Estados (*Island of the States*) and the eastern end of Tierra del Fuego, is 350 miles. We left the river on a sluicing ebb tide on 4th March and set sail to the southeast with a chilly but favourable westerly wind. By 7th March we were 80 miles off the eastern entrance to Estrecho de Magellanes. The barometer began to fall rapidly and the wind rose. By evening it was blowing a full gale from the west. We were now in 53 degrees south latitude and the wind was cold.

Before the gale

We hove-to under bare poles and I set a drogue from *Harrier's* bow. She rode over the four and occasionally five metre seas like a duck.

Everyone finds that his first gale at sea in a small boat is a memorable experience. Stephen was greatly impressed by the raw power that is stored in a train of large wind-driven waves. After the wind had moderated and backed to the southwest we remained hove-to in order to allow the seas to go down. Seas resulting from a gale are at their most dangerous as the wind moderates, when a shift in the direction of the wind can produce a large and very confused cross-swell.

After the gale

Early in the morning of 11th March the skyline of the Peninsula Mitre at the eastern end of the island of Tierra del Fuego was in sight. We drew near to scenery very different from Patagonia. In place of sterile plains we saw high mountains covered with forests of Antarctic beech. After sailing round Cabo San Vicente we anchored for the night in the sheltered water of Bahía Thetis.

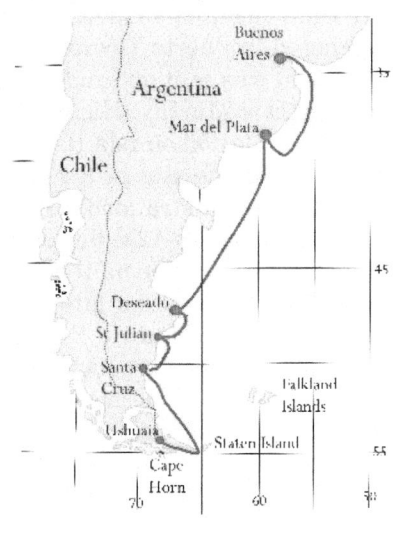

The next morning brought us fair weather. Conditions were reminiscent of a fine autumn day on the west coast of Scotland. The jagged profile of Isla de los Estados on our port hand was partly wreathed in cloud. We motored round Cabo San Diego and into Bahía Buen Suceso (*Good Success Bay*).

York Minster    Jemmy Button    Fuegia Basket

In the jargon of the Admiralty a supernumerary is a person aboard a naval vessel who is accommodated at public expense but who is not a member of the ship's crew. Darwin was one such, as was the ship's artist Conrad Martens and a young Anglican catechist, Richard Matthews.

Three other supernumeraries on board the *Beagle* at this time were a young man York Minster, a teenager Jemmy Button and Fuegia Basket, a girl about nine years old. These were the Fuegian Indians whom FitzRoy had taken captive during the first visit of the *Beagle* to Tierra del Fuego at the beginning of 1830.

FitzRoy had been appointed captain of the *Beagle* in December 1828 after the suicide of Pringle Stokes. In January 1830 the *Beagle* was anchored in Puerto Townsend at the eastern end of Isla London. A whaleboat was sent out under the command of the master of the *Beagle*, Matthew Murray. His task was to survey the neighbourhood of Cabo Desolatión on Isla Basket. One night the boat was stolen by Indians from the site of a remote bivouac on the island Murray and his men were stranded with little food and they were separated from the *Beagle* by 12 miles of exposed water. By making use of tree branches and a canvas tent they were able to devise a basket-like raft. Hence the name later given to the island and by extension the name given to Fuegia Basket. Aboard this improvised coracle, Murray and his crew were lucky enough to regain the *Beagle*.

FitzRoy searched for the stolen whaleboat for three weeks. Finally he took four young Fuegians onto the *Beagle* as hostages for its return. But their fellows ashore kept the boat in preference to the return of their compatriots. While awaiting the recovery of the whaleboat, which was never found, FitzRoy became interested in his captives. He formed the idea of taking them to England, educating them in 'English, and the plainer truths of Christianity, as the first objective: and the use of common tools, a slight acquaintance with husbandry, gardening and mechanism, as the second'.[4] They would then be returned to Terra del Fuego as the advance guard of civilisation. FitzRoy's plan was patterned on the traditional missionary recipe of the Bible and the plough.

Not long after their arrival in England, in 1830 one of the Fuegians, Boat Memory, died in Plymouth Royal Naval Hospital. His smallpox vaccination had failed to take. The remaining three, Jemmy Button, York Minster and Fuegia Basket escaped infection and took up board and lodging with the master of an infant school in Walthamstow. FitzRoy met all their expenses from his own pocket. Apart from an audience with King William IV and Queen Adelaide, their life in England was that of any school child. Jemmy Button and Fuegia Basket liked the life, but York Minster retreated into himself. He hated being taught to read and would only take a desultory interest in handiwork. Doubtless he felt self-conscious, at the age of about 26, at being included in a group of small school children.

While FitzRoy was pre-occupied with completing his *Beagle* duties and with providing for the Fuegians, a change of government policy took place at Westminster. In May 1831 he discovered that 'to my great disappointment an entire change has take place in the views of the Lords of the Admiralty, and that there was now no intention to prosecute the survey.'[5] Then, as today, Treasury cheeseparing damages the armed services as much as does enemy action. However, FitzRoy was willing and able to fight his corner.

His mother's elder brother Lord Londonderry, the third earl and a half-brother of Lord Castlereagh, may have been the 'kind uncle' who came to FitzRoy's rescue. The unidentified uncle pulled strings at the Admiralty to good effect. Another South American surveying voyage was quickly decided upon and on 27th June 1831 Londonderry's nephew was re-appointed to the command. The *Beagle* was re-commissioned and a thorough refit under FitzRoy's direction began at the Royal Naval Dockyard at Devonport. Six months later she sailed out into the English Channel at the beginning of her second, and most famous, surveying voyage. On board were the three Fuegian indians bound for their distant homeland.

When the *Beagle* entered Bahía Buen Suceso on 17th December 1832, on her second voyage south from the Rio de la Plata, she was greeted by stentorian shouts and many signal fires from Haush Indians on the hills on the north side of the anchorage. When he landed on the open beach the next day, Darwin encountered unacultured Fuegian Indians, their faces painted red and black, for the first time. He had admired the plains Indians of the Pampas but he was dismayed by the Haush.

> As soon as the boat came within hail, one of the four men who advanced to receive us began to shout most vehemently, & at the same time pointed out a good landing place. – The women & children had all disappeared. – When we landed the party looked rather alarmed, but continued talking and making gestures with great rapidity. – It was without exception the most curious & interesting spectacle I ever beheld - I would not have believed how entire the difference between savage and civilized man is. - It is greater than between a wild and domesticated animal, in as much as in man there is a greater power of improvement.[6]

It was unfortunate for Darwin's understanding that his first meeting with the Indians of the extreme south was with members of a destitute tribe. The Haush then numbered about 300 people[7] who eked out a living in the extreme southeast corner of Tierra del Fuego. They had been pushed from their ancestral territory by their more aggressive and successful neighbours, the Ona, to the west and north.[7] The Ona were also the hereditary enemies of the Yamana and the Alacaloof, the tribe to which the three supernumeraries belonged. FitzRoy records that while the *Beagle* was coasting further north they were hailed from the shore by parties of Ona Indians. 'York Minster and Jemmy Button asked me to fire at them, saying that they were "Oens-men - very bad men."'[8]

Fuegian Indian and his dog

    The year 1832 marked a turning point in Darwin's life. So many vivid observations of plants, animals, humans and nature generally had a powerful effect upon his inner life. In his autobiography he wrote that 'I remember when in Good Success Bay, in Tierra del Fuego, thinking (and I believe that I wrote home to the effect) that I could not employ my life better than in adding a little to Natural Science. This I have done to the best of my abilities, and critics may say what they like, but they cannot destroy this conviction.'[9] It was in the bleak environment of Tierra del Fuego that Darwin resolved his role in life as a scientist. Bahía Buen Suceso is an important locus in the history of science.

    The B*eagle* remained at Buen Suceso for four days. On 21st December 1832 she departed for the southern islands. A fair wind carried her to Cabo de Hornos (*Cape Horn*) where deteriorating weather persuaded FitzRoy to seek shelter in Bahía Saint Martin at the eastern end of Isla Hermite.

> Notwithstanding violent squalls and cold damp weather we kept our Christmas merrily: certainly, not the less so, in consequence of feeling that we were in a secure position, instead of being exposed to the effects of a high sea and heavy gale.[10]

Six days later, a year out from Barn Pool in Plymouth Sound, the *Beagle* left her snug anchorage and steered west towards Seno Christmas in an attempt to reach the home territory of York Minster and Fuegia Basket. After two weeks of struggling against strong westerly winds, the weather again deteriorated. FitzRoy records that during a violent storm;

> three huge rollers approached, whose size and steepness at once told me that our sea-boat, good as she was, would be sorely tried. ... the third great sea, taking her right abeam, turned her so far over, that all the lee bulwark, from the cat-head to the stern davit, was two or three feet under water. ... Had another sea then struck her the little ship might have been numbered among the many of her class which have disappeared: [11]

Beagle sorely tried

FitzRoy prudently decided to take the *Beagle* north to Paso Goree, a safe anchorage lying between Isla Navarino and Isla Lennox. The ship could be left at anchor there while the three Indians were taken to their homelands by boat through the sheltered waters of Canal Beagle and other channels westward.

When Stephen and I entered Bahía Buen Suceso 174 years after the *Beagle* there was no shouting nor any smoke signals from the shore. The radio carried a greetings message, at a normal speaking volume, from the five bored squadies who manned a small Armada Argentina station built just behind the beach at the head of the bay. *Harrier* spent two days at anchor in the bay. Stephen rowed ashore while I remained aboard to guard the boat. He discovered that the faces of the marines were painted neither red nor black, but his own face was smeared with sun-block. He walked up one of the surrounding hills, gave the marines a change of company and was presented with a piece of fresh beef from their freezer.

For all of my life I have been blessed with extremely sharp eyesight. However, during my vigil aboard *Harrier*, while Stephen explored ashore, I noticed for the first time that I could not focus my right eye clearly on distant objects. Things near at hand, such as a book being read, remained in clear view but the shore of the bay or the skyline further away above, appeared blurred when my left eye was shut. I recalled that the life of the mariner subjects him to a double dose of ultra-violet light. At sea solar radiation arrives directly through the air and it is also reflected onto one's body and eyes from the surface of the water. Ultra violet light is very bad for the lens and the retina of one's eyes and sunglasses do not provide a complete defense.

During a period of light winds and calms, Stephen and I motored *Harrier* along the south coast of Tierra del Fuego from Buen Suceso to Puerto Español and then on to Bahía Sloggett. Both bays provided reasonable shelter for the night. When we reached Cabo San Pío on 15th March, some ten miles west of Sloggett, the westerly wind became too strong to motor against. We anchored near the foot of some wooded cliffs just off a small stream, where I spent the night listening to gale force gusts of wind coming down from the land and howling through *Harrier's* rigging.

Calmer conditions returned by noon the next day. We got under way and soon we were abreast of the eastern end of Isla Picton and entering Canal Beagle. Away on the port hand Paso Goree came into view. In my mind's eye I saw the ghost of the *Beagle* lying there to her spectral anchor. More motoring brought us to the safe bay sheltering the historic estancia of Harberton. Although Harberton has nothing to do with the voyage of the Beagle, it was our first anchorage safe in all winds since Stephen had come aboard *Harrier*.

Harrier at Harberton

    Harberton was the first permanent European settlement to be made in Tierra del Fuego. An Anglican missionary, Thomas Bridges, established the estancia in 1886. His children, including his second son Lucas, were born in Tierra del Fuego. Lucas, together with his brothers and sisters, grew up with Yamana Indian children as playmates. After his father's early death he was adopted as an orphan by the fearsome Ona, whose territory lay in the forests just over the mountains to the north of Harberton.

    Lucas Bridges' autobiography, ***Uttermost Part of the Earth***, is one of the great books of the world. It includes an authoritative account of the life of the Ona, one of the last unacultured hunter/gatherer tribes to survive on the face of the earth. The estancia at Harberton remains in the possession of Thomas Bridge's descendants.

In the time of the *Beagle* the city of Ushuaia (a Yamana Indian name meaning *Bay Penetrating to the Westward*), did not exist. Today it is a busy tourist centre of 50,000 inhabitants. When the *Beagle* was in these waters the entire Indian population of Tierra del Fuego amounted to fewer than 10,000 people.

We took 24 hours to motor *Harrier* from Harberton to Ushuaia. As we approached the town before dawn we were blinded by the lights stretching across the head of the bay beneath the towering snowy mountains.

As Bill Tilman said of his approach to Montevideo aboard *Mischief* in 1955 'we began to experience one of the problems of entering a strange harbour at night, the picking out of the aids to navigation from among the even brighter aids to dissipation, the neon signs and coloured lights of bars, night clubs, and such like.'[12] At last we made out the port and starboard lights of the bay at Ushuaia and at 1000 we came alongside the pier maintained by the Asociacion Fueguina de Actividades Subacuaticas y Nautica, known for the sake of brevity as the Club AFASyN. Stephen threw a line ashore that was taken by Noel Marshall, a member of my club, the Royal Cruising Club, whose beautiful aluminium cutter *Sadko* was moored at the pier.

Stephen, alas, now had to leave Ushuaia and return to work. Aboard *Harrier* he was resourceful, tough and a good-humoured shipmate. I was sorry to see him leave - we made a good team.

Chapter 10
In the South

*Having a taste for strange country, I had long nursed
a strong desire to visit Southern Patagonia*
Eric Shipton, *Land of Tempest*, 1963

Ushuaia is the largest town on Isla Grande de Tierra del Fuego. It lies only 35 kilometres east of the Argentine border with Chile. The inhabitants of Ushuaia are largely occupied with fishing and catering for visitors. Skiers come in the winter and in the summer yachtsmen, yacht charterers and lovers of wild country arrive. The town itself is of little intrinsic interest, but it is the only place for hundreds of miles where a yacht can be repaired and maintained. I had intended to remain in Ushuaia for only three weeks.

Harrier and her equipment performed well on the voyage south from the Río de la Plata. In Tierra del Fuego, however, things started to go wrong. Troubles with the motor, the cooker and the cabin heater took many weeks to put right. Combustion machines are troublesome contraptions. After repairs I tried to leave Ushuaia in mid-July 2006 but further trouble with the motor's fuel system obliged me to return to the anchorage the same day. I then had the motor checked over thoroughly by the best diesel workshop in Ushuaia.

My time ashore and in the repair shops at the end of the world had its harsh moments. As my diary reveals.

1 April 2006
It was not a joke. Harrier was moored at the pier of the Club Nautico AFASyN in Ushuaia, outside a large steel ketch called Northanger. Northanger is about 15 metres long and a strong heavy boat. It was a fine autumn morning as I crossed Northanger's foredeck on my way ashore for some shopping and lunch in the town.

The pier of the AFASyN is a steel structure supporting a wooden boardwalk. Along either side of the boardwalk, at about 15 metre intervals, is a row of lamp-posts. Each consisted of a steel tube about 10 centimetres in diameter and some three metres high. On top of each was a glass globe containing a 100 watt light bulb.

Northanger was buffered from the dockside by large red fenders. In order to step ashore I had to pull her nearer to the dock. This is done by using your weight. By standing on her mooring lines, between her and the dock, you pull her sideways and this movement enables you to step ashore. So, while standing on one of Northanger's lines, I leaned over and grabbed a convenient lamp-post as a purchase to help me to step up onto the dock. A moment later I was struck a heavy glancing blow on the left side of my head as the lamp-post fell over and crashed onto Northanger's deck.

I was stunned but not so badly that I could not regain *Northanger's* deck. There I sat down, feeling slightly sick, on one of her deck boxes. Her people appeared, and not realising that I had received a nasty blow, they anxiously examined their damaged lifelines. They also noted that the welding at the base of the lamppost was rusted almost entirely away. After some 10 minutes I regained Harrier's cabin, where I lay down and rested. A large bump appeared on the side of my head and my left ear was slightly torn and was bleeding.

It was several days before I recovered my composure. I had time to grasp that had the lamp-post struck my head squarely, rather than with a glancing blow, I should probably have been knocked out. In that case I would have fallen unconscious into the water and drowned. A close call.

11 May 2006
This time I got ashore before fate struck her blow. It was just after dark on a day of thin drizzling rain. The downtown area of Ushuaia is cut off from the water of the bay by a busy road, Calle Maipu. Maipu is known locally as *la ruta*, the highway. I was standing at the edge of the pavement on the water side of Maipu before crossing the road and making my way uphill to an Internet café in the main street of the town, Calle San Martin.

I looked carefully to my left and right and, when there was a sufficient gap in the traffic in both directions, I crossed over the near lane. In the middle of the road, where there is no central reservation, I saw that the second lane of traffic was travelling towards me faster than I had expected. I turned to go back to the pavement. As I did so I realised that a small Ford Ka was upon me, and only three feet away. As the front bumper hit me the driver, a woman of about 30, managed to brake to a stop. I was thrown backwards onto the bonnet of the car and then, on a rebound, down onto the road. People immediately appeared from all directions and willing hands helped me to get back onto the pavement. I felt shaken, but in my mind I realised that I was lucky to be alive. Had the car stopped only one second later I should surely have been killed.

In a very short time the fire brigade, the police and an ambulance arrived. In retrospect I am impressed by the speed and efficiency of the Ushuaia emergency services. The ambulance parked just by me. I stood up, walked the few paces to the door of the ambulance and sat down in front of a doctor or paramedic. Despite our having few words in common, we were able to understand one another. He took my pulse and said that it was too rapid and that I should go with him to the hospital. He was a well-set-up man and I knew that I ought to pay attention to his opinion. But I also knew that, despite receiving a bad blow, I was not injured. I decided not to go to the hospital but instead to walk over to some friends, Nick and Jay, on their boat nearby and to look for some sympathy from them.

Before leaving the site of the accident I spoke to the driver, who was quite distraught. I said that I had made a mistake and that I did not blame her. A policeman took my name and passport number, and the crowd dispersed. I am writing this account in *Harrier's* cabin four days later. My bruises are still painful, but they get a little better each day. Upon reflection, I think that I had misjudged the flow of traffic because the cataract in my right eye has the effect of reducing my surroundings to a two-dimensional picture.

I have sometimes been asked by landsmen if it is not rather dangerous to be crossing the oceans in a small boat like *Harrier*. Next time that I receive this enquiry I shall tell of my near escapes in Ushuaia. I must get out of this town before I am struck by a meteorite or the sky falls down upon my head.

Eventually, recovered from my injuries and with an apparently fully functioning motor, *Harrier* and I departed eastward on 10th October 2006 for Puerto Williams, 25 miles away on the south side of Canal Beagle. I was escorted out of Argentine waters by a party of some 20 seals playing about the boat. In Darwin's time whales were commonly seen in these waters. Alas, they are rarely to be seen nowadays.

Puerto Williams on the northeastern corner of Isla Navarino is a port of entry to Chile. It was founded in 1953 as a base for the Armada de Chile in order to face down an Argentine claim to the small Chilean islands of Picton, Lennox and Nueva. Early in the afternoon I tied up alongside the small beached cargo ship that now houses the Yacht Club Micalvi. In 55 degrees south, it is the southernmost yacht club in the world. At Puerto Williams I was introduced to the onerous maritime bureaucracy administered by the Armada. There are very restrictive rules about where a yacht may go in these waters, an elaborate radio ritual is demanded and, of course, many pieces of paper must be signed, moved about and accounted for. Fortunately, compliance with these procedures is only casually supervised and the chinks in the system give the yachtsman room in which to breathe.

In 1833 on 19th January a party consisting of 27 people, including FitzRoy, Darwin, Matthews and the three Fuegians departed from the *Beagle*, leaving her anchored at the eastern end of Navarino. They travelled aboard three whaleboats and the yawl. The first night they spent in the cove that lies alongside the present Puerto Williams. The creek was known to the *Beagle* as Cutfinger Cove. 'This name was given because one of our party, Robinson by name, almost deprived himself of two fingers by an axe slipping with which he was cutting wood.'[1] The little fleet was rowed against the prevailing west wind from Paso Goree to Cutfinger Cove and on to Wulaia, a total distance of 75 miles, in four days.

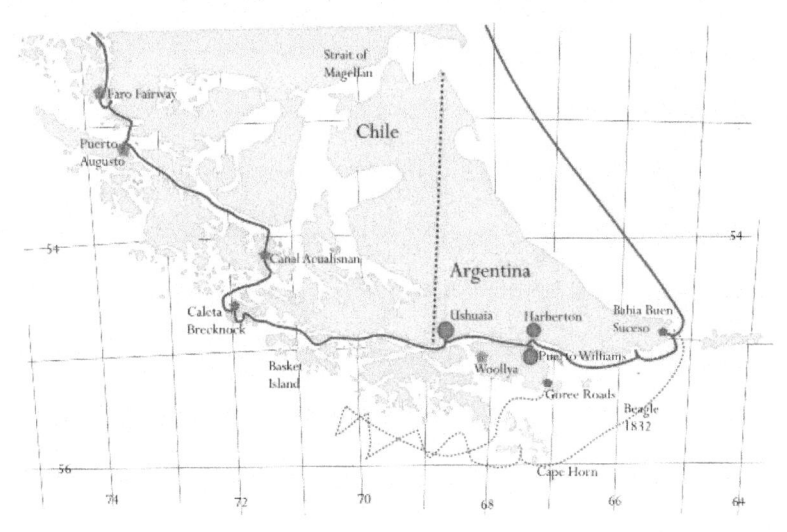

I was now ready to work my way westward through a maze of islands and intricate, rock strewn channels. After departing from Puerto Williams on 17th October 2006 I motored against a light westerly wind for a mere 18 miles to Caleta Melliones. A large cemetery lies on the east side of this bay where the land slopes gently down to the water. It is a melancholy monument to the encounter between a native population and the viruses of European diseases. Melliones is the last resting place of the Yamana people. The final graves there date from the 1950s.

Woollya, where the *Beagle* party arrived on 23rd January, is on Seno Ponsonby at the western end of Isla Navarino. It is, by Fuegian standards, well drained and well wooded. Woollya was Jemmy Button's home territory but not that of York Minster or Fuegia Basket. However, York Minster said to FitzRoy that he and Fuegia would rather stay at Woollya with Jemmy than return to their own country further westward. FitzRoy was pleased to think that his three protégés would remain together. 'I little thought', he records, 'how deep a scheme master York had in contemplation.'[2]

A camp of tents was established ashore. The Fuegians together with Richard Matthews landed, a vegetable garden was planted and three timber cabins built. One was for Matthews, one for Jemmy Button and the other for York Minster and Fuegia Basket. They had become attached to one another and intended to marry. At Woollya, York Minster began to build himself an unusually large canoe.

Woollya at the time of the *Beagle*

For some bizarre reason the Armada today will let only Chilean yachts enter Canal Murray or Seno Ponsonby. I was consequently prevented from visiting one of the most important sites to do with the voyage of the *Beagle*. Wulaia was an important location in the voyage of the *Beagle* and would very much liked to have seen it with my own eyes. However, I was obliged to sail by this piece of water and to go on westward to anchor for the night in Caleta Olla on the mainland of Tierra del Fuego. The next day the weather continued fine as I entered the Brazo Nordeste of Canal Beagle, leaving Isla del Diablo to port. I do not know how this island got its name - it does not look particularly devilish. Brazo Nordeste (*Northeastern Arm*) is on the itinerary of every cruise ship and charter boat in the south. It is between one and two miles wide and it runs in an almost straight line to the west for about 30 miles. Several spectacular beryl blue glaciers come down to the edge of its north shore.

Brazo nordeste, canal Beagle

I made good progress all morning along this scenic highway and arrived at Seno Pía in the middle of the afternoon. No sign of humanity was visible, while the surrounding mountains blocked VHF radio communications. I was now truly in the wilds. From my anchorage I looked north to the snout of the Ventisquero Romanche across half a mile of water strewn with small lumps of ice. Beyond the glacier, the mountainside rose into the clouds that hid the summits of the Cordillera Darwin from my view. I scooped a piece of glacier ice the size of a loaf of bread from the water. That evening I drank a whisky on some very old rocks.

Seno Pía, Ventiquero and the Cordilla Darwin

From Woollya FitzRoy sent the yawl and one of the whaleboats back to the *Beagle* at Paso Goree. He, Darwin and 12 men embarked in the other two whaleboats to row into the western channels. It was probably in Seno Pía that the voyage of the *Beagle* nearly came to an end. On 29th January the two whaleboats were drawn up on a beach near the snout of a glacier. The people were 200 yards away gathered round a fire cooking their lunch;

> when a thundering crash shook us - down came the whole front of the icy cliff - and the sea surged up in a vast heap of foam. ..... our whole attention was immediately called to great rolling waves which came so rapidly that there was scarcely time for the most active of our party to run and seize the boats before they were tossed along the beach like empty calabashes. .... had not Mr Darwin, and two or three of the men, run to them instantly they would have been swept away from us irrecoverably. Wind and tide would soon have drifted them beyond the distance a man could swim; and then, what prizes they would have been for the Fuegians.[3]

The *Beagle* was 100 miles away from Seno Pía. The nearest source of outside help was in the Falkland Islands more than 500 miles to the east. To the north, the inhabited island of Chiloe was 700 miles distant. Had the whaleboats been swept away and lost we would nowadays be speaking of the Wallacean rather than the Darwinian theory of evolution by natural selection.

From Seno Pía the two whaleboats rowed around the western end of Isla Gordon and back to Woollya through the Brazo Sudeste of Canal Beagle. They travelled about 250 miles through the water – the crew of the *Beagle* were the proverbial iron men in wooden ships.

At Woollya FitzRoy found that Jemmy Button had lost some of his possessions to thieves, one of whom was his own brother. 'what fashion do you call that?', Jemmy asked. Still, the cabins were in good order and the vegetable garden was beginning to sprout. York Minster and Fuegia Basket were getting on well together. Matthews, however, had lost a great many things and parties of visiting Yamana had threatened him with violence. He and FitzRoy decided that his life would be in danger if he remained. He abandoned his ministry and returned to the *Beagle* at Paso Goree with the whaleboats. From there, the ship sailed back to Bahía Buen Suceso and then to the Falkland Islands. She returned to the Río de la Plata to complete her second trip to the south on 26th April 1832.

Harrier and I pressed on westward from the anchorage at Seno Pía. We crossed Seno Darwin and motored down Canal O'Brien. We emerged into Seno Ballenero (*Whaleboat Sound*) and into another and a more rugged land. Some bushes and small trees could grow in sheltered spots near the shore but the great beech woods of Canal Beagle were no more. From just above the shoreline the surface of these islands consisted of naked rock. Only bare rock could withstand the force of the winds. In 1829, Seno Ballenero was the theatre that saw the drama of the theft of and the unsuccessful search for Matthew Murray's whaleboat. Modern names such as Cabo Longchase, Isla Leadline and Seno Ladrones (*Thieves' Sound*) commemorate incidents in the search. The Indians who then lived on these now uninhabited slabs of rock may have been dedicated thieves, but they must also have been among the toughest people in the world.

In these bleak surroundings I discovered that all was not well with *Harrier's* engine. Fuel was somehow leaking into the sump and even at low speed the engine began to overrun. I limped into Puerto Atracadro on Isla Brecknock where I pumped out the contaminated oil and put in two litres of fresh. It was only 15 miles to my next anchorage at Caleta Brecknock but the engine oil warning light had switched itself on before I arrived. Brecknock is one of the showpiece anchorages of the south. It is surrounded on all sides by steep walls of bare rock up to the skyline at about 400 metres. Once a boat is secured, Caleta Brecknock is a well-sheltered and safe harbour. I took two lines from the stern ashore and tied them to stunted trees just above the waterline. Anchor and chain held *Harrier's* bow steady in clear water ahead. My first task was to change the engine oil again with the last of my reserve supply. My second was to consider retreating all the way back to Ushuaia for diagnosis of the engine trouble and to make repairs.

I debated the next move with myself for three days. Winter returned, wind from the west blew over the anchorage, rain fell in torrents and showers of hail rattled on the deck. I decided that I would go north to Punta Arenas, on the strait of Magellan, to buy oil and obtain help for the ailing motor. Early in the morning of the fourth day the weather seemed to abate. An attempt to motor through Paso Gonzalez, which requires intricate pilotage, and out into Canal Cockburn had to be abandoned because of the arrival of more heavy rain and poor visibility. Back at the anchorage I fell asleep after lunch.

Vaihere and *Harrier* in Caleta Brecknock

Two hours later I was awoken by the sound of an outboard motor. A large steel schooner, *Vaihere*, flying a Belgian ensign had anchored just ahead of me and was laying out her shore lines. Her French crew and charter party were very hospitable and I had several meals in her spacious saloon. *Vaihere*, at 29 metres, was almost exactly the same length as the *Beagle*.

One of her crew, Henri, was a professional diesel mechanic. He diagnosed my engine trouble as a faulty fuel lift pump. Henri helped me to make a temporary repair and *Vaihere* gave me six litres of engine oil. This was a lucky meeting for me and I was very grateful to them for their help. Two days later *Vaihere* departed east for Ushuaia while I settled down in the caleta again to await the right weather for going to the west.

After eight days of inactivity I became restless. I made another attempt to leave Brecknock and get through Paso Gonzalez. This time I was driven back by a blizzard from the west so powerful that I was unable even to look to windward. Back at the anchorage I found the mountains and cliffs covered with a thin dusting of fresh snow. I began to feel as if I were marooned on the southern icecap of planet Mars.

Circumstances such as these encourage introspection. I found myself reflecting upon the many promising paths in life I had not taken and on the numerous dead-ends that I had tried and which had lead nowhere. It had been my misfortune to live in the time of feminism and political correctness, and I had never earned much money. On the other hand, I had lived my allotted span with health of mind and body, which is the greatest of all blessings. Furthermore I had been lucky to spend my adult life in the period of comparative peace between the end of the Second World War and the coming war with Islam. I reviewed in my mind the sunshine and shadows of a life.

The next day the weather again seemed to moderate. This time I was able to motor through Paso Gonzalez and out into Canal Cockburn in light wind and with good visibility. Here I found the wind to be in the southwest and I had a fine sail north for 20 miles to Caleta Luis on Isla Clarence. In Canal Cockburn I again crossed the path of the *Beagle*. At the end of her third return to the south she left Tierra del Fuego for good via Canal Cockburn in very different weather conditions. She and the *Adventure* sailed out into the Pacific on 10th June 1834

> between the 'East & West Furies'; a little further to the North, the Captain from the number of breakers called the sea the 'Milky Way'. - The sight of such a coast is enough to make a landsman dream for a week about death, peril, & shipwreck.[4]

FitzRoy intended to take the *Beagle* north in the Pacific Ocean as far as Coquimbo in 30 degrees south. On passage they had much bad weather, including two force 10 storms and one of force 11, from the northwest. Darwin commented that 'Such weather utterly destroys for every good end the precious time during which it lasts.'[5] After 17 days of winter weather, the *Beagle* put into San Carlos at the northern end of Isla Chiloe. The day before she arrived, her purser, George Rowlett, died. 'he had been for some time gradually sinking under a complication of diseases, the fatal termination of which were only a little hastened by the bad weather of the Southern countries.'[6]

At the time of the voyage of the *Beagle* San Carlos, which has been known as Ancud since 1834, was the capital and the largest settlement on the island of Chiloe. I planned to reach Chiloé and the north without an ocean passage by going through the more sheltered channels that lie inside the islands of the Chilean archipelago.

Three and a half months before transiting Canal Cockburn, the *Beagle* had revisited Woollya. There they found that Jemmy Button was well but he had lost all his possessions. York Minster had invited Jemmy and his family to accompany him, together with Fuegia Basket, on a visit to his own country near Seno Christmas. At Isla del Diablo he turned on them and robbed them of everything they had. He loaded his loot into his conveniently large canoe and disappeared with Fuegia into the west. Jemmy and his family were left naked and alone on the island. They had made their way back to Woollya with great difficulty.

On the *Beagle's* last night in Seno Ponsonby Darwin records that:

> Jemmy staid on board until the ship got under weigh, which frightened his wife so that she did not cease crying till he was safe out of the ship with all his valuable presents. - Every soul on board was sorry to shake hands with poor Jemmy for the last time, as we were very glad to have seen him. - I hope & have little doubt that he will be as happy as if he had never left his country; which is much more than I formerly thought.[7]

After crossing Canal Cockburn, I spent one night in Caleta Luis on Isla Clarence before motoring north through Canal Acualisnan and into the wider waters of the western portion of the strait of Magellan. The Acualisnan was unknown to the *Beagle*. It is named after a Yamana friend of Thomas Bridges who took him through the channel in 1885. This safe and well-charted passage is, for some unknown reason, placed off limits to visitors by the Armada. Fortunately for yachtsmen the prohibition is rarely monitored. The officers and ratings of the Armada de Chile are a fine body of men. It is a pity that they are obliged to administer so many pointless regulations and futile restrictions.

It would be repetitive to enumerate each of the several anchorages that I used while working my way westward through the strait of Magellan. On 12th November I entered Puerto Angusto on the large island that forms the south side of the estrecho. It is aptly named Isla Desolación. I was confined here by the wind for three days but fellow circumnavigator Joshua Slocum, on board his *Spray*, spent a month sheltering in Angusto on his second, and ultimately successful, attempt to escape into the Pacific in April 1896.

Slocum was working on deck at Angusto, 'a dreary enough place', when one day he:

> heard the swish of something through he air, and heard a 'zip'-like sound in the water, but saw nothing. Presently, however, I suspected that it was an arrow of some sort, for just then one passing not far from me struck the mainmast, where it stuck fast, vibrating from the shock - a Fuegian autograph. .... I threw up my old Martini-Henry and the first shot uncovered three Fuegians, who scampered from a clump of bushes where they had been concealed, and made over the hill ... [they] put Fuego real estate between themselves and the Spray as fast as their legs could carry them.[8]

At Angusto I was well sheltered by the trees and bushes at the edge of the water. I had only rain and contrary winds to cope with, for Isla Desolación is nowadays uninhabited except by lighthouse keepers. They have to spend their working hours in an augmented flux of ultra violet light under the Antarctic hole in the ozone layer. They too must also suffer from cataracts of the eye.

I was now getting near the point at which I could leave the strait of Magellan and go north into the channels of southwestern Chile. The turning point is Puerto Tamar where I arrived shortly after dark on 16th November. Like many other 'puertos' Tamar has only the port facilities that are provided by nature. It is protected from the sea by a long reef and it would, as I thought, be sheltered from the prevailing wind by a range of high hills to the northwest. I dropped my anchor 100 metres off a sandy beach and settled down for the night. By morning, the north wind was coming over the hill, down the slope and across the beach at Force 9. Despite the short fetch, small waves were slapping against *Harrier's* hull while furious gusts raised clouds of spume and blew them across the water. All day and all the next night we were blown back and forth by shifting gusts which often heeled *Harrier* down to her gunwhales. At Tamar I had good reason to be glad that I carry a heavy anchor and plenty of chain.

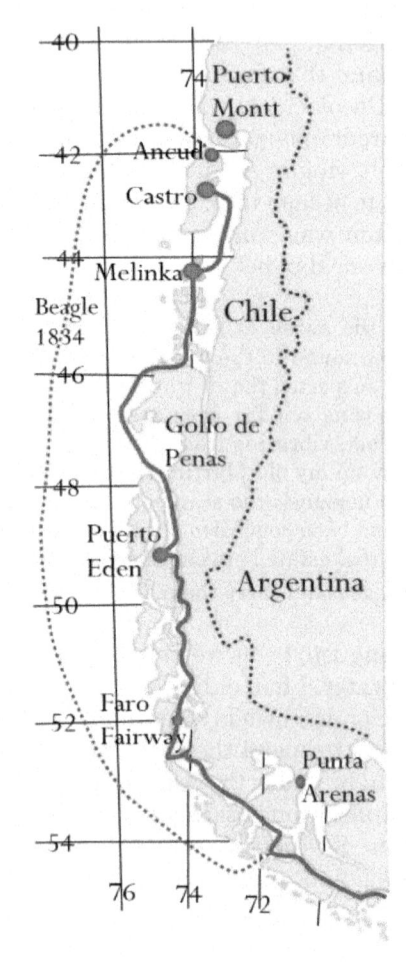

The following day the wind moderated. I investigated Paso Roda but I found that the northern exit into Paso Tamar was encumbered with too many unmarked rocks and shoals. I retreated to Caleta Rachas that, for once, did not live up to its name. Next day I could motor round the southwest side of Isla Tamar and then for 12 miles northward to Faro Fairway. The lighthouse was on an islet lying in the middle of the southern entrance to Canal Smyth. It was kept by Roberto together with his wife and daughter. Visiting yachtsmen such as me were a welcome change for them from the isolation and monotony of life on Fairway.

I was grateful to Roberto for supplying me with yet more lubricating oil for my ailing motor. The anchorage at Fairway is open to the northwest and my visit therefore had to be a short one. Before dark I crossed the channel and secured *Harrier* in another somewhat underdeveloped 'puerto', this time named Profundo. Before me lay 600 miles of intricate waterways, hidden caletas and wild mountainous country.

Day after day I plugged north against the never-ending contrary wind. I waited out spells of bad weather and I nursed *Harrier's* motor by never using it at its full power. I was conscious that so much use of the motor was against the principles of a simple-lifer such as myself.

I will not describe every anchorage I entered on this passage since this would merely be to assemble a catalogue of unfamiliar place names. I threaded my way through the narrows of Canal Smyth and emerged into Canal Sarmiento. Here I passed close aboard the rusting hulk of a small steamer, the *Hazel Branch*, high and dry on Islotes Adelaide. She had been there for more than a century, a monument to an engine failure, a steering breakdown or just a plain mistake. Canal Sarmiento was succeeded to the north by Canal Wide. Under a leaden sky, the mountains away on the eastern shore fell back behind one another in a sequence of blue ridges. In the far distance snow covered peaks could be glimpsed through the mist. On and over the water there were large numbers of diving petrels, white-chinned petrels and a few steamer ducks.

I saw no ships or other yachts for days at a time. In an anchorage, when the wind abated in the evening, the silence was absolute. No artificial lights, or glow of lights, were to be seen. I had a feeling that *Harrier* and I were intruding into some vast place that lay beyond the proper sphere of humankind. It may be possible, when standing on the deck of a large and comfortable cruise ship, to regard these surroundings as beautiful and wonderful. The scene before me was full of wonder but, when viewed from the cockpit of a small yacht with a faulty motor, the term beautiful was lame. I did not feel threatened by my situation but I knew that I could not afford to make a mistake. I was filled with strong sense of awe. I began to understand the distinction that Edmund Burke drew more than 250 years ago between the beautiful and the sublime. 'the sublime', he wrote, 'is an idea belonging to self-preservation.'[9]

In the canales

When I reached Caleta Bolina on Canal Concepción I again changed *Harrier's* engine oil with the last of the stock given to me at Fairway. When we emerged from the caleta into the canal it was by a piece of luck that the first vessel that I had encountered for days turned out to be an Armada patrol boat. They assisted me with a gift of more oil for the engine. This supply enabled me to motor through the narrow and spectacular Paso Piloto Pardo between Isla Angle and Isla Saumarez. On 10th December I anchored in Caleta Río Frio. Are they all not so in these parts? In the morning the motor refused to start at all. Luckily it was a fine day with a gentle north wind. For the first time in nearly two months I hoisted *Harrier's* sails and late in the afternoon I entered the enclosed bay that shelters the small fishing village of Puerto Eden. I anchored in the northeastern part of the harbour in front of the school and the post office.

Puerto Eden

Puerto Eden is in 49 degrees south latitude. Because of its location, it is a staging post for yachts travelling both north and south, and a stop-over for the commercial ferry ship that plies between Puerto Montt to the north and Puerto Natales in the south. One of the yachts anchored nearby, and bound for the south, was *Shanty*. She was owned by Peter, a professional mechanical engineer who had many year's experience of maintaining diesel motors. He spent an entire morning aboard *Harrier* where he showed me how a true expert goes about diagnosing an ailing engine. He tracked the problem down to a tiny hole in the diaphragm of the diesel lift pump. Fuel was leaking through this almost invisible hole and contaminating the oil in the engine's sump. I had no spare pump or pump diaphragm. I therefore got on board the Navimag ferry, the Magellanes, and travelled north to Puerto Montt. There I bought a replacement pump and ferried back to Puerto Eden a week later. With a new lift pump installed the engine started immediately and ran perfectly.

During my absence at Puerto Montt, the large yacht *Oasis* arrived in Puerto Eden. She anchored near *Harrier* and she was, like *Shanty*, southbound. On the last day of the year 2006 I joined her cheerful young Danish crew for an uproarious party. We let off so many rockets and flares that I was surprised that we did not manage to set *Oasis* alight. At three o'clock in the morning I rowed back to *Harrier* ready to sober up and continue my cruise northward in the New Year.

Only nine miles north of Puerto Eden the navigable channel between Isla Wellington on the west and the mainland to the east is reduced to the narrow Angostura Inglésa (*English Narrows*). This channel was discovered by the *Beagle* during her first surveying voyage in Chilean waters in the 1820s. I caught the north-going tide through the narrows and on account of a strong north wind I came to anchor for the night in Caleta Hoskyn a further three miles on. Two days later I was at anchor in Caleta Hale on Isla Orlebar, within sight of Faro San Pedro on the far western side of the channel.

Faro San Pedro is situated at the southern entrance to one of the gates in the passage north or south through the Chilean Channels. This is the notorious Golfo de Penas (*Gulf of Sorrow*). The gulf is roughly circular in plan and about 70 miles in diameter. To the west it is open to the Pacific Ocean for some 40 miles. A perpetual ocean swell enters the gulf and is reflected from its concave shores to form a complex pattern of interference waves. *Harrier's* motor purred comfortably for 16 hours as I travelled north-northwest across the gulf towards the turning point of Cabo Tres Montes. The water of the gulf was much more disturbed than the force 4 west wind would justify. I arrived five miles off Cabo Raper, the western extremity of Peninsula de Taitao, at 0400 feeling rather battered by *Harrier's* violent motion. At the end of the second day, in poor visibility, I could turn east and run before the wind into Bahía Anna Pink. The night was too dark to enter an anchorage and I was forced to stand off-and-on in narrow water until dawn. Caleta Saudade on Isla Guerrero was a secure refuge for the weary mariner. I spent 18th January at rest there while I reflected upon my introduction to the ocean misnamed Pacific.

Only later I learned that during the first third of the year some hundreds of earth tremors had disrupted the district of Puerto Aysén, which lies some 130 kilometres to the east of my anchorage at Isla Guerrero. I felt none of the shocks aboard *Harrier*. In April, four months after my departure from Guerrero, not a tremor but a massive earthquake struck Aysén. Tsunami waves of 10 metres caused great destruction in the neighbourhood and at the nearby small port of Chacabuco. By that time I had reached Valdivia, well to the north and clear of this episode of seismic mayhem.

The Archipelago de los Chonos is an intricate group of islands and channels lying between Golfo de Penas and Golfo Corcovado some 180 miles to the north. Today the Chonos are the centre of the Chilean salmon and mussel farming industries. Enormous floating cages fill many of the bays and a procession of small service ships ply the channels. In the Chonos I was back in civilisation and I could consider myself to be yachting, rather than voyaging, again.

The *Beagle* made the first accurate charts of the Chonos on a trip south from Valparaiso in November and December 1834 and January 1835. I motored north with Isla Ribero to the west and a tangle of islands on my eastern side. On 26th January I went through Canal Scorpio, a narrow waterway about seven miles long between Isla Royas and Isla Jechica. Its steep banks on either hand were densely wooded down to the water. This was how the west coast of Scotland must have looked before all the trees were cut down.

The Chonos archipelago is divided from the mainland by Canal Morelada. The Morelada was as much as 12 miles wide in places and it offered few convenient anchorages. I therefore decided to make my way north through the smaller and more sheltered Perez Sur and Perez Norte channels westward of the Morelada. The names of the islands on the seaward side of this part of my passage included James, Kent, Rowlett, Stokes, Benjamin, Forsyth, Midhurst, Mellersh, Arthur and Simpson - all names from the *Beagle's* list of officers. Edward Chafers, the master of the *Beagle*, had both an island and a canal named after him. The ship's carpenter, Jonathan May, gave his name to an island here and Isla Williams was named in memory of Corporal Williams, the marine who drowned in the Río Negro in Argentina. Eight miles offshore, the names of a pair of small islets commemorated the two gallant little schooners of the Atlantic survey, the *Paz* and the *Liebre*.

On 27th January I arrived at the small town and busy port of Melinka on Isla Ascension. Melinka was the hub of the Chilean fish farming industry. Every day a sizable ship would arrive bringing in supplies and taking out tanks of live fish. One morning a kayak came alongside *Harrier* paddled by a fit-looking grey-haired woman who spoke with a French accent. Karine Huet told me that she had written a book about her kayak journey through the Iles Tuamotu in the South Pacific and that she was now on her way south to explore the Chilean channels. Her cheerful demeanour in her tiny kayak made *Harrier* seem like a heavy and solemn cruise ship.

The last day of January dawned fine. I left Melinka in the early morning sunshine and motored all day across Golfo Corcovado. The sea was quiet with barely a ripple from a gentle northerly breeze. Huge flocks of sooty shearwaters skimmed over the water or rested on it in large rafts. After spending the night in Caleta Ichuac on Isla Lemuy I went on to Castro and dropped my anchor just in front of the Armada jetty.

Harrier at Castro

Castro is the capital of Isla Chiloé and today it is the largest town on the island. Chiloé means *Place of Seagulls* in the language of the Araucanian Indians. I warmed myself in the sun and looked across to the works of civilisation. The long voyage from Ushuaia through the channels and islands was the most arduous passage of my entire sailing career.

Chapter 11
Chile and Peru

the veil
Thrown back a moment with the glancing hand
While the o'erpowering eye that turns you pale
Flushes into the heart.
   Lord Byron, *Don Juan,* Canto II, 1819

For three centuries, Isla Chiloé was the extreme southern settlement of the Spanish Indies. Its people now have an ancient mixture of European and Indian blood in their veins and they speak Spanish with a characteristic local accent. At the time of the *Beagle's* visit, the island was a continuous dense forest with cottages and their gardens widely scattered among the trees. It was a peasant economy and the people 'widely differ from almost every other set of Spaniards in not being Gauchos.'[1] Darwin travelled in peace and tranquility the length and breadth of Chiloé by horse and rowing boat. He remarked that 'one may here enjoy the privilege, so rare in S America, of travelling without firearms.'[2] Despite our present-day worries about street crime we do not have to carry a pistol with us everywhere we go in South America.

Today the Chilote landscape is about equally divided between forest and cleared pasture land. The great Alerces (*Fitzroya cupressoides*), the South American equivalent of the Californian Sequoias, are all gone. The tallest trees I saw on Chiloé, apart from a few Eucalyptus, were Lombardy poplars, the punctuation marks of man.

FitzRoy does not mention, and Darwin barely refers to, the feature of the Chilote landscape that today inspires worldwide interest. In the year 2000, UNESCO declared 16 of the 60 timber churches of Chiloé to constitute a World Heritage Site. Almost every village and hamlet on the island has one of these remarkable buildings.

Church at Achao

A Chilote church usually consists of a nave and aisles of equal height with an arcaded and pedimented portico surmounted by a central tower at the west end. Sometimes a church, such as that at Castro, will have two west towers while those at San José and Tenaun have three. Chilote churches are, in effect, large rustic timber barns raised to a high level of architecture. The noble simplicity of these buildings is a fitting expression of, and monument to, the mestizo culture of the island.

Achao church cladding

To the east of Chiloé there is an extensive archipelago of inhabited islands and uninhabited islets. They are set in waters that are sheltered from the Pacific ocean swell. I spent four days exploring this comfortable cruising ground. My view of the beautiful timber church at Achao is an enduring memory.

In December Darwin experienced a spell of good weather when he was among these islands on board a whaleboat from the *Beagle* 1834:

> I fancied Chiloe never experienced a day such as this; I cannot imagine a more beautiful scene, than the snowy cones of the Cordilleras seen over an inland sea of glass; only here & there rippled by a Porpoise or a logger-headed Duck. And I admired this view from a cliff adorned with sweet-smelling evergreens, where the bright coloured, smooth trunks, the parasitical plants, the ferns, the arborescent grasses, all reminded me of the Tropics; neither did the temperature recall me to the reality.[3]

He noticed that the snowy volcanoes across the water in the Cordillera Andes were in full activity.

On 24th February 2007 I arrived at Ancud and once again joined the track of the *Beagle* and the *Adventure*. The name of the town, which was the capital of Chiloé in the nineteenth century, was changed from San Carlos to Ancud during the time that the *Beagle* was surveying the island. The anchorage off the town is exposed to winds from the north but the bay in the lee of Punta Arenas (*Sandy Point*) three miles westward, used by the *Beagle* during her visits, is secure in all winds.

The island of Chiloé lies on the boundary between the north winds which prevail in the south of Chile and the southerly and southwesterly winds produced by the south Pacific high pressure area centred on Isla Pascua (*Easter Island*). I sailed from Ancud on 26th February. Strong winds from the south pushed me on rapidly to Bahía Coral where I arrived the next day at noon. I felt my way into a shallow but secure anchorage in the lee of the islet of Mancera. In the time of the Spanish empire, Mancera was heavily fortified against pirates and buccaneers, most of whom were English. The ruins of the fortress and the church are still to be seen on the island.

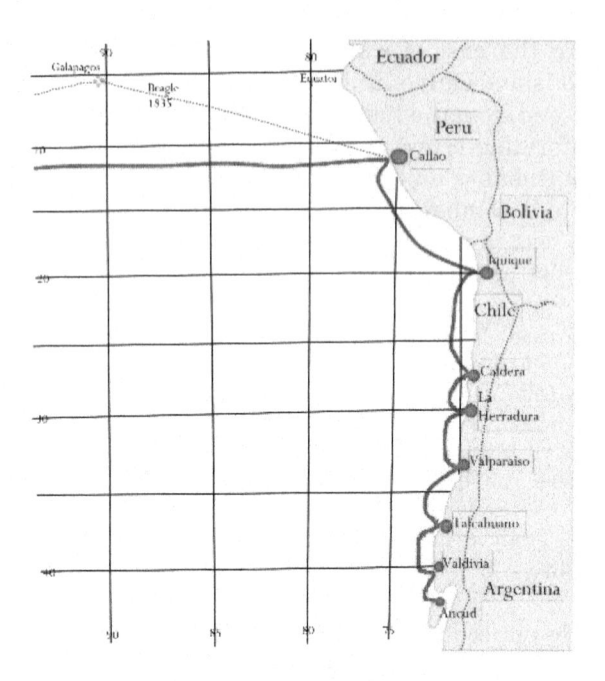

This passage was one of the few for which my time was shorter than that of the *Beagle*. She arrived at Puerto Coral on 8th January 1835, three days out from Ancud. She remained at anchor there for two weeks while Darwin and FitzRoy travelled up the Río Valdivia by boat. They found that 'The town of Valdivia is seated on the low banks of the river: it is completely hidden in a wood of Apple trees; the streets are merely paths in an orchard - I never saw this fruit in such abundance.'[4]

Valdivia in 39 degrees south was founded in 1552 by one of Francisco Pizarro's lieutenants, Pedro de Valdivia. A year later he was rash enough to offer battle to the redoubtable Araucanian Indians. The Indians under their chieftain Lautaro won the battle of Tucapel. They slaughtered the little Spanish army and took Valdivia prisoner. He was tortured with refined cruelty and was finally killed by having molten gold poured down his throat.

Pedro de Valdivia

    Three centuries later, at the time of the *Beagle's* visit, the town of Valdivia was still a Spanish enclave in Indian territory. As FitzRoy records, 'About Valdivia there are only a few leagues of ground held by Chile, excepting which all that magnificent tract of country, reaching from the Gulf of Ancud nearly to the Río Bio Bio, probably the finest district in all South America, is still kept by the brave Araucanians.'[5]

Lautaro

On 20th February 1835 Darwin was ashore in Valdivia resting amongst the apple trees and perhaps congratulating himself for not having to try to stand on the heaving deck of the *Beagle*. He wrote;

> It came on suddenly & lasted two minutes (but appeared much longer). The rocking was most sensible; The undulation appeared both to me & my servant to travel from due East. There was no difficulty in standing upright; but the motion made me giddy. - I can compare it to skating on very thin ice or to the motion of a ship in a little cross ripple.[6]

He was experiencing one of the most violent earthquakes to strike Chile during the nineteenth century. Valdivia, where most of the buildings were constructed of timber, survived with little harm. For other cities in the region the earthquake was a catastrophe.

On 28th February 2007, 172 years later, I followed Darwin and FitzRoy on a visit to Valdivia. Aboard **Harrier** I motored ten miles up the beautiful wooded river to reach the modern, charming, sleepy university town. Here I rented a berth for **Harrier** at the marina of the Club de Yates. She had now been in the water for more than a year, so I took the opportunity to have her slipped, cleaned, repainted and refloated at the club. The centre of the present town had been rebuilt in a routine commercial style after another disastrous earthquake, this time in May 1960. However, the road leading north from the club to the central Plaza de la República still had many fine timber houses dating from the time of the German settlers in the second half of the nineteenth century. They built, and no doubt lived, very well.

Río Valdivia

I am often asked if I do not find single-handed voyaging to be lonely. Occasionally I do, but the pattern of my life aboard *Harrier* generally alternates between solitude at sea and sociability ashore. Valdivia, both at the club and in the town, turned out to be one of my most sociable ports.

Late on a fine evening in March I was sitting at a café table on a first floor balcony overlooking the Río Valdivia. I was drinking coffee and reading a novel in English. Three people seated at the next table were discussing something, with a lot of laughter and much rapid-fire Spanish. Presently the two elder people left. The third, a woman with an intelligent, open face, turned to me. She was petite, with a head of glossy black ringlets and dark brown eyes. She could have stepped out of a fresco in the palace of King Minos at Knossos. Glancing towards my book she said,

> 'Que pais?'
> 'England, Inglaterra', I replied.
> 'Hablas usted castellano?'
> 'Poco.'
> 'And I have poco inglése,

So began a conversation in the composite language known as Spanglish. I learned that her name was Maria and that she was a teacher of art at a secondary school in the city. She discovered that I was a sailor who was going around the world in a small yacht. For an hour we tried to learn, with the aid of my dictionary, something of one another's language. By then the sun had set behind the trees on the far side of the river.

> 'Will you come to my house for some supper?'
> 'Si.'

We took a taxi to her flat in an inner suburb of the town. It was on the first floor of one of the timber terrace houses that survived the 1960 earthquake. This was the most powerful earthquake ever recorded. The floors and walls were no longer straight or level but thanks to the flexibility of timber construction the building stood securely. The dining table in her kitchen was soon covered with plates, food, dictionaries, writing pads, and pens and pencils. After a while we tired of learning new words and phrases in an unfamiliar language.

'Can you walk back to your boat at this time of night?', she asked. 'Puedes caminar?' '
Yes', I answered, 'but I would rather stay here with you.'

She looked at me carefully. Then, 'Yes', she said, 'OK'. She took me across the landing of her flat and into her bedroom. There she put me naked into her bed and got in beside me dressed only in thin pyjamas. She was soft and warm and fragrant.

And so Maria was asleep with her head on my shoulder, my hand on her bottom and her breasts pressed against the side of my chest. She had entrusted her life to a stranger from another land. How could she pay me a greater compliment? I felt as much her protector as her lover.

At breakfast she asked me,

Am I the first Latino woman that you have been to bed with?'.
'Yes, in fact you are the first woman of any kind that I
have slept with for more than five years. I have almost
forgotten what to do.'

We met many times during the next three weeks. We twice visited the land of the Araucanians, which is now the Chilean lake district. FitzRoy called it 'the finest country I had ever seen.'[6] Today it is a land of forests, pastures and lakes, all set before a backdrop of snow-covered mountains and volcanoes. It is one of the most beautiful landscapes I have ever seen. However, my meetings with Maria were overshadowed by the knowledge that I would be in Valdivia for only a short time. She kept herself at a greater emotional distance from me than I did from her. She was preserving herself from hurt.

Maria was a great admirer of the Chilean surrealist poet Pablo Neruda. She loved the tumultuous mixture of sentiment, sensuality and images from nature contained in his work. I have on a bookshelf aboard *Harrier* a bilingual edition of Neruda's *Twenty Love Poems and a Song of Despair*. It is signed on the title page by Maria.

After two months in Valdivia the seasons were starting to change and autumn mists were gathering in the trees about the marina. On 3rd May I cast off my warps and motored back down the river to the anchorage at Isla Mancera. Here I prepared *Harrier* and myself for the next stage of my passage north.

On the first day out from Bahía Coral, the wind was from the south but it was hardly strong enough to operate *Harrier's* wind-vane steering gear. During the night it strengthened and I then had favourable sailing conditions all the way to Bahía Concepción. I passed Isla Mocha to port and the morning before I arrived I saw the Río Leubu abeam to starboard. In June 1835 FitzRoy had made a dramatic ride from Concepción to the Leubu.

Bahía Concepción is a large body of water sheltered from the Pacific by Peninsula Tumbes and Isla Quiriquina. Puerto de Talcahuano lies in the southwest corner of the bay. Talcahuano and the city of Concepción, ten kilometres away on the Río Bío Bío, relate to one another in much the same way as do Devonport and Plymouth in Devon. Concepción and Talcahuano were in good shape during my visit, but things were not so when the *Beagle* was anchored in the bay.

> I went on shore to Talcuano & afterwards rode with the Captain to Concepcion.- The two towns presented the most awful yet interesting spectacle I ever beheld.- To any person who had formerly known them it must be still more so; for the ruins are so confused & mingled & the scene has so little the air of an habitable place that it is difficult to understand how great the damage has been. .... In Concepcion each house or row of houses stood by itself a heap or a line of ruins; in Talcuano, owing to the great wave little more was left than one layer of bricks, tiles & timber, with here & there part of a wall yet standing up. .... The earthquake took place, as we have seen at Valdivia, at half past eleven. It is generally thought if it had happened in the night, at least ¾ of the inhabitants would have perished. .... It is a bitter & humiliating thing to see works which have cost men so much time & labour overthrown in one minute;[7]

The whole of Chile is seismic and every coastal town in the country lives with the threat of sudden destruction by earthquake, tsunami or by both. In his diary Darwin, speculated on the subterranean connection between earthquakes and volcanism. His thoughts were an adumbration of the modern theory of plate tectonics.

At the Club Marina el Manzano at Talcahuano I waited until 23rd May in conditions of geological tranquillity for the arrival of mail from England. My next passage north was made over a calm sea and in light winds, as was that of the *Beagle* in 1835. The 170 miles took me five days' sailing. The *Beagle* anchored on 11th March 1835 in Bahía de Valparaíso immediately in front of the town. Nowadays this is the site of the largest port installation in Chile and in the bay there are no facilities for yachts. I went a further 12 miles north and entered the marina belonging to the Yacht Club Higuerillas at Concón. The coast between Valparaíso and Concón is now occupied by the resort town of Viña del Mar, the Brighton of Chile.

Bahía de Valparaíso at the time of the *Beagle*

My time at Concón was uneventful, unlike the first and last of the three visits the *Beagle* made to Valparaiso. FitzRoy recorded that when she and the *Adventure* arrived in the port from Chiloé for the first time in June 1834.

> I was made to feel and endure a bitter disappointment; the mortification it caused preyed deeply, and the regret is still vivid. I found that it would be impossible for me to maintain the Adventure much longer; my own means had been taxed, even to involving myself in difficulties, and as the Lords Commissioners of the Admiralty did not think it proper to give me any assistance, I saw that all my cherished hopes of examining many groups of islands in the Pacific, besides making a complete survey of the Chilian and Peruvian shores, must utterly fail. I had asked to be allowed to bear twenty additional seamen on the Beagle's books, whose pay and provisions would then be provided by the Government, being willing to defray every other expense myself; but even this was refused. As soon as my mind was made up, after a most painful struggle, I discharged the Adventure's crew, took the officers back to the Beagle, and sold the vessel.[8]

The *Adventure* was sold at a loss. The shabby conduct of the Admiralty affected FitzRoy's health and left him with money worries. He tried to forget his disappointment by losing himself in work. He became thin and gloomy. Fearing that he might succumb to his hereditary malaise of melancholia he resigned his position as captain and appointed his first lieutenant John Wickham to take his place. Wickham showed his generosity of spirit by refusing the promotion. He persuaded FitzRoy to resume his command of the *Beagle*.

Darwin was absent from the *Beagle* during these events. He returned from a six-week trip into the country and a visit to Santiago, suffering from the first serious illness of his life. For a month ashore he had been ill in bed. Shortly before the *Beagle* departed south for the survey of Chiloé and the Chonos the two young men were back on board. They were both depressed, in poor health and they had both contemplated abandoning the voyage and returning to England in a commercial ship.

Darwin and FitzRoy usually got on well together, but at this time their morale broke down. They had a furious row over a trifling matter of etiquette. FitzRoy thought that he was obliged to give an expensive party on board the *Beagle* in return for the hospitality that they had all received ashore during the last months. Darwin countered that perhaps there was no need.

> He then burst out into a fury, declaring that I was the sort of man who would receive any favours and make no return. I got up and left the cabin without saying a word, and returned to Concepcion [Valparaiso, in fact] where I was then lodging. After a few days I came back to the ship and was received by the Captain as cordially as ever, for the storm had by that time quite blown over.[9]

FitzRoy knew that he had a quick temper and he also knew that he must be careful not to bear grudges. A few days later the *Beagle*, with Darwin on board, left for a return trip to the south. She surveyed Chiloé, the Chonos archipelago and the coast of the mainland as far south as the Golfo de Penas before returning to Valparaiso on 14th February 1835. Three months of travel and hard work in the open air put both men back on their feet.

The second half of March and the months of April, May and June 1835 were a busy time in Darwin's life. On 18th March he left Santiago with Mariano Gonzales as guide and companion, a muleteer and eleven mules. For three days they travelled steadily eastward while gradually ascending. At the foot of the western ridge of the Andes;

> We began the tedious ascent, & first experienced some little difficulty in respiration. ... upon finding fossil shells on the highest ridge, in my delight I entirely forgot the Puna. ... Certainly the labour of walking is excessive, & in breathing deep & difficult; & it is nearly incomprehensible to me how Humboldt (& others subsequently) have reached 19000 ft.[10]

They hurried onward to the Paso Portillo at some risk of being caught in a high-altitude autumn snowstorm. On the 22nd they walked over the perpetual snow on the Portillo at 2867 metres above sea level and began a slow descent onto the plains of Argentina. Five days later they entered the ancient city of Mendoza. Darwin was not impressed with the place. 'the happy doom of the Mendozinos is to eat, sleep & be idle.'[11] Today Mendoza is a large busy city and the centre of the Argentine wine industry.

After only a day in Mendoza, they left to return to Chile by crossing the less elevated Paso Uspallata to the north of the Portillo. While walking up to the pass, Darwin made one of his most important geological discoveries. At Vicensio he found a grove of between 50 and 60 fossilised tree trunks embedded in sandstone. This was incontrovertible proof that the spot on which he stood, at an elevation of 1800 metres above the sea, had once been dry land at a lower elevation. It had subsequently been submerged under a deep ocean for an age. Then it was elevated to its present height where an aeon of atmospheric erosion exposed the fossils. His observations clearly corroborated Charles Lyell's uniformitarianism. Darwin became convinced about geological evolution long before he published his theory of evolution in the living world.

In July 2007 I followed Darwin across the Andes, not on the saddle of a mule but sitting in an air-conditioned coach. The modern road from Santiago over the mountains to Mendoza went through a tunnel cut beneath the Paso Portillo. As the bus ascended through the bleak landscape I looked out of the window and thought of Darwin and his mule train slogging slowly upwards through the thin, cold air. From Mendoza I took a bus across the Pampas to visit friends in Buenos Aires.

While in the capital city, I consulted an optician about the failing vision of my right eye. My left eye was functioning well enough, but without visual input from the right eye I had lost a three-dimensional view of my surroundings. She diagnosed a cataract in the lens, caused probably by the intense ultra-violet radiation that reaches high southern latitudes through the hole in the ozone layer of the earth's atmosphere. I would need an operation upon my return to England. Meanwhile, my visual world remained restricted. The rest of my circumnavigation was a voyage through a two-dimensional world.

After a week in Buenos Aires I learnt that the Andean road tunnels and passes were blocked by snow. I returned to Santiago in a jet airliner, the cop-out of the modern traveller.

Darwin and Gonzales got back to Santiago on 10th April. Two weeks later they set out from Valparaiso on Darwin's longest land journey in South America. Their route as far as Coquimbo followed roughly the course of the modern Carretera Panamericana. Further north, their journey was complex because Darwin made several geological detours inland. After riding for 420 miles from Valparaiso they arrived at Copiapó on 1st July to meet the *Beagle*. At that time FitzRoy was absent on his mission south to help the men of HMS *Challenger*.

On her way north from Valparaiso to La Herradura in April and May 1835 the *Beagle* briefly surveyed a number of the bays and coves that indent the coastline of Chile. At Bahía Conchali the local people did not believe that story about surveying the coast and making charts. FitzRoy records;

> My reception was very hospitable; but the people made sure I was a smuggler; and some of the principal inhabitants rode with me several miles next morning to the place where my boat was hauled ashore, thinking all the time that I was only waiting for a favourable opportunity to tell them my secret, and make advantageous terms.[12]

Darwin commented that 'A person who could possibly mistake Captain FitzRoy for a smuggler, would never perceive any difference between a Lord Chesterfield and his valet.'[13]

So far as possible I reserved maintenance work on *Harrier* for the times when she was alongside a floating pier. At Higuerillas I refurbished my headsail sheet winches and improved the chassis of the wind-vane steering gear. The Higuerillas marina is one of only two in the vicinity of Valparaiso that offered shelter in all winds. The moorings have scarcity value and the daily rates, even for a small yacht, were sufficient to bring tears to one's eyes. I therefore departed as soon as I could. I had another light weather passage of 190 miles north to Bahía La Herradura. The Municipio of La Herradura is today a suburb of the port town of Coquimbo.

Bahía La Herradura (*Horseshoe Bay*), in 30 degrees south, is the most northerly naturally secure anchorage on the coast of Chile. The bay is long and deep, and the narrow entrance excludes the Pacific swell. In May 1835 FitzRoy and the *Beagle* made good use of the calm waters of this bay.

> It was my intention to refit there thoroughly, and prepare the *Beagle* for receiving a large supply of stores and provisions at Valparaiso, which would enable her to run down the coast to the Galapagos, and thence across the Pacific to Sydney in Australia.[14]

All her people moved ashore to a camp of tents on what is now a beach popular with holiday makers and local people walking their dogs. In the course of a month the ship was stripped, cleaned, repainted and refurbished. *Harrier* and I remained at La Herradura for nearly six months. I was awaiting the season for crossing the Pacific. I occupied my time with writing the first half of this book about my voyage.

It had nothing to do with my voyage nor with that of the *Beagle*, but the 27th of December was a red-letter day in my life. Clear dry air, productive of what astronomers call 'good seeing', has attracted a number of giant astronomical telescopes to the mountains of central and northern Chile. The northern of the two eight metre diameter telescopes that constitute the international Gemini project is on Mauna Kea volcano on the island of Hawaii. The other has been built on Cerro Pachón in Chile. The two telescopes can together observe the entire sky. I was fortunate to be invited to take part in a visit to Gemini Sul.

We drove for two hours up a specially-constructed road to arrive on top of Cerro Pachón at mid-day. The telescope is housed in a 40 metre diameter dome at an altitude of 2700 metres. Inside were offices, the control room and large workshops. Above, on the first floor, was the mighty instrument itself. The structure of an eight metre diameter telescope is on the scale of a steel railway bridge, but it moves as smoothly and accurately as the mechanism of a fine watch. The dome was opened and the telescope rotated to show us its motion. Every night Gemini North and Gemini South look far out into the universe. They receive data to help us to answer the questions

'What is out there?', 'Where are we?', 'Where are we going?'. I shall long remember my visit to the great eye of wondering mankind.

Looking at the great mirror of Gemini Sul

    While Darwin was travelling ashore in the north, the *Beagle* returned south for her third and final visit to Valparaiso to buy stores for the crossing of the Pacific. Here FitzRoy learned that HMS *Challenger*, a three-masted barque under the command of his friend Michael Seymour, had gone aground in thick weather at a remote spot on the coast south of Talcahuano and had been wrecked.

    From Valparaiso, FitzRoy sent the *Beagle* north under the command of John Wickham to continue the survey, to meet Darwin at Copiapó and to rendezvous later at Callao, the port of Lima in Peru. At Valparaiso, FitzRoy cajoled Commander Mason, an elderly and cautious officer, into taking his ship HMS *Blonde*, south to Talcahano. They arrived in Bahía Concepción on 14th June 1835. At Concepción, FitzRoy hired horses and, accompanied by a guide and a local acquaintance, Anthony Vogelberg, he crossed the Río Bío Bío into Indian territory. For two days they rode at a furious pace through wind and rain across the beautiful country of the unconquerable Araucanians.

At the *Challenger's* camp near the mouth of the Río Leubu, FitzRoy and Seymour quickly worked out a plan of rescue. The wreck had occurred more than a month before and time was running short. Sickness had appeared in the camp and Seymour had received news of the approach of a hostile band of Indians. FitzRoy and Vogelberg then galloped back to Talcahuano through more foul weather. Shortly afterwards FitzRoy went south aboard the *Blonde* to the Río Leubu where he played an important part in taking off and saving the crew of the *Challenger*.

Two chapters of FitzRoy's *Narrative* are devoted to a vivid description of his hurrying ride to and from the Leubu, through wind and rain, by day and night, through forests, over rivers and across dangerous country on a desperate mission of life and death. Robert FitzRoy was a High Romantic to the core.

On 16th January 2008 *Harrier* and I sailed from La Herradura. We had been at anchor there for so long that I felt I had become an honourary citizen of the town. The 350 mile passage north to Puerto Caldera took *Harrier* six days of easy sailing before a gentle south wind. Mineral ores are exported through Caldera and it is the port of the the city of Copiapó, 80 kilometres inland. The southern summer of 2007-2008 brought a drought to central and northern Chile. Crops suffered and the bed of the Río Copiapó had run dry.

Darwin and Gonzales were glad to ride into Copiapó at the beginning of July 1835 - 'the smell of the fresh clover was quite delightful after the scentless air of the dry sterile Despoblado'[15] - but Puerto Caldera did not impress him. 'It is a miserable assemblage of a few houses, situated at the foot of some sterile plains & hills.'[16] He returned aboard the *Beagle* and 'In the evening I gave my "adios" with a hearty goodwill to my companion, Mariano Gonzales, with whom I had ridden so many leagues in Chile.'[17] Mariano Gonzales is another of the unsung heroes of the voyage of the *Beagle*.

When the *Beagle* called at Puerto de Iquique, 400 miles north of Caldera, in July 1835 the small town was part of Peru. In later times, between 1879 and 1883, Bolivia and Peru allied themselves to fight a war with Chile, now known as the War of the Pacific. Chile won and she extended her border north to the 18 degrees south parallel at the expense of the losers. Inland, the war brought her possession of the only large surface deposit in the world of sodium nitrate ore. For the next 40 years an export trade of nitrate as an agricultural fertiliser made Chile rich. The fine mansions and grand opera house at Iquique date from the days of the Chilean nitrate boom.

Opera house at Iquique

In 1835 the *Beagle* anchored in Bahía de Iquique for eight days (the name means *sleep* or *laziness*, in the Aymara Indian language). One hundred and seventy three years later I remained tied up at the quay of the Club de Yates y Botes for five days. On the Sunday I morphed myself into a tourist and bought a day ticket to travel in a comfortable bus to see something of the Atacama desert. The Atacama and the Gobi deserts are rivals for the title of the driest places on earth. In parts of the Atacama no rain has ever fallen.

The bus took us to see some large petroglyphs of unknown antiquity on the stony hillsides of Cerro Pintado. If these works really are landing beacons for visiting UFOs then the Martians like to set themselves down at very dry locations. In the middle of the day we drove through sparse but extensive plantations of Tamarugal trees. Their deep roots can somehow obtain sufficient water for life from beneath an apparently desiccated landscape. In the foothills of the Andes, a copious spring of good water emerges from the ground in the middle of the little oasis town of Pica. The irrigated orchards of Pica supply Iquique with its fruit.

The Atacama desert is dotted with abandoned nitrate workings, known as oficinas. What is now the ghost of a nitrate company town can be seen and explored at Humberstone. In its heyday more than 3000 people lived and worked here. The church, cinema, market and housing areas stand empty and forlorn. In the distance the abandoned nitrate oficina of Santa Laura crouches on the desert horizon like a rusting dinosaur. All is redolent of exile and decay.

Oficina Santa Laura

My passage of 600 miles north from Iquique to Callao was a delivery trip accomplished in good weather with a gentle following breeze. I kept at least 30 miles offshore in order to avoid fleets of fishermen and the occasional marauding Peruvian patrol boat. I benefited from the Humboldt ocean current flowing steadily to the north. It was a peaceful ten days and a good time to read. I tried once again to make sense of Georg Hegel and his philosophy. At dawn on 3rd March I motored around the north end of Isla San Lorenzo and into Bahía Callao in a flat calm. In the middle of the morning I moved to pick up a mooring buoy off the buildings of the Yacht Club Peruano in the suburb of La Punta. Callao lies in 12 degrees south and is the principal port of Peru. Peruvian boobies, a cousin of the European gannet, plunged from a height into the smooth sea. Flocks of band-tailed gulls, Inca terns and

Peruvian pelicans patrolled the bay at a lower altitude. The seafowl left no doubt about the name of the country at which I had arrived.

Inca terns

    The *Beagle* anchored in the roadstead of Callao on the 19th of July 1835. Nearly three weeks later FitzRoy arrived with Commodore Mason aboard HMS *Blonde.* There FitzRoy 'enjoyed the satisfaction of finding all well on board the Beagle.'[17] At Lima Commodore Mason handed over a letter of instruction that later involved FitzRoy in some tricky negotiations in Tahiti.

    For three hundred years before the arrival of the *Beagle* the city of Lima, together with its port of Callao, had been the rich and proud metropolis of the Spanish Indies. When, early in the nineteenth century, the Spanish empire broke into a number of independent nations Lima lost its central purpose and the city went into decline. By 1835 Lima was in a sad state. Darwin recorded that 'The city of Lima is now in a wretched state of decay; the streets are nearly unpaved & in all directions heaps of filth are piled up.'[18] Nevertheless Captain Carrasco, the director of the nautical school in Lima, welcomed the visit of the *Beagle* and he gave FitzRoy every possible assistance with the *Beagle's* survey.

    Darwin, while FitzRoy was busy with his duties in Lima, interested himself in girls and in exotic fruit.

> The close elastic gown fits the figure closely & obliges the ladies to walk with small steps which they do very elegantly & display very white silk stockings & very pretty feet. – They wear a black silk veil, which is fixed round the waist behind, is brought over the head, & held by the hands before the face, allowing only one eye to remain uncovered · But then that one eye is so black & brilliant & has such powers of motion & expression, that its effect is very powerful. ...

Secondly for the Chilimoya, which is a very delicious fruit, but the flavour is about as difficult to describe, as it would be to a Blind man some particular shade or colour; it is neither a nutritive fruit like the banana, or a crude fruit like the Apple, or refreshing fruit like the Orange or Peach, but it is a very good & large fruit & that is all I have to say about it.[19]

Chilimoya (custard apple)

     While waiting the season for sailing across the Pacific Ocean I reflected on my long sojourn in South America. I came to realise that the cult of feminism has made only slight inroads into their culture. To this day the men and women of South America regard themselves as complementary to one another rather than as antagonists.

Lima girl in 1835

Every inhabitant of the continent has, throughout the centuries, received more than a fair share of dictatorial and self-defeating government, economic trouble and petty criminals in the street. But despite it all the *savoir faire* and the innate good manners of the Spanish-speaking peoples survive undimmed in every country that I visited. We in Britain, where doctrinaire sexuality and industrial barbarism are rife, have much to learn from the wise, hospitable and civilised people of South America.

Chapter 12
Pacific Ocean

I find that it is somewhat more tolerable to be always alone than never able to be so.
     Michel de Montaigne, *On three kinds of social intercourse*, 1580

A well-found yacht, even one so small as *Harrier*, need have no fear of a gale at sea provided that she has no land close to leeward. A wind of force 8 may raise seas as high as five metres but in the open ocean the seas will rarely tumble over and break. A gale in deep water is wet and uncomfortable but is not dangerous for her. The same is not true of a tropical revolving storm. These meteorological convulsions are known in the various oceans as hurricanes, typhoons, cyclones or willy-willys. They occur in the tropical latitudes of the oceans of the world during the summer season. Only the South Atlantic Ocean is quite free of tropical revolving storms.

In these mighty storms wind speeds can exceed 100 knots. Waves are mountainous, confused and breaking. Large and fully crewed ships have foundered in tropical revolving storms and no yacht can expect to survive the violence of a full hurricane or cyclone at sea. Tahiti lies in the path of the cyclones that occur between November and May in the western part of the tropical South Pacific. I therefore delayed my departure from Peru until the beginning of the southern winter in mid-June 2008.

In September 1835, the *Beagle* departed Callao for the South Pacific on a north-western course. Her surveying duties were now at an end. Her principle remaining task was to make a connected chain of meridian distances around the world and to test the accuracy and reliability of the many types of chronometer that were available by the 1830s. The rate of the 22 chronometers on board were checked by means of lunar distance calculations. Lunar distances are very accurate but they are difficult to observe from the moving deck of a ship at sea. FitzRoy and Stokes, the two most competent astronomers on board the *Beagle*, measured lunar distances from the stability of sites ashore.

After a passage of six days the *Beagle* sighted Chatham Island, the most eastern of the Galápagos. Chatham is now called Isla San Cristóbal, while the Galápagos Islands are now known in Spanish as the Archipielago de Colón. The *Beagle* spent just over a month exploring and charting this unique group of islands. Before the arrival there of man in the sixteenth century the Galápagos were the last place on earth where reptiles rather than mammals were the dominant land fauna. In 1835 the human population only amounted to some 300 political prisoners banished there from Ecuador.

FitzRoy devoted 22 pages of his *Narrative* to their time in the Galápagos. The *Beagle* made a circuit of the archipelago during which she visited most of the main islands. My purpose among these islands was not to spend a lot of money just to gawp at tortoises and iguanas. I intended to follow the track of HMS *Beagle*, to see the places that she visited and to compare the state of the islands then with the conditions that prevail now. In addition I wanted to observe as many as possible of the 13 species of finch that are indigenous to the Galápagos. The attempt that Darwin later made to explain the geographical distribution of these birds had an influence on his mature thinking in later life. They have become known to the world as 'Darwin's Finches'.

While the *Beagle* was carrying out her survey work in the Galápagos Darwin contrived to spend four days ashore collecting specimens on Charles Island, now known as Isla Floreana. He was as keen as ever to have stable land, rather than the rocking deck of a ship, under his feet. He records that;

> I industriously collected all the animals, plants, insects & reptiles from this Island. – It will be very interesting to find from future comparison to what district or "centre of creation" the organized beings of this archipelago must be attached.[1]

Darwin did not formulate his theory of evolution by natural selection while he was aboard the *Beagle*. During the time when he was in the Galápagos he still believed in a slightly modified version of biblical special creation. According to this interpretation of events, God did not create all of life in only one place. Rather, on the fourth day He exercised his inventive faculty in a number of separate places scattered about the face of the brand new earth. These innovative hot spots were known as centres of creation. However, the observations and collections which Darwin made among the islands started him thinking about what he later called 'the species question'. His ideas came to fruition 23 years after the end of the voyage of the *Beagle* with the publication of his *Origin of Species* in 1859.

HMS *Beagle* in the Galápagos. James Island in the background.

My proposed itinerary in the Galápagos would occupy a month and required a special dispensation from Quito. However, letters to the Ecuadorian government went unanswered and the Charles Darwin Research Station on Isla Santa Cruz proved to be impotent and evasive. I therefore decided, very reluctantly, to sail from Peru directly across the Pacific Ocean to Tahiti. Following the advice that is given to navigators in *Ocean Passages for the World* I set a course from Callao due west for 2600 miles to a point in the ocean at 12 degrees south and 120 degrees west. I departed from Callao on 19th June on a course that took me well to the south of the Galápagos Islands.

Missing out the Galápagos was the greatest disappointment of my voyage. It is an unfortunate fact that the modern Ecuadorian government has become hostile to the independent traveller, and particularly to the independent traveller who wants to explore the Galápagos. The authorities nowadays regard foreign visitors merely as cash cows and in the Galápagos they have their most esteemed milking parlour. The preferred consignment is a party of rich tourists neatly packaged in a large cruise ship. This facilitates the process of taxation, it is convenient for the collection of fees and it ensures a rapid turnover of punters. There is evidently no longer scope for an independent traveller to study the early development of Darwin's thought nor to illuminate the nineteenth century history of the Galápagos Islands.

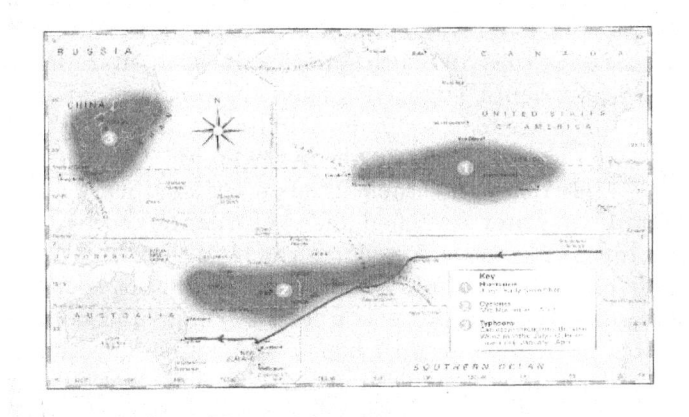

Pacific Ocean. Areas shown red are subject to tropical revolving storms.

The Pacific Ocean is very large. An observer on the moon, when positioned over the earth's equator in longitude 160 degrees west, would see no land except for New Zealand, bits of Australia, New Guinea and the extreme western margin of North America. The earth would look to him like an almost completely blue planet.

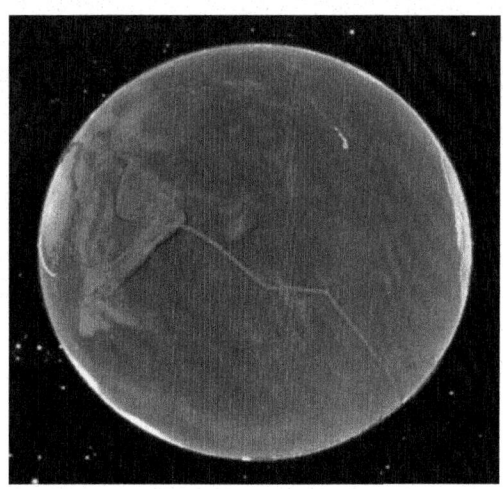

Blue planet. The red line is my track across the Pacific Ocean.

One of the most important ocean currents in the world, named after Alexander von Humboldt, flows in the South Pacific Ocean north along the west coast of South America. Its cool antarctic water, which is rich in nutrients, supports one of the world's greatest commercial fisheries. *Harrier* took seven days, in fine weather and light southerly winds, to cross this mighty river in the ocean.

The trade wind then filled in the southeast and more than 4000 miles of water stretched ahead of *Harrier's* bow. My days settled into a routine. In the open ocean away from shipping lanes the chance of colliding with a ship is so small that I did not keep a continuous watch while the weather was fine. The wind-vane self-steering gear mounted on *Harrier's* stern kept us on course day and night. Each evening I got into my bunk at about 2230 and slept all night. At 0730 in the morning I got up and made a breakfast of tea or coffee, a bowl of porridge and an orange. Small jobs of cleaning or boat maintenance occupied the morning. At noon I read my position from a hand-held GPS receiver and plotted it on a paper chart. *Harrier* is not equipped with electronic charts and a chart plotter. Lunch was a light meal, while dinner consisted of pulses cooked in a pressure cooker accompanied by bread made in *Harrier's* galley.

During my crossing the trade winds were lighter than I had expected. *Harrier* proceeded steadily westward at an average of 80 miles a day. She is capable of a hull speed of slightly more than six knots in smooth water and in a fresh breeze. However, spray begins to come on deck at speeds of more than four knots, she heels under the press of her sails and life on board becomes uncomfortable. On an ocean voyage, I set no more sail than is sufficient to keep *Harrier* going through the water at four knots, giving a progress of 100 miles in a day.

Occasionally gusts of wind, heralding the arrival of a shower of rain, would oblige me to go forward to the mast and reef the mainsail. An hour later the sail would have to be shaken out again. In general, our progress was steady and my life crossing the Pacific was gentle and peaceful.

Sailing on the Pacific Ocean

    A long ocean passage is an opportunity to read some of those books whose great length, when busy with life ashore, can seem to be intimidating. I had all six volumes of Marcel Proust's *A la Recherche du Temps Perdu* on my bookshelf for the passage of the Pacific. *La Recherche* turned out to be an extraordinarily vivid and sustained piece of writing. In it Proust scrutinised his past life through the lens of memory. I admired the book but I did not like it. He depicted the fashionable world of late nineteenth and early twentieth century Paris as self-absorbed, snobbish, bi-sexual and over-heated. Reading Proust's six volumes kept me hypnotised during my afternoons, but when I had finished them I felt that I was free to emerge into mental fresh air again.

    After 35 days at sea I had reached a point in the ocean 130 degrees west of Greenwich. I estimated that if *Harrier's* average speed lessened when I reached the Tuamotu archipelago I might begin to run short of water. I therefore decided to divert west-north-west to the Îles Marquises. Early in the afternoon of 3rd August the mountainous island of Hiva Oa appeared in the distance directly over the bow. There are no coral reefs about Hiva Oa but, in a spirit of caution, I delayed closing the coast until daylight next day. By 1400

I was at anchor in the sheltered bay a short distance by road from the chief town of Atuona.

The *Beagle* never visited the Marquises. *Harrier* and I remained at Atuona only long enough to get water, re-provision my galley and see something of the island. Shops at Atuona were quite well stocked but French Polynesia must be the most expensive location on earth. The fact that a British passport is also a European Union passport spared me from having to pay the sizeable bond that is imposed on visitors from non-EU countries. This is the only advantage that I have ever received, or expect to receive, from the dreaded European Union.

On the crest of a hill overlooking Atuona the Cimentière Calvaire contains the grave of Paul Gauguin. He arrived in Polynesia in 1891 as an emotional and artistic refugee from the Paris of Marcel Proust. He was fleeing from the stultifying atmosphere of the Parisian Belle Epoch. 'I had reached the point where I told myself it was time for me to set off for a Simpler Country .... I was thinking of packing my trunks and going to the Marquises, the Promised Land where there are more acres than one knows what to do with.'[2] In the South Seas he could make his famous paintings of lovely, brown, naked girls at their ease in the tropical sunshine. I vote with Paul Gauguin.

Aha Oe Feii (*What? Are you Jealous?*)

The South Pacific Ocean is rarely entirely quiet. An ocean swell penetrates into the bay of Atuona but the surrounding hills exclude nearly all wind. I drifted out of the anchorage on tiny zephyrs on the morning of 19th August. Once clear of the headlands *Harrier's* sails felt the breeze and I turned to starboard to go west through Canal Haava before turning southwest for Tahiti, 800 miles distant. The great coral archipelago of Îles Tuamotu, which stretches some 900 miles from east to west and covers an area larger than Western Europe, lay across my course from Hiva Oa to Tahiti. The islands are difficult to see from an offing because no part of the Tuamotu archipelago is more than three metres above sea level. The Tuamotus have been known for centuries as the Dangerous Archipelago.

I laid a course for the strait between the coral islands of Rangiroa and Arutua. This strait is 15 miles wide but I would not have dared to negotiate it at night without the aid of the GPS system. The *Beagle* transited the same strait in November 1835 with only a lead line and a sharp lookout to rely upon. After two more days of easy sailing with a favourable wind the green, mountainous island of Tahiti (from the Tahitian verb *to transplant*) came in sight. I sailed through the Passe de Papeete and brought up at the municipal moorings in the heart of the town.

Papeete in 1835

Papeete is the capital city of Tahiti and of French Polynesia. In the eighteenth century Tahiti was an exotic land of noble savages and free love. Nowadays it resembles a suburb of a mid-sized metropolitan French city that has been moved into a tropical climate.

Modern Papeete

While I awaited the arrival of a parcel of mail from England I moved eight kilometres to the east and brought up at an anchorage under the shelter of Pointe Venus, which was used by the *Beagle*, in Baie de Matavai. A small monument near the lighthouse commemorates the visit of Captain James Cook and the astronomer Charles Green aboard the *Endeavour* in 1769. The observatory on Pointe Venus was one of about 12 set up at various places in the world to observe simultaneously the transit of Venus across the face of the sun. This project was the first worldwide collaborative scientific investigation. The distance that the observations established between the earth and the sun was equivalent to 151 million kilometres. This is remarkably close to the accepted modern figure for what is known as the astronomical unit, or AU.

Tahiti and Moorea (*Yellow Lizard*) are, like the Îles Marquises, of volcanic origin. In the centre of Tahiti, Mont Orohena rises to 2241 metres. Its peak is usually hidden in cloud. The valley of the Rivier Tuauru leads south from Baie Matavai into the heart of Orohena. While FitzRoy was busy with official duties, Darwin made one of his most venturesome land journeys. He walked up the Tuauru with two Tahitian guides and a dog. They carried ropes and some provisions. After three hours they reached a point where the valley floor was scarcely wider than the stream and further progress was blocked by a series of steep waterfalls. On either hand the walls of the valley were nearly vertical.

With the assistance of his agile guides and the rope, Darwin ascended one of these precipices, probably that on the west side of the valley. The supplies and dog were hauled up the steep places with the rope. By evening they had reached a small flat spot where they built a shelter of bamboo and banana leaves, and bivouacked.

> The Tahitians, having made a small fire of sticks, placed a score of stones about the size of cricket balls on the burning wood. In about ten minutes time, the sticks were consumed & the stones hot. They had previously folded up in small parcels made of leaves, pieces of beef, fish, ripe and unripe bananas, & the tops of the wild Arum. – These green parcels were laid in a layer between two of the hot stones & the whole then covered up by earth so that no smoke or steam escaped. – In about a quarter of an hour the whole was most deliciously cooked; the choice green parcels were laid on a cloth of Banana leaves; with a Cocoa nut shell we drank the cool water of the running stream & thus enjoyed our rustic meal.[3]

They descended by steep tracks along narrow ridges, no doubt lowering the long-suffering dog by rope down the steeper places. After a second bivouac on the mountainside they reached Matavai at noon on their third day out.

Four years before the arrival of the *Beagle* at Tahiti a British trading vessel, the *Truro*, had called at the nearby island of Aura, now named Anaa. The inhabitants of Aura were known for their ferocity. The master and mate of the ship were murdered by them and the *Truro* was ransacked. At that time, Aura came under the jurisdiction of Queen Pomare of Tahiti. FitzRoy obtained an audience with the queen and some of her chiefs. He handed her the letter from the British government that had been given to him by Commodor Mason at Lima. It demanded compensation from the kingdom of Tahiti for the attack on the *Truro*.

The chiefs & people resolved to subscribe & complete the sum which was wanting. – Capt. FitzRoy urged that it was hard that their private property should be sacrificed for the crimes of distant Islanders. They replied that they were grateful for his consideration, but that Pomare was their queen, & they were determined to help her in this her difficulty.[4]

With this diplomatic errand completed the *Beagle* departed for New Zealand on 26th November. Darwin was sad to be leaving 'the island to which every traveller has offered up his tribute of admiration.'[5]

The *Beagle* sailed past the neighbouring island of Moorea without stopping but I called in at Baie de Cook for the sake of its extraordinary mountainous skyline. In past times these jagged forested mountains were said to be the haunt of the lizard men. When lizard men were hungry they would come down to a valley, kidnap some unfortunate person and return uphill to hold a cannibal feast. Should the sound of drums be heard in the hills above Baie de Cook it might, perhaps, behove the modern yachtsman to set an especially alert anchor watch.

Harrier in Baia de Cook, Moorea. The land of the lizard men in the background.

The distance from Tahiti to New Zealand is 2600 miles. Although the passage is only part of the crossing of the south Pacific, it is nearly the whole length of a voyage across the North Atlantic Ocean. I sailed southwest to pass east of Tonga and to the west of the Kermadec Islands. My daily routine for the next 41 days was much the same as it was during my 44 solitary days from Callao to Atuona. As before I was busy with navigation, cleaning and maintenance and with managing the yacht. I was not bored, for solitude on a voyage is not the same thing as loneliness.

When only a day out from the north island of New Zealand I encountered my first episode of bad weather at sea since experiencing the gale off the Atlantic entrance to the strait of Magellan in March 2006. The wind came in from the southwest at force 7 and gusting force 8. I was carrying aboard *Harrier* a new nine-foot diameter parachute type sea anchor. *Harrier* will ride out a normal gale when she is simply hove-to under her triple-reefed mainsail. A sea anchor would only be required in earnest in a storm, but I decided to deploy it for the first time in any case. Now was the time to test the sea anchor in conditions that were less than extreme. *Harrier* lay to her sea anchor quietly for 18 hours as powerful three metre high seas swept past us on their way towards the northeast.

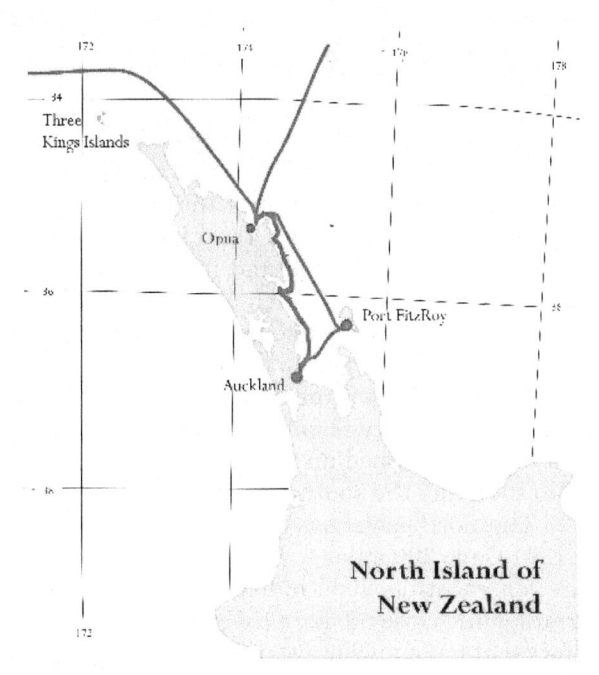

At 0430 on the 30th of October, in calmer weather, I got sight of the powerful New Zealand lighthouse on Cape Brett. During the morning I crossed the sheltered waters of the Bay of Islands before entering the North Island of New Zealand at the village of Opua on Inlet Waikari. Waikari means "*rippling water*". There must be several thousand yachts afloat in the Bay of Islands. Nearly everybody in New Zealand has a boat and is an active sailor. This helps to explain how a nation of fewer than five million inhabitants can be such a powerful player in international competitive yachting.

The *Beagle* spent ten days in the Bay of Islands in December 1835. At that time the English population of the district was only some 200 or 300 people. The villages of Kerikeri and Pahia were orderly missionary settlements but Kororarika (*flesh of Blue Penguin*), now known as Russell, on the south shore of the river, was quite otherwise. The English residents, Darwin reported:

> are of the most worthless character; & amongst them are many run away convicts from New South Wales. ... This little village is the very strong-hold of vice; ... In such places the missionaries are held in little esteem; but they complain much more of the conduct of their countrymen than of the natives. It is strange, but I have heard these worthy men say that the only protection which they need & on which they rely is from the native Chiefs against Englishmen![6]

The modern Opua has three capable boatyards devoted to maintaining the fleet of local boats. I arranged to have *Harrier* laid ashore at Ashby's Boatyard for a thorough refit. At Ashby's *Harrier* was found to need more work than I had anticipated. The refit cost twice as much as I expected and it took three times as long to complete. Other yachtsmen, when I commented on this, gave me an indulgent smile. 'So what else is new? Boats, don't you love them?' By the time she was returned to the water the summer season for crossing the Tasman Sea to Australia had passed. Furthermore, summer weather would be needed for crossing the Great Australian Bight from east to west. I obtained an extension to my visitor's visa and settled down to spending the southern winter in New Zealand.

The northeastern coast of the North Island of New Zealand, from East Cape 200 miles to North Cape, could have been designed by nature for yachting. It is indented by innumerable bays and small harbours while close offshore there are many islands and islets offering the yachtsman anchorage and unspoiled open country. In summer the weather is benign and the prevailing west winds provide hundreds of square miles of sheltered water. Should the charms of nature pall an anchorage at the large city of Auckland is not far away overlooking Waitemata Harbour.

One winter day in July the weather service broadcast a warning of the approach of a storm with winds of as much as 100 knots. I moved *Harrier* to a more sheltered corner of the marina with the assistance of Graeme from *Chiquita*. The move went without a hitch. When *Harrier* was securely tied up in her new position I remarked 'Well Graeme, we seem to have done that in a seamanlike manner.' 'Yes', he replied, 'we didn't hit anything, and that is what I call seamanlike.' During the night the storm arrived. Next morning the wind was blowing so strongly that I could not get off *Harrier's* deck onto the marina pontoon.

Auckland skyline

During the winter I explored much of this coast including a visit to the anchorage off Herald Island at the western border of Auckland city. Everywhere in New Zealand the resources of a modern country are available, while at the same time the worst aspects of the capitalist fashion for greed have been kept at arms length. People are skilled and well educated, and they permit themselves the leisure to consider each other's interests, and to look after wandering visitors. New Zealand has not been entirely preserved from the worldwide rising tide of violence nor can it be insulated from the sinking miasma of globalisation. But the general tenor of life in New Zealand remains calm, egalitarian and informed by good sense. Would that every country in the world were as sane as New Zealand.

November 2009 came round and on the 6th of the month I cleared customs and immigration at Opua and set off from the Bay of Islands bound for the Tasman Sea and Australia. Spring is a time of easterly winds in the Tasman and I looked forward to a quiet, prosperous passage. A south-easterly wind took me up the east coast of North Island in good style. From a position 30 miles north of the Three Kings Islands I set a course due west for Lord Howe Island, 750 miles distant. The fair land of New Zealand faded from sight astern. Why did I not just stay there? Perhaps I should have appealed to the authorities for political asylum from the European Union.

From Lord Howe Island a course south of west would get me into the south-going East Australian Current and ought to lead me comfortably into Port Jackson and Sydney. The weather gods had other ideas, however. For 12 days the wind blew strongly from the northwest. *Harrier* was set as far as latitude 35 south. Here I encountered days of calm and contrary ocean currents that sometimes flowed at as much as three knots.

On the morning of 10th of November the morning radio communiqué broadcast on short wave by RadioNewZealand gave news of a submarine earthquake to the north near Tonga. On this occasion no destructive tsunami had been reported from the islands. That morning, after breakfast, I was cleaning *Harrier's* galley. I felt the boat surge and move rather as if we were in a rapidly ascending lift. I looked out and saw the surface of the sea apparently sloping downward and away from us astern. I immediately doubted myself. Were my eyes deceiving me? Had something gone wrong with my sense of balance? Or was it that a tsunami wave was passing beneath us? A second surge passed by almost immediately. In the open ocean a tsunami wave does not break – it simply propagates itself rapidly across the surface of the sea in the form of a long-wavelength undulation. However, when a tsunami wave reaches shallow water it tumbles over itself to form a large and destructive breaking wave. If the earthquake really had sent a tsunami in my direction then I was glad to have encountered it in deep water.

Until the time that I was 30 miles away from Sydney Heads the weather and the ocean current continued to be contrary. As the coast came into view in the distance on a clear morning the warming of the great continent of Australia induced a mighty sea breeze. This carried me to a position off the entrance to Port Jackson between Sydney Heads. The passage across the Tasman had been hard work all the way. Next morning I motored into the harbour where the morning light showed the Sydney Opera House, the great bridge and the towers of the Sydney central business district to best advantage. With the last of my fuel I crept into Neutral Bay and cleared with the Australian Customs Service on December 11th 2009.

The next day I went to the Internet where a message from my son James gave me the worst news that I have ever received. Readers will recall that I met my stepmother, the travel writer Anne Mustoe, at Viedma on the Argentine Río Negro in February 2004. That was to be the next to the last time that we were to see one another. She had been taken ill while bicycling in Syria. She died on the 10th of November in the Armenian hospital in Aleppo. Anne was my best friend for more than 30 years. With her death I lost the most important reference point in my life. The world felt smaller and colder without her.

Chapter 13
Australia

Australia, the lucky country.
    Popular saying

Port Jackson in New South Wales was discovered less than fifty years before the *Beagle* arrived in Australia. In 1788 Arthur Phillip, governor of the penal colony at Botany Bay, sailed into the great bay and founded the city of Sydney. 'It is', he wrote,' the finest harbour in the world, in which a thousand sail of the line may ride in the most perfect safety[1]. On 12th January 1836, two weeks out from New Zealand, the *Beagle* sailed into Port Jackson and anchored in Sydney Cove.

Both FitzRoy and Darwin were struck by the vigour and prosperity of the new city. In the *Narrative* Robert FitzRoy quotes a poem published in 1789 by Erasmus Darwin, forecasting Australia's future greatness.

> Where Sydney Cove her lucid bosom swells,
> Courts her young navies and the storm repels,
> High on a rock, amid the troubled air,
> Hope stood sublime, and waved her golden hair,
>   ....
>
> 'Hear me,' she cried, 'ye rising realms!' record
> Times opening scenes, and truth's unerring word-
> There shall broad streets their stately walls extend,
> The circus wide, and the crescent bend;
>   ....
>
> Here ceased the nymph – tumultuous echoes roar,
> And Joy's loud voice was heard from shore to shore-
> Her graceful steps descending pressed the plain;
> And Peace, and Art, and Labour, joined her train.[2]

Sydney Cove in the 1830s

Darwin was proud to contemplate the realisation of his grandfather's prophecy.

> In the evening I walked through the town & returned full of admiration at the whole scene. - It is a most magnificent testimony to the power of the British nation; here, in a less promising country, scores of years have effected many times more than centuries in South America.- My first feeling was to congratulate myself that I was born an Englishman.[3]

Darwin would be amazed were he to return and visit the magnificent modern city of Sydney. But what, I wonder, would he make of the harbour bridge and Bjorn Utzon's heroic Sydney Opera House?

Modern Sydney

Port Jackson is nowadays the home water of countless thousands of yachts. I based *Harrier* at the Cammeray Marina located in a sheltered cove off Middle Harbour, a 20 minute bus ride from downtown Sydney. The little yellow boat from England quickly became an object of local interest. Noel and Jean arrived alongside in their dinghy one warm weekend evening, and they came aboard for a glass of wine and a yarn. Noel was an experienced master mariner, a yachtsman and a busy skipper of charter yachts. His profession gave him a lively interest in maritime safety. Overhead, flocks of sulphur-crested cockatoos flew past, screeching loudly.

> 'My crossing of the Tasman was uphill all the way', I complained. 'I intended to keep north close to Lord Howe Island but 12 days of northwest wind forced me down to 35 south. Then the East Australian Current headed me as I slowly worked north again towards Port Jackson. I began to fear that Australian Customs would get worried and post me as overdue.'
> 'Don't you have an SSB radio?', asked Noel.
> 'No. Just a VHF set.'
> 'Do you carry a rescue beacon, an EPIRB?'
> 'No. You see, I am a simple-lifer afloat.'

'What? No EPRIB? You're mad!'
'Well, *Harrier* is the first boat that I have ever owned which carries even a radio. Years ago I sailed twice across the North Atlantic in a boat the size of *Harrier* that had no radio and no engine either. As I say, I am a simple-lifer.'
'But nowadays you can have an EPIRB. With it you can summon help to any part of the world', said Noel.
'True, but I think that a yachtsman ought to be self-sufficient at sea. Nobody makes me go sailing, so what right do I have to call anybody out to rescue me?'
'But an EPIRB costs only a few hundred dollars.'
'I know, but just as you do not play football by picking up the ball and running with it, so the rules of the game that I play afloat do not call for an SSB or an EPIRB. If *Harrier* suddenly sinks under my feet then my luck has run out and I must expect to drown like a gentleman.'
Jean interjected. 'If that happens we shall never be able to read your book! It would be mean of you to disappear before it was published.'
'I still think you're mad', said Noel.

And the conversation passed on to other topics.

The *Beagle* spent nearly three weeks in Port Jackson. Then, after a passage south of only a week, she came to anchor in the harbour of Hobart in Tasmania. My attempt to follow the track of the *Beagle* in Australian waters was neither a happy nor a successful experience. *Harrier* and I arrived at Port Jackson in early December and I intended to depart the Cocos Keeling Islands for Mauritius in the following June, at the end of the southern summer. The South Indian Ocean, like nearly all tropical waters, is subject to cyclones during the summer months. This schedule would, furthermore, give me time to travel in Australia, repeat Darwin's journey to Bathurst and to see something of the interior of the country. However, I reckoned without the surprisingly hostile attitude of the Australian government towards the independent traveller.

In New Zealand I had obtained a tourist visa valid for six months and I had extended it for a further six months without trouble. An extension to the standard Australian visa of three months would, I was told, be available upon arrival in Australian territory. No conditions as to health, solvency or otherwise would be required for the extra time. However, once in Sydney I found myself charged a hefty fee for a compulsory interview at the central offices of the Australian Department of Immigration and Citizenship. After being kept waiting for nearly an hour I was escorted to a chair which was set before a large desk. A middle-aged oriental woman behind the desk began to interrogate me. Why do I want more time in Australia? Where do I want to go? Why do I want to go there? Can I prove that I own my boat? With the aid of a map and Harrier's certificate of registration I was eventually able to make my case.

The conditions that were imposed for a time extension to my visa included an exhaustive and very expensive health investigation. I was required to prove that I was not infirm, diseased or mentally deficient. Apparently it was hygienic for me to spend an initial three months in Australia, healthy or otherwise, but it was dangerous and insanitary for me to remain in the country for a further five months without an exhaustive health check. The people who thought up this one were evidently untrained in logic.

Australian government policy virtually invites illegal immigrants masquerading as 'asylum seekers' but it repels the independent traveller who merely wants to see the country. Such are the absurdities of political correctness. My circumnavigation was being made on a modest teacher's pension and I could not afford so much expensive and foolish bureaucracy. The rules turned out to be deeply entrenched and it was clear that there was no point in disputing them. I therefore decided to leave Sydney for Hobart promptly and to hurry from Australian waters as quickly as possible.

I departed Sydney on 4th February 2010. Twelve days of fine summer weather, one windy rainy day apart, accompanied me to Storm Bay and the city of Hobart, the capital of the state of Tasmania. Hobart lies on the land between the River Derwent and slopes of Mount Wellington to the west. I think that a medium-sized city can provide the optimum environment for human life. Cities like Copenhagen, Amsterdam, Auckland or Hobart possesses nearly all the facilities of a metropolis but without the hectic pursuit of money and glamour that characterizes the globalised life of a large city such as London, New York, Sydney or Paris. I spent three weeks in Tasmania in and around the inhabitable city of Hobart.

The *Beagle* and her crew remained at anchor in Sullivan's Cove, the harbour of Hobart, where they were occupied with surveying and longitude observations. Darwin stepped off the moving deck of his ship onto solid, stable ground. He stayed ashore for 11 days. Mount Wellington, towering above the town at 1270 metres, was an obvious challenge to him, and to me.

At the time of the *Beagle's* visit Hobart was a new and flourishing town. There were, however, no convenient buses from the town to the mountain. Darwin, together with Symes Covington and a guide, walked five kilometres from Hobart to the beginning of the climb up Mount Wellington. By this stage in the voyage Covington was Darwin's assistant rather than simply his servant. They found that 'the vegetation was very luxurious & from the number of dead trees & branches, the labour of ascent was almost as great as in T. del Fuego or Chiloe.'[4] From the summit they had to walk all the way back to town 'after a severe day's work.'[5]

On a fine early autumn morning I took a bus to the base of the mountain at the western Hobart suburb of Fern Tree. A rough but well-established path wound steadily up the lower slopes of the mountain from the roadside. After three hours of hot work, I emerged onto the rocky summit of Mount Wellington. With my last reserves of energy I joined a group of tourists on top of the large summit cairn. The whole of the southern part of Tasmania was spread out below us. As far as the eye could see, the landscape consisted of rolling hills and small mountains covered with eucalyptus forest. There is still space for both man and nature in Tasmania. Once upon a time I could, without prior training, walk out of my door and go straight up a mountain without getting tired. Today I was glad when some visitors offered me a lift in their car back down the mountain and on to Hobart.

The distance from Hobart westward to King George's Sound in Western Australia is 2400 miles. My copy of *Ocean Passages for the World* showed a sailing ship track westward from Adelaide to Cape Leeuwin, but only east-going tracks to Tasmania further to the south. Nevertheless, I convinced myself that *Harrier* and I could make it south about Australia from Hobart. I sailed down the D'Entrecasteaux Channel and emerged into the Southern Ocean on 13th March in 43 degrees south. I had hoped to get changeable weather during the passage, but for the next ten days the wind blew steadily and strongly from the north and northwest. When I arrived at the latitude of the Bass Strait, and still near to the coast of Tasmania, I realised that I could make no progress to the west under these conditions.

I recalled that in 1897, because of contrary winds, Joshua Slocum aboard the *Spray* had abandoned his attempt to sail westwards south about Australia. The *Spray* was twice the length of *Harrier* and nearly three time her displacement. A large and powerful yacht could follow the course of the *Beagle* but *Harrier* turned out to be too small and light for the job. I would have to get past Australia to the north rather than to the south.

I therefore turned east and after negotiating the islands and channels between Tasmania and the mainland of Australia I arrived at the fishing port of Eden at the south-eastern corner of New South Wales. The *Beagle*, however, had managed to cross the Great Australian Bight in 18 days of windward sailing in 1836. Darwin lamented that 'to me, from the long Westerly swell, the time has passed with no little misery.'[6]

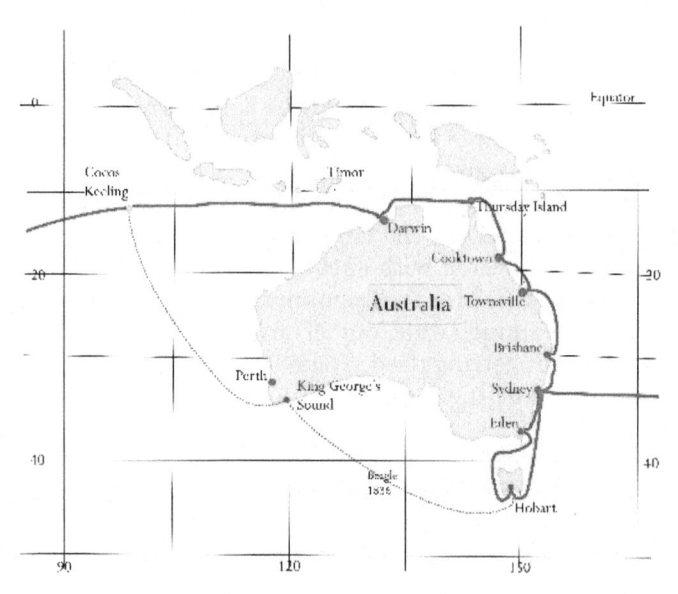

On the way north up the east coast of Australia I stopped at another fishing port, Bermagui, in order to repair an electrical fault in the motor starting circuit. This gave me the opportunity to visit the nearby small town of Pambula.

Symes Covington remained in the employ of Darwin after their return to England in 1836. He assisted Darwin with preserving, cataloguing and publishing his geological and natural history collections. After Darwin's marriage to Emma Wedgwood in 1839 Covington emigrated to Australia. Five years later he was appointed as Pambula's second postmaster. He died there in 1861 and is buried in the town cemetery. His gravestone carries the inscription 'Assistant to Charles Darwin's Voyage in HMS Beagle 1831 – 1835'.

Covington remained in contact with Darwin by letter until the end of his life. In 1850, in the shadow of the Hungry Forties, Darwin wrote to Covington to say that 'when I think of the future I very often ardently wish I was settled in one of our Colonies, for I have now four sons and what on earth to bring them up to I do not know. ..... Whenever you write again tell me how far you think a gentleman with capital would get on in New South Wales.'[7]

Charles Darwin remained living in England but one of his great-great grandsons, Chris Darwin, emigrated to Australia in 1986. He lives with his Australian wife Jacquie and their three small children in a secluded house on the edge of a wooded valley in the Blue Mountains of New South Wales.

In mid-June I travelled by train a few miles west from Sydney to meet them. I arrived to find the house filled with the gleeful miniature anarchy that only a group of small children can create. They reminded me of the time, long ago, when my two children were little. Chris works in Australia as a tour guide. His family connections and his location in the Blue Mountains put him in a good position to show visitors the places that are associated with the *Beagle's* visit to Sydney. The bicentenary in 2009 of the birth of Charles Darwin prompted an expansion in Darwin-Beagle tourism in Australia.

Chris Darwin and a group of like-minded friends met from time to time to preserve the memory of an earlier ancestor, Erasmus Darwin, and the eighteenth century Lunar Society. An original paper is read to the modern Lunar Society to be followed by a discussion on topics that are of current interest. Most of their papers and discussions are concerned with historical, scientific or environmental matters. The eighteenth century English Lunar Society held its meetings in the houses of its members in Staffordshire. In New South Wales meetings also took place, at full moon if possible, in the Sundeck Cave on one of the Blue Mountains, Mount Victoria. The tradition of the original Lunar Society is alive and well in Australia.

I had reached Port Jackson from the south in mid-April and returned to a mooring at the Cammeray Marina in Middle Harbour. Here I made a number of time-consuming improvements and repairs to *Harrier*. It has been well said that you do not sail a yacht around the world - you repair her around the world. I was finally ready to leave for the north, the Torres Strait and the South Indian Ocean at the end of June. I wanted to make my crossing of the Indian Ocean as soon as possible so I decided to treat the passage north to Darwin as a delivery trip rather than an exploration.

The distance from Sydney to Darwin via the Torres Strait is some 2300 miles. The first part of the passage was a coastal trip in rough water on the leeward side of the Coral Sea. North of Bundaberg I entered the channel inside Fraser Island, the world's largest sand island, and put into the yacht harbour of Urangan on the mainland. Here I was in water that was sheltered by one of the natural wonders of the world. The Great Barrier Reef is the largest coral reef in the world. It extends 1400 miles along almost the whole of the coast of the state of Queensland. The reef is the largest object ever made by living creatures. Inside the reef there is an intricate navigable passage all the way north to Thursday Island on the Torres Strait.

When he was bound north in these waters in 1897 Joshua Slocum rejoiced that 'the best of admiralty charts made it possible to keep on sailing night and day. Indeed, with a fair wind, and in the clear weather of that season, the way through the Barrier Reef Cannal, in all sincerity, was clearer than a highway in a busy city, and by all odds less dangerous.'[8] His blithe confidence was misplaced, for one night north of Cooktown, while she was running under full sail he put the *Spray* onto a coral reef. He was lucky that she came off almost immediately and sustained no damage. Even in this age of the GPS system I proceeded through the channel more slowly and cautiously. Apart from the cities of Brisbane, Gladstone, Townsville and Cairns I anchored in 28 rivers and anchorages along the way. By anchoring frequently, I avoided sailing in intricate waters at night.

The passage from Thursday Island across the Gulf of Carpentaria took 12 days of motor-sailing in calm, sultry weather. Van Diemen Gulf provides a shortcut inside Melville Island and at its western end there is a snug anchorage in the lee of Cape Hotham. I took the fair tide through the Vernon Islands on the morning of 17th October and emerged into Beagle Gulf. The name of this piece of water commemorates the *Beagle's* third surveying voyage made to northern Australia in the 1840s.

Cullen Bay, Darwin

    Shortly after dark I anchored *Harrier* off Emery Point, at the entrance to Port Darwin, in four metres. This is an adequate depth of water at neaps, when the tidal range is only a metre, but at springs the range increases to seven metres. On account of the large springs range the marinas at Darwin are situated behind lock gates. At mid-day on 18th October I locked into the Cullen Bay marina and tied up at the boatyard operated by Geoff and his wife Kaye. Here I had *Harrier* slipped, cleaned and anti-fouled in preparation for a passage across the South Indian Ocean to South Africa.

    The east, south and west shores of Australia are well protected by large tracts of ocean. Her northern border with New Guinea and Indonesia, however, is guarded only by the Arafura and Timor Seas. These stretches of water are narrow. The distance south from Timor to the coast of Australia is only about 300 miles.

    In recent years the Australian government has come to operate a foolish and supine policy of border protection. The consequence has been the development of an active trade in people smuggling from the north, particularly across the Timor Sea. Every year thousands of illegal immigrants arrive in Australia aboard makeshift Indonesian boats. The Timor Sea is also a busy highway for terrorist traffic and for the smuggling of illegal drugs. I set off from Darwin on 31st

October 2010 into these troubled waters with a certain feeling of trepidation.

During the southern summer, the doldrums move south of the equator to cover nearly the whole of the Timor Sea. I sailed and motorsailed in light winds over a smooth sea. Once or twice a day a large cloud towering overhead would bring a heavy rain shower and a strong blast of wind, calling for a reef to be put into the sails.

On day three I experienced my first encounter with smugglers. On the northern horizon I sighted what seemed to be a fishing boat apparently hove-to beside a large dark but unidentified object floating alongside her. Presently she left her station and came steadily towards me. She proved to be some 25 metres long and carrying a crew of at least four men. I started my motor, advanced the throttle and kept on course to the west. The boat looked powerful but she was either unable or unwilling to overtake me. To my relief she soon bore away to the north towards her previous position.

My voyage returned to tranquillity for the next two days. In the morning I sighted a group of three large fishing boats some two miles to the south of my course. I could see through binoculars that they were circling closely round a large, bright red floating object as if they were guarding it. The object of their interest consisted of four square packages, each about three metres long on a side, and evidently lashed together. It looked very much like a drugs rendezvous. The three boats confined themselves to their tight patrol while I sailed by as inconspicuously as I could.

On day seven I sighted yet another large boat, apparently a fisherman, about two miles away. She was on course to pass well astern of us. The sea was calm and visibility was good. I left the cockpit and went below to make a cup of tea. Before the kettle had boiled I heard and felt a great crash from aft. On deck I found that *Harrier's* stern was overhung by the bows of the boat. She had collided with my stern gantry, which now had a bent stanchion. On her deck were six rough-looking aborigines, all staring straight at me. One man, on the foredeck, looked like a hobgoblin. He was barefoot and dressed only in a pair of ragged cotton trousers. His entire head was painted white apart from the eyes and mouth. This individual bade me, with a contemptuous gesture, to 'Clear off!!'. Their boat then departed towards the north with the six crew laughing together loudly.

I had been deliberately rammed. Fear is, proverbially, part of prudence. I started my motor quickly and moved off as rapidly as possible to the west. I was lucky that the six men were intent upon intimidation rather than being determined to rob or murder me. Had they rammed me at speed amidships, *Harrier* would have been stove and we would have sunk. And nobody would ever have known.

I presume that my assailants were outriders for a smuggling gang. Their task was to keep their routes and rendezvous clear of inconvenient passing boats. I have no photographs of this incident. I am sure that, had I pointed a camera at my assailants, I would have been shot.

The rest of the passage was uneventful. I sighted South Keeling, the main island of the Cocos Islands, on 22nd November. South Keeling is a coral atoll consisting of a chain of low islands arranged in a near circle some eight miles in diameter around a shallow lagoon. A gap in the reefs on the north side gives entrance to Port Refuge and to sheltered water in the lee of Direction Island. Direction is a classic tropical island – white coral sand beaches, limpid turquoise water and groves of palm trees swaying in the warm wind. Here *Harrier* remained for a week.

The Cocos Islands were uninhabited until John Clunies-Ross, a Shetland sea captain, arrived with a party of Malays in 1825 to establish a coconut farming settlement. The enterprise flourished for 150 years from the sale of coconut oil and dried coconut meat, or copra. But circumstances changed and after World War II it had become impossible for the settlement to earn a living from its coconut plantations. The ownership of the islands was transferred from Britain to Australia and in 1977 the Australian government bought out John Cecil Clunies-Ross, the last king of Cocos.

South Keeling

When the *Beagle* anchored in Port Refuge in April 1836, John Clunies-Ross was away on an excursion to sell his coconut oil. While FitzRoy made a marine survey of the atoll, Darwin studied its geology. At that time the accepted geological explanation of an atoll was that it was composed of coral polyps built upon the rim of a submerged volcano. At South Keeling Darwin developed an alternative account. He had observed the elevation and subsidence of geological formations from his visit in 1832 to Santiago in the Cape Verde Islands and during his later travels in the Chilean Andes. At South Keeling, he discovered that the edge of the atoll fell away to great depths only a short distance offshore, and that the coral rock continued as far down as the *Beagle's* leadline could reach. He reasoned that the coral structure must have been built up over the lapse of time as the foundation rocks subsided. Darwin was true to the encyclopedic principles of his mentor, Alexander von Humboldt, when he wrote that;

> such formations surely rank high amongst the wonderful objects of this world. ... We feel surprised when travellers relate accounts of the vast piles & extent of some ancient ruins; but how insignificant are the greatest of them, when compared to the matter here accumulated by various small animals.[8]

His account, *The structure and distribution of coral reefs*, published in 1842 was his first original contribution to geological science. Darwin's theory was well received at the time and it remains the accepted explanation of the formation of coral reefs and islands.

The circumnavigation of Joshua Slocum very nearly came to an end in 1897 at Keeling Cocos. Slocum wrote that;

> within sight of the village, I came near to losing "the crew of the Spray" – not from putting my foot in a man-trap shell, however, but from carelessly neglecting to look after the details of a trip across the harbour in a boat. I have sailed over the oceans; I have since completed a course over them all, and sailed round the whole world without so nearly meeting a fatality as on that trip across a lagoon, where I trusted all to some one else, and he, weak mortal that he was, perhaps trusted all to me. However that may be, I found myself with a thoughtless African negro in a rickety bateau that was fitted with a rotten sail, and this blew away in mid-channel in a squall, that set us drifting helplessly to sea, where we should have been incontinently lost. With the whole ocean before us to leeward, I was dismayed

to see, while we drifted, that there was not a paddle or an oar in the boat! There was an anchor, to be sure, but not enough rope to tie a cat, and we were already in deep water. By good fortune, however, there was a pole. Plying with this as a paddle with the utmost energy, and by the merest accidental flaw in the wind to favour us, the trap of a boat was worked into shoal water, where we could touch bottom and push her ashore. With Africa, the nearest coast to leeward, three thousand miles away, with not so much as a drop of water in the boat, and a lean and hungry negro – well, cast the lot as one might, the crew of the Spray in a little while would have been hard to find.[9]

If Slocum had been swept out to sea and lost at Keeling Cocos the first solo circumnavigation would have been postponed for a quarter of a century. Between 1921 and 1925 the American yachtsman and photographer Harry Pigeon sailed his 34 foot yawl *Islander* singlehanded around the world. His route took him through the then new Panama Canal. Since that time many boats have followed the example of Slocum and Pigeon. I do not know the ordinal number of my circumnavigation.

The Cocos Islands are now the westernmost piece of Australia. They are technically an Australian Ocean Island Territory. Life is very quiet on South Keeling and the feeling there is of being in the sunshine at the very edge of the inhabited world. It is a fitting location for one of the most beautiful birds in the world. From *Harrier's* deck I watched a party of fairy terns circling over the beach and among the palm trees. It is a small tern with completely white plumage. It flies with all the buoyancy and elegance of the tern family. A fairy tern contemplates the world through two large dark eyes, as if it were the aerial spirit of some departed poet.

Fairy tern

In 1836 this ethereal creature made a similar impression on Charles Darwin;

> there is one charming bird, it is a small and snow white tern, which smoothly hovers at the distance of an arm's length from ones head, its large black eye scanning with quiet curiosity your expression. Little imagination is required to fancy that so light & delicate a body must be tenanted by some wandering fairy spirit.[10]

Chapter 14
South about Africa

The cloud may stoop from heaven and take the shape
With fold to fold, of mountain or of cape
Alfred Tennyson, *The Princess,* 1847

The stretch of the South Indian Ocean between Cocos Keeling and South Africa is tranquil, at least politically. It lies to the south of the sea area threatened by pirates operating from the coast of Somalia, and it is free from the smugglers who infest the Timor Sea. It is not, however, immune to troublesome weather. In the southern summer the whole of this ocean, and particularly the western part near Madagascar, is subject to cyclones. I departed from Cocos Keeling on 29th November 2010 at the beginning of the cyclone season.

The *Beagle* crossed this piece of ocean at the recommended time of the year. In April 1836 the *Beagle's* 'passage to the Mauritius was slow, but in smooth water.'[1] She was now homeward bound and the minds of her people were preoccupied with getting back to England as soon as possible. Darwin had written to his sister Caroline from Hobart that: 'There never was a ship so full of homesick heroes, as the Beagle. – We ought all to be ashamed of ourselves.'[2]

My luck with the right weather at the wrong season held, and I arrived within sight of Mauritius on 30th December after an uneventful passage with favourable winds. At 0300 next day I anchored in sheltered water at the entrance to the capital, Port Louis. In the morning I motored *Harrier* into the port, cleared customs and immigration, and then moored at the marina near the centre of the city.

Sailor's yarns in Port Louis

Mauritius is a fertile island measuring some 25 by 35 kilometres in extent. Its area is slightly larger than that of Greater London. The scenery consists of wide, rolling plains backed by exotic mountains of volcanic origin. More than 1.2 million people live on Mauritius. The island is dependent on the cultivation of sugar cane and the export of sugar, as well as tourism and some vanilla farms. For two and a half weeks I relaxed in its peaceful, tropical ambience. No Tennysonian lotuses grow amongst the sugar cane, but in Mauritius it is easy to forget the troubled outside world and to dream away the days.

Had it survived the arrival of man in the early sixteenth century the Dodo would today be a world class tourist attraction for Mauritius. This flightless bird, larger in size than a goose, became extinct in the late seventeenth century. The Dodo fell victim, as do so many wild creatures nowadays, to habitat loss, hunting and the animals introduced by man. It is hard to believe, when judging by the appearance of the Dodo, that it is related to the pigeons and the doves.

The dodo

A secluded valley in the interior of the island is the setting of the novel *Paul et Virginie* that was published by Bernardine de Saint-Pierre in 1787. The story tells of two children who grew up in a state of natural charity in a rustic location in the centre of the island, far from the influence of the wicked world. When she was twelve, Virginie was uprooted and sent alone to Paris to obtain an inheritance and acquire some cultural polish. The ship in which she returned two years later was wrecked on the north coast of Mauritius. Virginie had been so corrupted by the false values of civilisation that she would not take off her clothes in order to swim to the beach. She was drowned and Paul, who loved her, died soon after of a broken heart.

Paul et Virginie

Both Darwin and FitzRoy, by now homesick and lovelorn, possessed their own copies of this famous tear-jerker, as did I. 'Oh,' lamented Darwin to his cousin William Darwin Fox, 'Oh, that I had a sweet Virginia to send an inspired epistle to.'[3]

I departed Port Louis on 24th January 2011in an intense tropical downpour. At a distance of less than three miles the island disappeared from view behind the falling rain. On the second day out, while motoring over a calm sea, *Harrier's* diesel motor stopped. The motor had run perfectly ever since the repairs that had been made at Puerto Eden in Chile in 2006. I drained the sump of the fuel tank and replaced both fuel filters, to no avail. The wind remained favourable, however, and I made good progress until I reached a point some 150 miles south of the large island of Madagascar. Here the mainsail halyard winch failed. I could reset the sail using a secondary emergency halyard, but the set of the mainsail was less than perfect. Then, to cap it all, the mainsail was further handicapped when the gooseneck fitting broke away from its position on the mast. We proceeded towards Africa under jury rig at a much reduced speed.

Two days later, the servo blade of the wind vane steering gear broke in half. I hauled the two pieces out of the water and into *Harrier's* cockpit. Fortunately I could induce *Harrier* to steer herself using only her sails, some extra control lines and a few pieces of shockcord. We got under way again and proceeded at an even slower speed towards the coast of South Africa.

From time to time somebody will ask if it worries me to be out on the wide ocean alone in a small boat. In fact I usually cross an ocean in an alert but at the same time tranquil state of mind. I find that a period of solitude, provided it is not prolonged, is refreshing. In addition, I have confidence in *Harrier* as a weatherly seaboat. The gear failures which occurred on this passage, however, affected my morale and I started to feel anxious. What, I began to wonder, would go wrong next? My destination on this passage was Simon's Town, near to the Cape of Good Hope. However, I decided that it was prudent to divert to the nearer port of East London and make repairs before going on to the west. On 21st February I sailed into the harbour and anchored near the clubhouse of the Buffalo River Yacht Club. The location was sheltered from the wind, the water in the river was calm and *Harrier's* deck became still. The state of my morale began to improve.

At a small boatyard on the left bank of the river I had *Harrier* hauled out of the water. The various repairs took four weeks to complete. The fuel system was found to be choked with dirt from the diesel fuel that I had bought at Cocos Keeling. During these weeks ashore I was sustained by the hospitality of the members of the Buffalo River Yacht Club. When I was afloat again, I departed East London for Simon's Town, calling on the way at St Francis Bay and Mossel Bay. *Harrier* herself was now in good shape but I, in a new country, had encountered a member of an unfamiliar population of viruses. I sailed out of the river with a severe cold in my head and on my chest.

In the early hours of 22nd March, I rounded Cape Agulhas, the southernmost point of the continent of Africa. Here a southeast wind set in and began to increase in strength. By the time I had reached Cape Hangklip, at the eastern entrance to False Bay, the wind was blowing a gale astern. Simon's Town was still 12 miles away across the bay. As the waters of the bay began to shallow, the waves became increasingly steep. Several waves rose up and broke over the deck. When only four miles from the shelter of Simon's Bay, an unusually large wave came aboard. It flooded the cockpit, soaked me and swamped the motor. I reached the bay under a shred of sail to find myself only partly under control and not far from a lee shore. Getting into shelter entailed sailing close to a fleet of yachts lying to their moorings in the strong wind. Under these conditions I realised that something would be bound to go wrong if I approached them closely. I swallowed my pride and radioed to the Simon's Town lifeboat for assistance. They came out promptly and towed me the short distance to the marina of the False Bay Yacht Club. I stepped onto the pontoon relieved to be moored but wet, tired, hungry and still suffering badly from the virulent cold in my head.

In June 1836 the *Beagle* spent 12 days anchored in Simon's Bay. In those days the town was according to Darwin 'a couple of hundred square whitewashed houses, with very few gardens & scarcely a tree'[4] He observed that 'The number of negroes is not very great, & the Hottentots, the ill-treated aboriginals of the country, are, I should think, in a still smaller proportion.'[5]. Today Simon's Town is a pretty, bustling, multi-racial and thriving seaside town.

Simon's Town main street.

Several ill-informed authors have put it about that, during the voyage of the *Beagle*, FitzRoy and Darwin were to be found pacing the deck while quarrelling about religion. This is idea is false.

In 1839, three years after the return of the *Beagle* to England, FitzRoy wrote that;

> While lead away by skeptical ideas, and knowing extremely little of the Bible, one of my remarks to a friend, on crossing vast plains composed of rolled stones bedded in diluvial detritus some hundred feet in depth, was 'this could never have been effected by a forty days flood'- an expression plainly indicative of the turn of mind and ignorance of Scripture. I was quite willing to disbelieve what I thought to be the Mosaic account, upon the evidence of a hasty glance, though knowing next to nothing of the record I doubted.[6]

For his part Darwin wrote, many years later, that;

> Whilst on board the Beagle I was quite orthodox, and I remember being heartily laughed at by several of the officers (though themselves orthodox) for quoting the Bible as an unanswerable authority on some point of morality. I suppose it was the novelty of the argument that amused them.[7]

While the *Beagle* was on passage from Simon's Town to St Helena, FitzRoy and Darwin collaborated on an article about the British Christian missionaries in Tahiti and New Zealand. The text interleaves passages written by FitzRoy with extracts from Darwin's diary. They wrote approvingly about the activities of the missionaries and the effects of their work, and they concluded that;

> On the whole, balancing all that we have heard, and all that we ourselves have seen concerning the missionaries in the Pacific, we are very much satisfied that they thoroughly deserve the warmest support, not only of individuals, but of the British Government.
> ROBT. FITZROY
> CHARLES DARWIN[8]

Their joint paper was published in Cape Town three months after it was written. In later life Darwin's and FitzRoy's opinions on religion diverged, but while aboard the *Beagle* their views coincided. At that time they were both conventional, orthodox Anglicans. The picture of angry quarrels between them about religion during the voyage is a myth.

The visit of the *Beagle* occurred at the time of one of the formative events in the history of South Africa. In the 1830s and 1840s, some 12,000 Boer farmers and tradesmen migrated north from the Cape Colony in what is known to history as the Great Trek. In their new lands, they and their descendants founded the new countries of Natalia, Transvaal and the Orange Free State. Here they encountered the final stages of another migration, the Bantu Expansion, coming down from central Africa to the north. The modern state of South Africa is the outcome of the meeting and intermingling of these two migrations. The original inhabitants of South Africa, the Koisan or bushmen, (the term 'Hottentot' is now considered to be derogatory) have been displaced and marginalized by both the black and the white immigrants. Their fate has been that of many indigenous peoples in north and south America, Australasia, Japan, China and other parts of Asia.

In 2006 Stephen Johnson had accompanied me on my passage on the coast of Patagonia south to Tierra del Fuego. That trip gave Stephen a taste for yachting and voyaging. On 12th May 2011 he arrived at the False Bay Yacht Club from Argentina carrying a watertight case full of impressive cameras, and with a wet suit and diving gear in his luggage. Stephen was as much at home on, or indeed under, the water as he was on dry land. His wife Alexa and their young son Elliot had travelled to a rented house near Salvador in Brazil to await our arrival.

Stephen in aquatic mode

According to Herodotus, Africa was circumnavigated by the Phoenicians in the seventh century BC. In modern times the Cape of Good Hope was first rounded from the Atlantic by Bartolomeu Dias in 1488 and then by Vasco da Gama in 1497 on his way to India. The *Beagle* sailed into the Atlantic from Simon's Town in 1836 and the *Harrier* followed in the tracks of these distinguished navigators around the tip of Cape of Good Hope in early June 2011. We put into the marina of the Royal Cape Yacht Club to provision and prepare for the passage of nearly 4000 miles across the South Atlantic ocean to Brazil.

Cape Town. Table Mountain with a grey tablecloth

More trouble with *Harrier's* motor delayed our departure from Cape Town a further week. At last, on 9th June, Stephen and I sailed out of Table Bay on our way to the island of St Helena, 1700 miles away to the northwest.

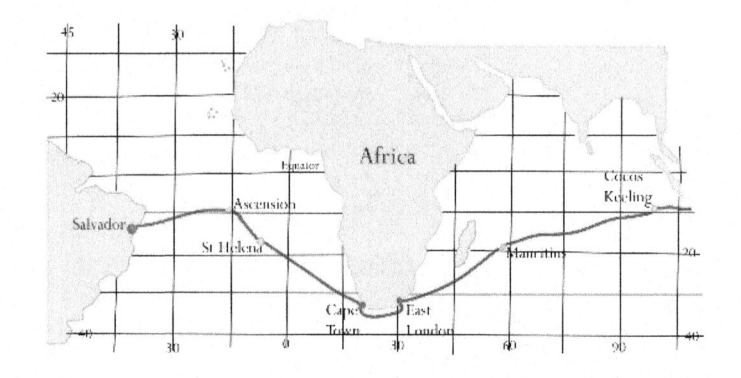

A window in the weather gave us favourable sailing conditions until, in 25 degrees south latitude, we escaped from the influence of westerly and northwesterly winds.

A bright full moon rose from the horizon in the east on the evening of 15th June. As we watched, the disk began to darken and the lower part became obscured. Presently our satellite was reduced to a dim russet blob in the sky and the track of moonlight on the sea diminished and turned dull red. We sailed on over a darkened sea for about 20 minutes while the moon slowly regained her brilliance. It is easy to understand why the ancients thought that an eclipse was a portent.

We motor-sailed through a broad band of changeable wind and weather until we encountered the southeast trade winds in 22 degrees south latitude. On this passage Stephen showed himself to be not only a diver and photographer, but also a most patient and skilful fisherman. On most evenings, we dined on fresh dorado (*golden*) or on tuna. Dorado are a fish that mate for life. Eating a dorado can make one feel guilty on account of its bereaved spouse. On one day we ate what we could of a full-sized Wahoo more than a metre long. On another day a monster from the deep arrived on deck.

Stephen and the wahoo

Stephen and the sea monster

The trades settled into the south and southeast, Force 3 or 4, the sea turned a deep blue with scattered white horses and the sky became a pale blue with flocks of fluffy white clouds. The benign trades carried us briskly to the anchorage off Jamestown, St Helena, where we arrived on the 29th of June. 'This island', remarks Darwin, 'rises like a huge castle from the ocean. A great wall, built of successive streams of black lava, forms around its whole circuit, a bold coast.'[9] The anchorage was sheltered from the wind but not from a perpetual ocean swell.

The most famous inhabitant of St Helena was Napoleon Bonaparte. He was exiled there in 1815 after his defeat at the Battle of Waterloo. He died at Longwood House in 1821 and was buried in the Valley of the Willows, in the interior of the island.

Napoleon's grave in 1838

His body, which was not repatriated until 1840, was still interred on the island when the *Beagle* made her visit. Darwin spent a week ashore living in a cottage near Napoleon's grave. He thought that 'a tomb situated close by cottages & a frequented road does not create feelings in unison with the imagined resting place of so great a spirit'.[10] Today the site of the grave is kept in good order and Longwood House is a well-maintained Napoleonic museum.

Napoleon's grave in 2011

For many months past, my solitary voyaging life aboard *Harrier* had been little harassed by the passage of time. Occasionally the season of the year hastened or retarded me, but I rarely needed to worry about timetables and deadlines. Matters stood otherwise at St Helena for Stephen. He looked up from the screen of his laptop, wearing a thoughtful expression.

'Alexa has e-mailed me from Brazil"', he said. 'The house we have rented has turned out to lack some of the things we expected, it is infested with mosquitoes and bats and is a 40 minute walk through dense tropical growth to the nearest store. Also, my three year old Eliot is missing me.'
'That's rotten luck, and tough on Eliot', I replied.
After a pause Stephen, looking slightly uneasy, asked me, 'Since things forced you to leave out a visit to the Galápagos and we had no time to go to the Falklands, would you consider missing Ascension Island as well? We could get to Brazil more quickly if we sailed there directly from here. Alexa isn't happy with her situation and I would like to help her out as soon as I can.'
I thought about the problem for several hours before replying that, 'The purpose of *Harrier's* voyage is to go to all the places that the *Beagle* visited. I've had to bypass some important places but I'm reluctant to miss out on another.'

To my great relief Stephen then agreed that we should try to complete the whole of our planned transit of the South Atlantic. We determined to sail to Brazil via Ascension as fast as *Harrier* could carry us.

The 700 mile passage to Ascension took us eight days of pleasant, rapid sailing. Ascension seemed like a smaller version of St Helena. Darwin quoted the people of St Helena as saying that; 'We know we live on a rock, but the poor people at Ascension live on a cinder.'[11] The anchorage off Georgetown was at least as disturbed by ocean swell as that at Jamestown. Nearly five years of voyaging had not reconciled Darwin to life on board a ship. 'The ocean is a raging monster, insult him a thousand miles distant, & his great carcase is stirred with anger through half an hemisphere.'[12] However, the interior landscape of Ascension, like the interior of St Helena, is green, fertile and tranquil. Both places felt blessedly removed from the aimless rush of life in the wider modern world.

FitzRoy took the *Beagle* on a south-southwest course from Ascension for Brazil in order to complete her chain of meridian distances around the world. This was 'a sore discomfort & surprise to those on board who were most anxious to reach England'.[13] Like the *Beagle*, *Harrier* had a rendezvous in Brazil. On 16th July we cut short our visit to Ascension, got our anchor on board and headed slightly south of west for Salvador de Bahia. The whole passage lay comfortably within the zone of the southeast trade winds. *Harrier* hurried onward before a brisk quartering breeze.

We found that the most comfortable daily routine on passage was to keep watches of four hours on and four off. Stephen liked to be awake at dawn, when he could see the sun appear in the east and watch it rise to fill the new day with light and warmth. I preferred to keep the evening watch, when the sun set behind banks of red and gold clouds, the stars came out and darkness spread over the deep. Differences of temperament manifest themselves in many ways, including as an attitude toward the rotation of the earth upon its axis.

The 29th of July 2011 was my 78th birthday. Soon after dark on that evening we were 40 miles from the coast of Brazil. Over the bow we could see the glow cast into the sky by the lights of the city of Salvador. Next day we left the Santo Antonio shoal and the Farol da Barra to starboard, and once again *Harrier* entered into the great inland sea of Baia de Todos os Santos.

The *Beagle* had done the same thing in 1836. She finished her journey around the world on the first day of August. I completed my circumnavigation at the same spot 175 years later, almost to the day.

Arrival in Salvador. Farol da Barra in the background.

Of the 22 chronometers with which the *Beagle* sailed in 1831 only two failed to complete the voyage. One of those that were still working was judged to be an indifferent performer, 14 were described as rather good, four were good and one, made by Murray, was described by FitzRoy as very good. During the circumnavigation, the readings from the 20 functioning instruments were averaged according to a careful arithmetical method. The chronometer times for the successive passages were carefully recorded. At Salvador in 1836 the times were summed at precisely the spot, the Fotro San Pedro, from which the *Beagle* had departed in 1832. The fort was sited near the present position of the Bahia Marina. FitzRoy was able to boast that; 'The whole chain exceeds twenty four hours by about thirty three seconds of time.'[14]

In 1839 FitzRoy wrote that;

> Mr G J Stebbing, of Portsmouth - who was engaged for the purpose, as well as to keep our instruments in repair, take care of our collection of books, assist in magnetic and other observations, and write for me - was of invaluable assistance; and, I may well say, contributed largely to whatever was obtained by the Beagle's voyage.[15]

Stebbing is another of the unsung heroes of the voyage of the *Beagle*. His work, together with the work of others on board the *Beagle*, helped to make possible accurate navigation by chronometer in South America and many other part of the world.

Chapter 15
Homeward Bound

A ship's voyage and human life are well compared, each being from a port to a port.

John Scott Hughes, *Sailing Through Life*, 1947

Harrier reached Brazil with, for Stephen, two days in hand. The day after our arrival he was reunited with Alexa and Elliot and on the following day they boarded a plane for their flight back to Buenos Aires. Stephen and I had crossed the South Atlantic in good style and in amity. If I come to part with *Harrier* I shall try to sell her to Stephen and he will try to buy her.

Salvador has the reputation of being, after São Paulo, the worst city in Brazil for criminal violence. Early in the afternoon on 8th August I was walking back to the Bahia Marina from Campo Grande along the main coastal highway of the city. It runs beneath a cliff face while on the seaward side a large *barrio* slopes down the water. I paused to take a photograph. I then noticed that I was being followed along the pavement two young men. They were tidily dressed and looked no different from many other people to be seen every day in the city streets. One overtook me, and as I turned to see where the other was walking I found myself looking at the pointed end of a large hunting knife. Simultaneously my rucsac was torn from my back. 'Hand over the camera!' This I did, whereupon the two ran back along the road with their loot before disappearing down a staircase leading into the lanes of the *barrio*. These two were not poverty stricken nor did they look degenerate – they were just plain criminals.

The experience of being robbed at knife point made me decide me to leave the streets of Salvador. An afternoon's sail north from the city brought me into the sheltered bay of Aratu. Before dark I picked up a mooring buoy off the well-remembered clubhouse belonging to the Aratu Iate Clube. Next day I was once again sitting on the club veranda, admiring the view and eating lunch. A smart middle-aged man wearing well-made casual clothes sat down at the next table. His calm, purposeful demeanour seemed to be familiar. Looking across at me, he asked in English,

175

'Have you just arrived?'
'Yes.'
'Where are you from?'
'I arrived last week from Ascension Island. Mine is the small yellow boat on the mooring over there.'
'That is interesting. A few years ago we had another small yellow boat here. Yes - I remember now - it was sailed by an Englishman named Julian.'
'That man was me. I am Julian and it was me aboard that boat. And I think you must be Otavio.'
For a moment Otavio looked at me in astonishment. Then his face broke into a broad smile of recognition. He got up and came over to my table. I stood and he gave me a warm Brazilian hug around the shoulders.
Welcome back to Aratu. How are you these days? I did not recognise you with a white beard.'
'Thanks, and I barely recognised you. You have put on weight around the middle.', I said.
'Afraid so.', he replied.

    I remained at Aratu for nine days while I decided on my next move. In 1836, on her homeward voyage, the *Beagle* sailed from Recife (*Reef*) in Pernambuco directly to the Cape Verdes against the north-east trade winds. The *Beagle* was 27 metres long and displaced 242 tons. *Harrier*, at eight metres and four tons, is too small a boat to beat across an ocean against the steady strength of the trade winds. I evolved a plan to sail north to Jacaré on the Rio Paraiba and to do some work on *Harrier* there. I would then sail from Jacare for the Arquipelago dos Açores (anglicized to *The Azores*) at the beginning of the next southern winter, in order to arrive in the North Atlantic in early spring.

    At Jacaré, on the south bank of the Rio Paraiba, there is a long-established boat yard owned by an ex-pat Englishman, Brian Stevens. I made a number of minor repairs and improvements to *Harrier* here during my stay at Jacaré. While there, I discovered that the Brazilian immigration bureaucracy would not allow me to remain in the country for longer than six months. I would have to depart before the end of January 2012. I therefore resolved to leave Brazil at the end of January and await the arrival of the northern spring in the neighbouring country of French Guiana.

    The Fleuve Mahury, on which Cayenne, the capital city of French Guiana is located, is an unsuitable place for yachts. Some 30 miles to the west of the Mahury, the Fleuve Kourou is smaller, better sheltered from the northeast wind and less commercial. In late March, after a prosperous passage from Jacaré, I arrived at the shelter of the three islands of the Îles du Salut, (*Salvation Islands*) where I dropped my anchor near a large cruise ship. The islands lie some 8 miles north of the entrance to the Fleuve Kourou.

The Îles du Salut, better known to English speakers under the name of 'Devil's Island', were part of an infamous prison colony for 100 years until its closure in 1954. They are the location of the novel, or memoir, *Papillon* written by Henri Charrière who was a prisoner for 14 years in the 1930s and 40s. The barracks building on Île Royale has been converted into a hotel and the islands are now a popular tourist destination. A faint atmosphere of exile and despair clings to the old stone buildings and continues to pervade the island. After two days I departed the islands and entered the Fleuve Kourou.

The yacht anchorage lies directly opposite the small town of Kourou, on the west bank of the river. At Kourou the river was about the width of the Thames at Teddington. It was bordered by dense mangrove swamp on both banks. From the anchorage the town was out of sight, hidden behind a high wall of mangrove. Flocks of black vultures were always to be seen gliding and soaring over the forest. In the evening the river water at the edge of the muddy banks was patrolled by black skimmers. This bird, which looks rather like a large tern, flew back and forth close above the water. With the elongated lower mandible of its bill it scooped up small fish and other creatures from just beneath the surface. A skimmer's method of feeding is unique.

A black skimmer

Kourou town itself may have been of little intrinsic interest but it lies lay than 30 kilometres from a place of international significance. In 1964, General de Gaulle moved the French rocket launching facilities from Algeria to the banks of the Fleuve Kourou. This was a sound move technically as well as politically. It is advantageous to launch a space rocket from a site in a low latitude. The centrifugal force generated by the rotation of the earth, and imparted to a space rocket at its launch, is greatest at the equator.

Port Spatial de l'Éurope. Ariane 5 rocket on the left.

Eleven years later, in 1975, the European Space Agency took responsibility for the site and since then under French leadership it has been developed into the Guiana Space Centre, also known as the Port Spatial de l'Europe. Britain contributes to the cost of the centre but the rockets themselves have been made in France. More recently, some rockets launched from Guiana are of Russian manufacture.

Early in the morning of 23rd February 2012 I was one of a crowd of about 500 people assembled on a hilltop seven kilometres from the rocket launch pad. Lift-off with a cargo of supplies for the International Space Station was scheduled for 0130 hours. The weather was overcast and settled, the wind was light and there were no reports of technical problems.

A thousand eyes were focused on the distant floodlit launch gantry as the public address loudspeaker counted down the seconds. On cue, the launch pad was engulfed in a sea of flame as the unmanned Ariane 5 rocket lifted off and rapidly gained speed. Twenty seconds after lift-off the throaty roar of the motor reached us. The Ariane accelerated steadily before disappearing into cloud. The clouds became illuminated from within, and it looked from below as if the sun had suddenly arisen overhead in the middle of the night. The roar of the motor grew fainter as the rocket sped away, propelled into space by its ball of fire. Presently the clouds reverted to their previous pattern of dark and light grey and the sky became silent. The launch of a space rocket at night is the ultimate *Son et Lumière*.

By the end of April I was ready to sail from Kourou for the Azores. I motored *Harrier* out of the Fleuve Kourou and, leaving Devil's Island to starboard, I headed north into the latitude of the north east trade winds. By the time I reached seven degrees north the wind was blowing from the east-northeast at a steady force 4. The next two weeks of sailing were a very tiring. The wind was forward of the beam, *Harrier's* motion was rough and uneven and the small breaking waves sent water and spray across the deck. I set two reefs in the mainsail and together with the staysail sheeted in forward of the mast I settled down to slog it out with the elements. Apart from squalls of rain, one day was like its predecessor and successor. The noon positions moved steadily northward up the chart until, in 30 degrees of north latitude, the wind eased towards the northwest and began to lose its strength.

I was entering the zone of calm and light winds is known as the Horse Latitudes. *Harrier* made slow, but very much more comfortable, progress through these waters and in 34 degrees north we entered the latitude of predominantly westerly winds. However, our entry into the westerlies coincided with a period of unsettled ocean weather. A sequence of complex depressions trailing long fronts was passing north of the Azores. I experienced strong winds from the north and the south together with some calms and much northeasterly wind. The last 180 miles of the passage took me six days of baffling sailing. On the morning of 21st June, the rocky western end of the island of Faial came into sight, looking grey and dismal beneath a layer of dense cloud, I remembered the words of Joshua Slocum aboard the *Spray* in 1895. 'Only those who have seen the Azores from the deck of vessel realize the beauty of the mid-ocean picture.'[1]

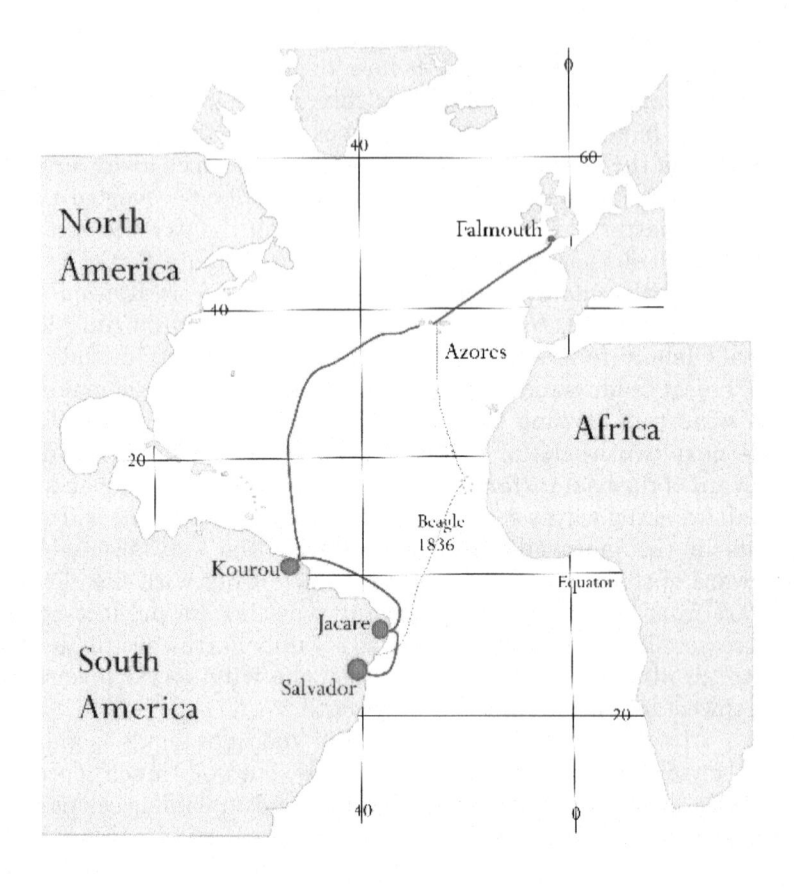

When I started *Harrier's* motor in order to enter the marina at Horta, I found that no power was being transmitted from the motor to the propeller. I entered the harbour under sail and anchored just inside the breakwater. Another yachtsman in his outboard powered inflatable dinghy towed us to the reception dock. The passage from Kourou had taken me 47 days. This was altogether too long a time to spend with only myself for company. Long passages have to be undertaken, but for me the ideal ocean passage lasts no longer than two weeks. One's own inner resources are apt to become exhausted on a very long ocean voyage.

Once the *Beagle* had sailed from Recife, Darwin no longer had active duties as the expedition naturalist. On passage to England, he and Covington occupied themselves with making fair copies of his notebooks and putting his papers into order. The work was often interrupted by his old affliction, sea-sickness. On passage to the Cape Verdes he records that;

> We lie close hauled to the wind, & therefore there is considerable pitching motion; I suffer very much from sea-sickness. – But it is on the road to England; in truth some such comfort is necessary to support the tedious misery of loss of time, health & comfort.[2]

The passage may have been uncomfortable but it was no small achievement, by FitzRoy and his crew, to take a small square-rigged ship such as the *Beagle* across an ocean against the force of a trade wind.

They arrived at Santiago on 31st August 1836 and after a stay of only five days, the *Beagle* departed for the Azores. This passage was a great deal easier than the earlier contest with the trade winds. After less than three weeks at sea, they were at anchor in the harbour of Angra under the lee of Monte Brasil.

Angra (*brook or stream*) on the island of Terceira was the capital of the Azores until 1835 when the government of the archipelago moved east to Isla São Miguel. The size and architecture of Angra reflect it past glory. While FitzRoy and the crew were busy with their surveying duties, Darwin moved ashore for the last of his land journeys.

The British consul in Angra lent Darwin the use of a horse and the services of guides. He rode along the southeast side of the island to the town of Praia da Vitória (*Victory Beach*). I distrust horses so I rode a small motor scooter along the same route. In Darwin's time, Praia was 'a quiet forlorn little place;'[3] I found it to be a flourishing seaside holiday location. He then rode on to the northeastern part of Terceira which he noted was 'particularly well cultivated, & produces a large quantity of fine wheat.'[4] This farmland is now submerged beneath an airport.

Like Darwin, I saw some old friends in the fields and hedgerows of the island. Chaffinches, starlings and blackbirds flew up at the noise created by the motor of my scooter. The Azorean blackbird seems to be a more slender affair than its plump British cousin.

Terceira reveals its volcanic nature at a small shallow valley in the centre of the island. Many vents of steam emerge from scattered clefts in the ground and the air about them is sulphurous. Darwin was lucky here, as he was in Chile, to find the volcano active.

'Throughout the island, the powers below have been unusually active during the last year; several small earthquakes have been caused, and during a few days a jet of steam issued from a bold precipice overhanging the sea, not far from the town of Angra.'[5]

During the final stage of the voyage of the *Beagle,* Darwin wrote down some reflections on his collections and his observations of the natural world. These thoughts evidently came to him while he and Covington were organizing and completing his ornithological notes.

> When I recollect the fact, that from the form of the body, shape of scales & general size, the Spaniards can at once pronounce from which Isd. [in the Galápagos] any tortoise may have been brought: - when I see these Islands in sight of each other and possessed of but a scanty stock of animals, tenanted by these birds but slightly differing in structure filling the same place in Nature, I must suspect that they are only varieties. The only fact of a similar kind of which I am aware is the constant asserted difference between the wolf-like Fox of East & West Falkland Isds. — If there is the slightest foundation for these remarks, the Zoology of Archipelagoes will be well worth examining: for such facts would undermine the stability of species.[6]

That autumn a spark occurred in Darwin's mind that changed the history of science. Reflecting on the geographical distribution of living creatures set him on a train of thought that would lead to the publication many years later of his *Origin of Species*. On board a Royal Navy 10-gun brig, sailing home across the North Atlantic Ocean in 1836, a new epoch in mankind's view of itself was initiated.

It took the *Beagle* only seven days to make the passage from the Azores to Falmouth Harbour in Cornwall. She arrived there in stormy weather on the 2nd of October 1836. She had been absent for just three months short of five years. The little ship had completed her most famous voyage in good style.

Falmouth in 1826

    Aboard *Harrier* I rejoined the track of the *Beagle* at Angra, after stopping briefly at Velas on the tranquil island of São Jorge. I had been away a long time and, like the crew of the *Beagle*, I was anxious to arrive back in England quickly, despite the fact that the Azores are an interesting yachtsman's cruising ground in their own right. Secure marinas have been built on most of the inhabited islands. There is much to enjoy in the archipelago, including verdant landscapes, a balmy climate, pretty towns and the gentle manners of the people.

    After a visit of 10 days, I departed from Angra and set off on the last leg of my voyage around the world. I had mostly grey overcast weather but the wind held in the southwest and *Harrier* hurried on towards England. The passage before a fair breeze was routine. Twenty three days out from Angra, on the morning of 4th September 2012 I sailed into the secure harbour of Falmouth and tied up in the municipal marina.

Modern Falmouth

Twelve days later I dropped *Harrier's* anchor at Barn Pool in Plymouth Harbour.

Harrier in Barn Pool. Summer 2012.

After more than 42,000 miles of sailing and 800 days at sea, I had returned to the exact spot from where I had begun my voyage 11 years earlier. Had my stepmother Anne lived she would have travelled down to Plymouth. There she would have given me, as a fellow circumnavigator of the world, a very big hug.

Chapter 16
After the Voyage
Meditation and water are wedded for ever
Herman Melville, *Moby Dick,* 1851

Darwin moved the short distance from the wooden deck of the *Beagle* to a stone quay at Falmouth on the very day of the *Beagle's* arrival. The same evening he took a coach to Shrewsbury and arrived at The Mount the next day. For Darwin the voyage of the *Beagle* was over and his engagement with the sea was at an end. With the solid ground of England firmly under his feet, he became a life-long land lubber. He never departed from the shores of Britain again. From Shrewsbury he wrote to FitzRoy that;

> I arrived here yesterday morning at Breakfast time, & thank God found all my dear good sisters & father quite well – My father appears more cheerful and very little older than when I left. My sisters assure me that I do not look the least different, & I am able to return the compliment. Indeed all England appears changed, excepting the good old town of Shrewsbury & its inhabitants – which for all I can see to the contrary may go on as they now are to Doomsday – I wish with all my heart, I was writing to you, amongst your friends instead of that horrid Plymouth. But the day will soon come and you will be as happy as I now am. ...... Good bye – God bless you – I hope you are as happy, but much wiser than your most sincere but unworthy Philos. Chas. Darwin [1]

For Darwin, the voyage was over but it was not so for FitzRoy. He sailed the *Beagle* from Plymouth to Portsmouth from where he wrote to Darwin that 'Fuller [FitzRoy's steward] told me that you looked very well and had on a good hat!' [2] He took the *Beagle* on to Greenwich on the River Thames. Here the chronometers could be finally calibrated by reference to the time-setting signal ball atop the Octagon Room at the Royal Observatory. The *Beagle* was then moved downriver to the Woolwich Dockyard where she had been launched 16 years earlier. Here the gallant little ship was paid off, or as we would say mothballed, on 17th November 1836.

Darwin and FitzRoy shared their lives aboard a small ship for five years. They had their ups and downs, mostly on account of

FitzRoy's mercurial temper. but they remained friends despite everything. However, during all that time they never discussed the state of their hearts. Shortly after their return to England, FitzRoy wrote to Darwin to announce that he was married to Mary O'Brien, the daughter of a retired Irish general. Darwin knew nothing of the fact that FitzRoy and O'Brien had become engaged before the departure of the *Beagle* in 1831.

While Darwin was occupied in London and Cambridge with editing his notebooks and documenting his collections, FitzRoy settled down to write his account of their voyage. The text of Volumes I and II and his compilation of Volume IV of the *Narrative* were published in 1839. By the date of publication FitzRoy had undergone a religious conversion – it may be that his wife had a part in turning him toward fundamentalist Christianity. For the rest of his life, FitzRoy held that the first chapter of Genesis was a factually correct scientific and historical text.

FitzRoy had no further voyages in prospect when, in 1841, he was offered the chance of election to parliament by his maternal uncle Lord Londonderry. After an acrimonious election, he took his seat in the House of Commons as the controversial member for the County of Durham. A year later his life took another turn.

The short visit of the *Beagle* to the Bay of Islands in 1835 qualified FitzRoy, in the opinion of the British government, to become the second Governor General of the expanding colony of New Zealand. He travelled with his wife and children to Auckland where he took up his new duties in 1843. At the time of his governorship the native Maoris outnumbered the English settlers by a factor of 1000. FitzRoy had much difficulty in preventing the more myopic settlers from provoking a war with the Maoris. The colony had no army or militia and its treasury was bankrupt. FitzRoy made his own position insecure by failing to keep his boss in London, the Secretary of State for the Colonies, properly informed about events in New Zealand. Lord Stanley sacked him after only two years in office. It is doubtful whether FitzRoy or any other man could have made a success of a deeply flawed situation. Upon his dismissal, FitzRoy wailed that: 'I am deeply and irreparably injured'[3]. For my part I confess to a fellow feeling for Robert FitzRoy – he was a man who was a good leader but a hopeless subordinate.

FitzRoy's naval career paused until 1848 when he was appointed Superintendent of Woolwich Dockyard. A part of his duties at Woolwich was to test and evaluate the Navy's first screw-driven steamship, HMS *Arrogant*. In 1851 Francis Beaufort and Charles Darwin were among the 13 Fellows who supported his election as a Fellow of the Royal Society. FitzRoy's high reputation as a mariner, hydrographer and scientist led to his being made the Meteorological Statist at the Board of Trade in 1855. In this role, which he occupied for the rest of his life, he made important contributions to the evolving technique of weather forecasting. In fact, the phrase 'weather forecast' was coined by FitzRoy. During these years he accumulated seniority in the Navy. He was promoted to Rear Admiral in 1857 an Vice Admiral in 1863.

Robert FitzRoy, aged about 57

Despite his worldly success and high reputation, FitzRoy was inwardly a haunted man. Together with his blue blood he had inherited a ghost from his mother's family, the Stewarts. All his life he suffered from a disposition towards melancholia. During his time aboard the *Beagle* he was subject to severe and debilitating bouts of depression. In middle life the family affliction receded from his consciousness to some extent but in later years it resurfaced and brought him to his end. His uncle Castlereagh had cut his throat with a penknife in 1822. Forty three years later, three months before his sixtieth birthday, his nephew Robert FitzRoy in a fit of depression and despair took up his razor and with it he slit his own throat.

The journal of the Life-boat Institution described FitzRoy in its obituary as 'the skilful sailor, the travelled naturalist, the earnest Christian and the best friend of the population which fringes our sea-girt isle.'[4] Everybody admired Robert FitzRoy but he was not liked by all. FitzRoy was a great and good man but, more than are most of us, he was his own worst enemy.

Charles Darwin discovered on his arrival in England in 1836 that he had an enormous publishing task ahead of him. His geological and zoological specimens had been carefully conserved by John Henslow in Cambridge. The work of having them examined by experts in the various natural history disciplines took several years. Darwin complained that; 'I find the geologists are all willing to render all assistance & exceedingly kind, - but the Zoologists seem to think a number of undescribed creatures rather a nuisance.'[5] Eventually, expert identifications and descriptions of his fossils, reptiles, birds and much of the other zoological material became available. Full publication of his *Zoology of the Voyage of the Beagle*, edited by Darwin, was spread over the three years 1840 to 1843.

During these years Darwin found time to write Volume III of the *Narrative*, a text that has become known to the world as *The Voyage of the Beagle*, get married to his cousin Emma Wedgwood, read widely and to frame his theory of evolution by natural selection. In September 1842 he and Emma, with their two children William and Anne, moved to the largest house in the Kentish village of Down, now known as Downe. The move was partly dictated by Darwin's increasingly poor health. He lived at Down for the rest of his life.

Several lines of thought about evolution in the natural world converged in Darwin's mind during the late 1830s. The ornithologist John Gould discovered that the finch specimens collected on the Galapagos Islands by Darwin and others constituted a group of 14 distinct and previously unknown species, which he grouped into four genera. They were not, as Darwin initially supposed, merely 12 varieties of a single species. Each island was tenanted by a particular set of the species, all of whom were endemic to the archipelago. The birds of this group were similar to some of the finches of South America. The most obvious explanation of this pattern of distribution in the Galápagos was that the 14 species were descended from a single immigrant ancestor species. The original birds diverged from one another as they spread onto the different Galápagos islands. These birds have become known to natural science a 'Darwin's Finches'.

By 1840, Darwin had come to doubt the reliability of the Old Testament as a historical document, the plausibility of New Testament miracles and the literal accuracy of the gospel narratives. While FitzRoy's mind was turning to religious fundamentalism, Darwin's ideas were moving towards religious scepticism. But despite the increasing divergence of their religious opinions, FitzRoy and Darwin remained in friendly contact. In 1840 Darwin wrote to FitzRoy to say that;

> I think it far the most favourable circumstance in my life that the chance afforded by your offer of taking a Naturalist fell on me. I often have the most vivid and delightful pictures of what I saw on board the Beagle pass before my eyes. These recollections, and what I learnt on Natural History, I would not exchange for twice ten thousand a year.[6]

After his move to Down House, Darwin took great interest in the methods of the breeders of domestic animals and plants. Selection by humans from the variations that spontaneously occur in nature had clearly brought into being a vast number of creatures that are useful to mankind. Human selection of animals could be observed in action and he 'soon perceived that selection was the keystone of man's success in making useful races of animals and plants. But how selection could be applied to organisms living in a state of nature remained for some time a mystery to me.'[7] Then;

> In October 1838, that is, fifteen months after I had begun my systematic enquiry, I happened to read for amusement Malthus on Population, and being well prepared to appreciate the struggle for existence which everywhere goes on from long-continued observation of the habits of animals and plants, it at once struck me that under these circumstances favourable variation would tend to be preserved and unfavourable ones to be destroyed. The result of this would be the formation of new species. Here, then, I had at last got a theory by which to work; but I was so anxious to avoid prejudice, that I determined not for some time to write even the briefest sketch of it. In June 1842 I first allowed myself the satisfaction of writing a very brief abstract of my theory in pencil in 35 pages; and this was

enlarged during the summer of 1844 into one of 230 pages, which I had fairly copied out and still possess.'[8]

For the following 10 years and more, Darwin worked to refine his ideas and bounce them off scientific friends and colleague, particularly Joseph Hooker at the Royal Botanic Gardens at Kew, Charles Lyell at the Royal Geological Society and his old mentor John Henslow at Cambridge. Eventually the patience of his friends wore thin. In 1856 Lyell persuaded him to settle down to writing a full account of his ideas. If he continued to procrastinate he would be forestalled. In May 1856 Darwin began to compose an enormous three volume, massively detailed book on his theory of evolution by natural selection.

Darwin did not originate the notion of evolution. By the middle of the nineteenth century the writings of the French naturalist Jean-Baptiste Lamarck, Robert Chambers in Edinburgh and Darwin's grandfather Erasmus Darwin had familiarised educated opinion to the idea that the natural world had developed and evolved. Darwin's contribution was to propose a mechanism by which evolution occurred and to show how it operated in nature.

Two years after beginning work on his tome, a letter arrived at Down from one of Darwin's correspondents, Alfred Russel Wallace. Wallace was a traveller and collector of natural history specimens. The letter had been posted in Ternate, an island in what is now Indonesia. While Wallace had been immobilized by a bout of malaria, he had hit upon the idea of evolution in the natural world by natural selection. He wrote his conclusions down in a short lucid essay and included a copy with his letter. If Darwin thought the essay was worthwhile, Wallace wrote, would he please send it to Charles Lyell to see if it might be published.

Darwin was thunderstruck. He wrote to Lyell that 'I never saw a more striking coincidence; if Wallace had had my MS. sketch written out in 1842, he could not have made a better short abstract! Even his terms now stand as heads of my chapters. .... So all my originality, whatever it may amount to, will be smashed,'[9] 'I should be extremely glad now to publish a sketch of my general views in about a dozen pages or so; but I cannot persuade myself that I can do so honourably. .... I would rather burn my whole book, than that he or any other man should think that I had behaved in a paltry spirit.'[10]

The month of June 1858 had brought Darwin a blow to his work and also anguish on account of the death from scarlet fever of his last child, his baby son Charles. While Darwin was prostrated by these two blows his friends took action. Hooker and Lyell arranged that Darwin's 1844 abstract and Wallace's essay, together with Darwin's letter of 1857 to the botanist Asa Gray at Harvard on the principle of divergence, should be read at a meeting of the Linnean Society that November. The meeting marked a turning point in the history of biology and in our ideas about ourselves and the natural world. A short time later Thomas Bell, the president of the Linnean, contrived to write that;

> the year that has passed ... has not, indeed, been marked by any of those striking discoveries which at once revolutionize, so to speak, the department of science on which they bear .... It is only at remote intervals that we can reasonably expect any sudden and brilliant innovation which shall .... confer a lasting and important service on mankind[11]

Disputes over scientific priority are often acrimonious, but at this point both Wallace and Darwin showed themselves to be honourable men. Darwin wrote to Wallace with the text of the Linnean meeting. He was relieved and also impressed by the reply. In a letter to Charles Lyell Wallace said that 'It would have caused me much pain & regret had Mr. Darwin's excess of generosity led him to make public my paper unaccompanied by his own much earlier & I doubt not much more complete views on the same subject,'[12] In later years Darwin was careful to acknowledge Wallace as the co-discoverer of the theory of evolution by natural selection, while for his part Wallace published his book *Darwinism* in 1889. Wallace and Darwin behaved to one another with admirable justice and candour.

The arrival of Wallace's essay at last prompted Darwin to put his ideas down on paper in a digestible form. In August 1858 he settled down to the most intensive spell of work in his life. The result was the publication in November 1859 of his ***On the Origin of Species by Means of Natural Selection, or the Preservation of Favoured Races in the Struggle for Life***. The book sold well and remained in demand. For the next 20 years Darwin took a background role in the progress of his book and in the spread of his ideas. The public conduct of the campaign was mainly in the hands of Charles Lyell, Joseph Hooker and Thomas Huxley. Huxley became known as 'Darwin's bulldog' on account of his forceful advocacy of Darwin's notions and for his pugnacious style of discourse.

It was at the time of his writing the *Origin* that Darwin finally abandoned his waning belief in religion. The implausibility of the arguments for the existence of God, the problem of evil and the finite lifetime of the universe led him to declare himself to be an agnostic. The term was coined by Thomas Huxley to describe those who, on account of the limited scope of human understanding, disclaim knowledge of immortality, the Godhead, destiny or transcendence. By the year 1860, 24 years after the return of the *Beagle* to England, Darwin's religious ideas had come to differ completely from the fundamentalist convictions of his old shipmate Robert FitzRoy.

In Darwin's lifetime there was no satisfactory answer to some of the more serious scientific objections that were soon raised to his theory. He wrote to Asa Gray at Harvard:

> Let me add that I fully admit that there are very many difficulties not satisfactorily explained by my theory of descent with modification, but I cannot possibly believe that a false theory would explain so many classes of facts, as I think it certainly does explain. – On these grounds I drop my anchor & believe that the difficulties will slowly disappear.[13]

Seven years after the publication of the *Origin*, the Scottish physicist William Thomson (later Lord Kelvin) objected that the energy of the sun would be exhausted long before Darwin's slow incremental processes could have become effective. Thomson estimated the age of the sun at 100 million years. Thomson's business partner, Fleeming Jenkin, observed that if inheritance was a matter of the blending of the characteristics of the parents, then the features of a novel individual would quickly become merged back into the general population and its uniqueness would be quite lost within a few generations.

The discovery in the late nineteenth century of radioactivity, and the re-discovery in the early twentieth century of the work of Gregor Mendel on inheritance, provided solutions to the difficulties raised by Thomson and Jenkin. In the middle of the twentieth century the realisation that the replication of DNA underlies reproduction in the whole of the living world, from bacteria to plants and animals, confirmed Darwin's conception of all living things being connected by a great network of inheritance. During the latter part of his life Darwin extended his evolutionary principles to include mankind, and he tried to understand the occurrence in nature of the variation of individuals within the same species. Near the end of his life he made important contributions to the knowledge of the physiology of plants.

Charles Darwin did not lay claim to the possession of a notably powerful intellect. He attributed his scientific success to a capacious memory, a talent for observation and a capacity for hard work. Darwin's mind was like a sunrise which slowly but surely casts a comprehensively bright light over a wide landscape. Thomas Huxley's mind, on the other hand, was like an intellectual searchlight. He could quickly cast a brilliantly illuminating light onto the most difficult areas of science. Huxley could instantly find the correct answer to a question but Darwin's central skill was to know how to ask the right question in the first place.

Our modern educational system rewards a candidate who can answer a given question quickly, fully and accurately. Nowadays we recognize and reward the Huxleys of our time, but we undervalue the talents of people who possess a creative and discursive mind of Darwin's type, at our peril.

Despite persistent ill health Darwin lived for 23 years after the publication of the *Origin*. The steady spread of his ideas destroyed the ancient and comforting image of a benevolent god who had created the natural world as a vast assembly of perfectly inter-related living creatures. The basic idea of natural theology, that the scientific study of the world was to understand the handiwork of God and thus to reveal the benevolent workings of the divine mind, was contradicted by the mechanistic notion of natural selection. Darwin's substitution of a natural for a celestial origin of living things was a profoundly disturbing notion for many millions of people. The *Origin* obliged all thinking people to revise many of their most cherished assumptions about life, time and destiny. For them, the world after Darwin became a bleaker and more abstract place in which to dwell.

Charles Darwin, aged about 70.

In 1881 Darwin finished writing an autobiographical memoir in which he summed up his life for the benefit of his family and friends. It was only published in full 50 years after his death. It contains character sketches of FitzRoy and many other people who played important parts in his life. He wrote that 'The voyage of the Beagle has been by far the most important event in my life and has determined my whole career; .... I have always felt that I owed to the voyage the first real training or education of my mind.'[14] His memories of his five years aboard the *Beagle* shadowed him for the rest of his life.

He was also dogged throughout his adult life by chronic ill-health. In the autobiography Darwin says of his wife Emma;

> in my whole life I have never heard her utter one word which I would rather have been unsaid. She has never failed in the kindest sympathy towards me, and has born with the utmost patience my frequent complaints from ill-health and discomfort. I do not believe that she has ever missed an opportunity of doing a kind action to anyone near her. I marvel at my good fortune that she, so infinitely my superior in every single moral quality, consented to be my wife. She has been my wise advisor and cheerful comforter throughout life, which without her would have been during a very long period a miserable one from ill-health.[15]

Without her Darwin could have achieved nothing. Emma is an unsung heroine of the Darwinian revolution.

By the time of his death in 1882 from heart failure Darwin had become generally recognised as one of the most distinguished Englishmen of all time. A group of men eminent in science, politics and religion wrote to the Dean of Westminster to say that 'it would be acceptable to a very large number of our countrymen of all classes and opinions that our illustrious countryman, Mr. Darwin, should be buried in Westminster Abbey.'[16] On 26th April he was lowered into his last berth in the north aisle of the nave of the abbey. His grave is near the monument of Isaac Newton, the grave of his critic Lord Kelvin and to that of Charles Lyell, his long-time friend and mentor.

It is remarkable how quickly Darwin's theory of evolution by natural selection became generally accepted. When he died, not quite 23 years after the publication of *Origin of Species*, his theory had been largely adopted by educated opinion. One of his obituaries said of him that he was 'the man of this generation who will be to it what Bacon and Locke and Newton were to theirs.'[17]

For my part I have found that the voyaging life on board a yacht is a varied one. In harbour, the days are full and busy with seeing new sights, making new friends and maintaining the boat. When at sea, the rhythm of life is quite different. Here there are no bosses or customers to placate, no telephones to answer, no e-mail messages to read and reply to, and no road traffic to evade. Aside from occasional episodes of bad weather, the daily routine is peaceful and one day is much like the previous day or the next. Time passes, the noon positions move slowly across the chart and one has leisure to read, think and reflect. Darwin, too, found life at sea conducive to thinking and working. In 1832 he wrote to his father that 'I find to my great surprise that a ship is singularly comfortable for all sorts of work. - Everything is so close at hand, & being cramped, makes one so methodical, that in the end I have been a gainer. .... If it was not for sea-sickness the whole world would be sailors.'[18]

It is for others to judge whether the experience of a circumnavigation aboard *Harrier* has much altered, for good or ill, my character or personality. However, my outlook on life did evolve over the course of more than 800 days at sea. By the end of the voyage I felt more distant than I did at the outset from the so-called 'real world' of business, politics, sport and competitive ambition. These things receded into the background of my consciousness while other preoccupations came to occupy the forefront of my mind.

The author aged 78

During long passages in the open ocean I found myself with leisure to dwell on an analogy between my boat and our planet earth. On an ocean passage I was entirely dependent upon *Harrier* for support, food, water, shelter, survival and arrival. The resources on board the boat were finite and I was obliged to use them with discretion, foresight and economy. If a piece of equipment failed, I tried to make a repair - I could not simply throw it away and get a new one. As *Harrier* sailed across the ocean I navigated and maintained her carefully, since she was the only 'sea capsule' that I had.

Yacht *Harrier* sailing across the wide ocean

The collective position of mankind on the earth is not dissimilar to my solo situation aboard *Harrier* at sea. We are all entirely dependent upon planet earth for support, food, water, shelter and survival. As with *Harrier*, the resources on board spaceship earth are finite. If the earth is to remain habitable it must be maintained and its resources used with foresight and discretion. The earth, as it spins through space, is the only 'survival capsule' that we have. My circumnavigation has left me with an enhanced appreciation of the precariousness of human life and with a more realistic understanding of the fragility of planet earth.

Planet earth spinning through limitless space

Appendix A
Map of the Voyage of the Beagle

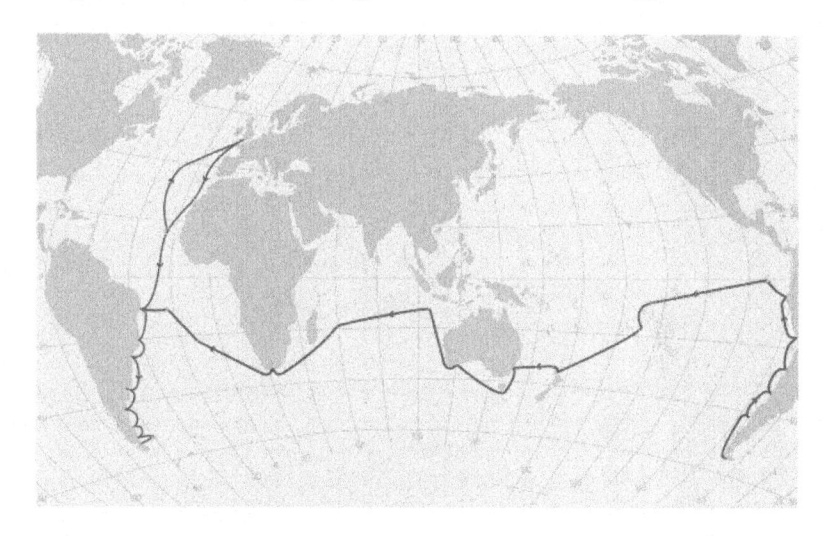

The voyage of the *Harrier* follows closely the track of the *Beagle* around the world from 1831 to 1836, which is shown on this map.

Appendix B
Map of the Voyage of the Harrier

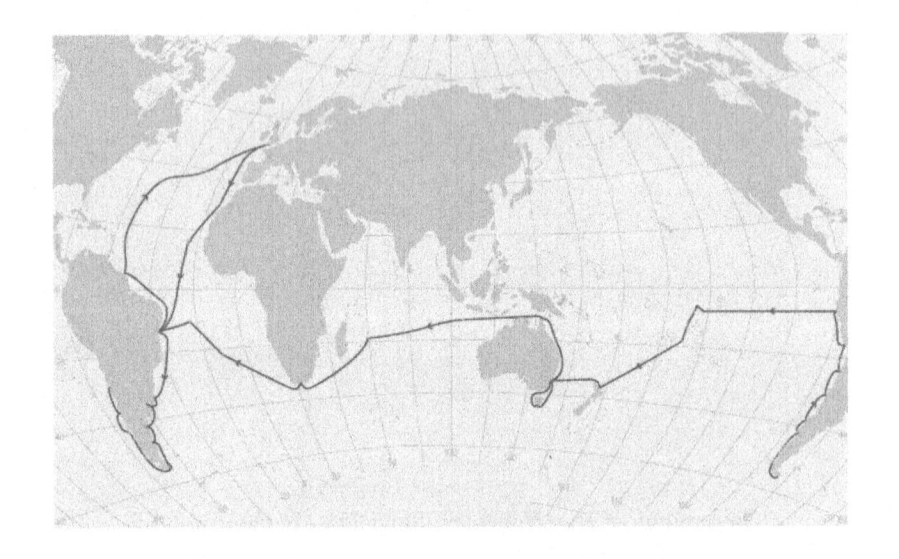

Appendix C
HMS Beagle

In the later stages of the Napoleonic wars a new class of small warship, the 10-gun Brig, was developed by the Royal Navy for communication, fleet supply and scouting purposes. The first 10-gun Brig was launched in 1807 and eventually some 100 were built. They were not well thought of. So many 10-gun brigs foundered at sea in bad weather that they acquired the reputation of 'coffin brigs'[1]. A later author described them as 'this worthless class[2].

HMS *Beagle*, a 10-gun Brig, was launched at Woolwich Royal Dockyard, on the river Thames, in 1820. She measured 27.75 metres overall on deck, 7.50 metres in beam and her draught aft was 4.00 metres. Despite the poor reputation of her class the *Beagle* survived the hazards of the sea for the next 50 years, and on account of her illustrious career she became one of the most famous ships ever to serve in the Royal Navy.

HMS *Beagle* rigged as a barque for her second surveying voyage

The *Beagle* was placed into the charge of Robert FitzRoy by the Admiralty in July 1831. He carried out a comprehensive refit at the Royal Naval Dockyard at Devonport on the river Tamar, around the corner from the city of Plymouth.

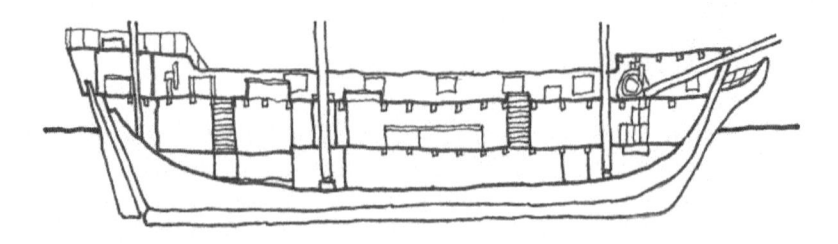

Longitudinal section of HMS *Beagle*

At the dockyard, many of her timbers were found to be rotten. During the course of rebuilding her hull, the ship's main deck was raised by eighteen inches. This increased the headroom in the main deck below from 1.40 metres to just over 1.70 metres and helped to keep her people moderately well accommodated and fed throughout her coming voyage. This improvement also had the effect of increasing the *Beagle's* freeboard and so making her more weatherly than the standard 10-gun brig. A mizzen mast was added aft so as to make her technically a barque rather than a brig. Modern features such as lightning conductors on the masts and a closed cast-iron galley stove just abaft the foremast were installed. A modern windlass was fitted forward for lifting her anchors. FitzRoy was very pleased with the work of the dockyard – 'all was as perfect as humanly possible'.[3]

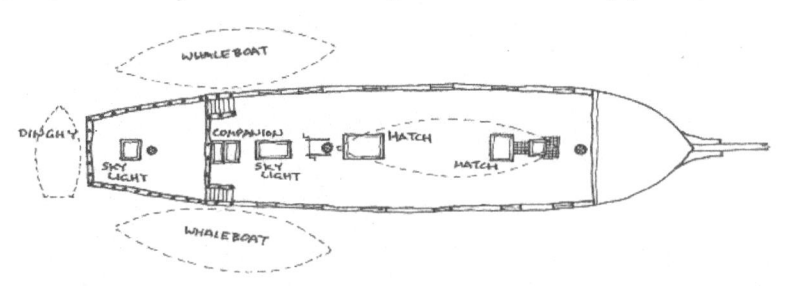

Main deck of HMS *Beagle*

Under FitzRoy's direction, a sheltered space was created aft on the main deck, immediately forward of the new poop cabin and drafting room, in which the helmsman stood to steer the ship. From here the *Beagle* was steered around the world. The drawing of the *Beagle's* wheel shown below was made from memory by Philip Gidley

King, who had served on the voyage of the *Beagle* as a midshipman fifty years before.

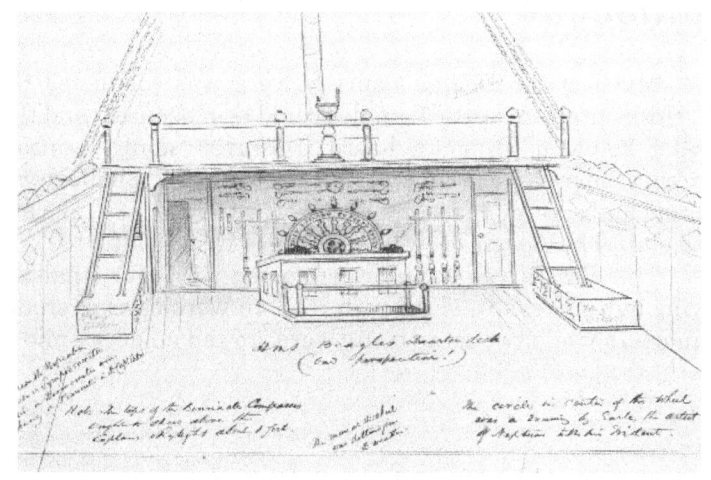

HMS *Beagle's* poop deck

The *Beagle* emerged from her refit at Devonport a more commodious and seaworthy vessel than before. Nevertheless, she remained a small ship to carry so many men so far on so arduous a voyage.

Scale model of HMS *Beagle*

Appendix D
Whaleboat

Much of the *Beagle's* survey work was conducted from her deck. Horizontal and vertical angles could be measured, and the depth of water sounded, from on board. However, many locations that required a survey were inaccessible to the ship. Shallow water, or water encumbered by reefs and shoals were no place to take a square-rigged ship. The *Beagle* drew as much as 4 metres aft.

The *Beagle* was therefore equipped with four whaleboats for carrying out surveys in shoal waters. Two were carried on davits at the quarters while two more boats were stowed on deck amidships.

The whaleboat class was evolved during the late eighteenth century for the New England whale fishery. They were typically 30 feet long and six foot in beam. They were rowed by four men working very long oars. The boat was often steered by a coxswain using a fifth long oar.

A whaleboat was double ended so that the whale could be approached conveniently, while the boat could retreat quickly if the whale showed fight. The design was found to be weatherly and versatile. Whaleboats were soon adopted by the Royal Navy for use as workboats and as ships' tenders.

The *Beagle's* whaleboats were as indispensable for her survey work as were her sextants, chronometers, compasses and leadlines.

Appendix E
Harrier of Down (the first)

With a war raging and Denmark and Norway under German military occupation, Scandinavia in 1942 was neither the time nor the place from which a popular design for a small sailing yacht might emerge. Nevertheless, in that year the Scandinavian Yacht Racing Union gave the Swedish yacht designer Tord Sunden the job of making sense of several similar, promising designs for a new, small cruising yacht. The result of his work was the Folkboat, or 'people's boat'. In the years immediately after the end of the Second World War, the Folkboat became one of the most popular small cruising and racing yachts in Scandinavia, Britain, many parts of Europe, Australia and the United States. Since that time, many thousands of Folkboats have been built in all parts of the world and the class remains active and in production today.

A Folkboat is 7.64 metres (25 feet) long, 2.20 metres (7 foot 3 inches) in beam and she draws 1.20 metres (3 foot 9 inches) of water. The hull of the original design was clinker built in softwood. She has a three-quarter Bermuda sloop rig, a tiny cabin and was intended to be sailed without an inboard engine. A Folkboat is a simple, seaworthy and economical boat that is affordable, capable of accommodating two people in modest comfort or four people in acute discomfort, and that is able to keep the sea.

A standard Folkboat under way.

The class became so popular that many yacht designers and builders throughout the world have made their own interpretations of the Folkboat specification. One of these was the fibreglass Folksong design built in Cheshire by Eric Bergquist. Early in 1997 I bought the Folksong *Zeta*. She departed from the standard Folksong, and indeed Folkboat, design in having a junk rig, rather than being rigged as a sloop.

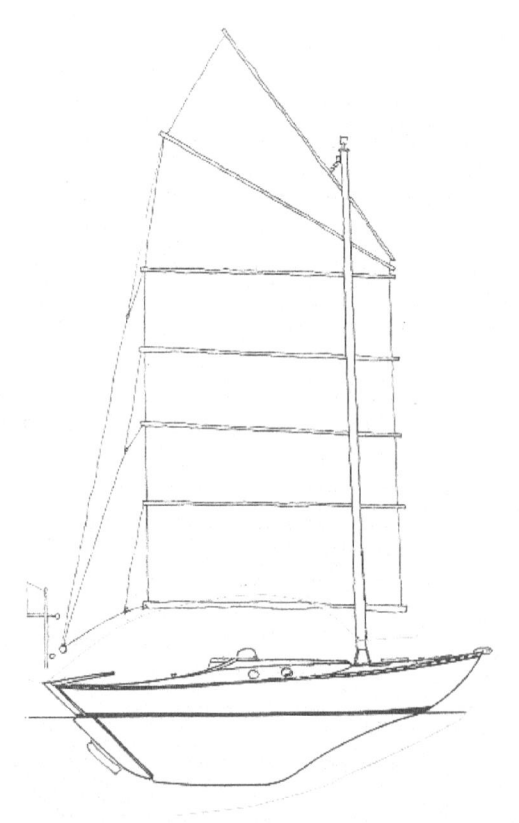

Zeta. A junk rigged Folksong

After buying her, I took *Zeta* to a boatyard at Pin Mill, on the river Orwell in Essex. I removed *Zeta's* flush deck and cabintop and replaced it with a raised turtle deck covering the whole length of her hull, including her cockpit. This provided me with three cabins below and full sitting, though not standing, headroom in the main and aft cabin. Her new shape was more seaworthy than the old, for the cabintop and cockpit are the features of a conventional sailing yacht that are most vulnerable to rough seas. I retained *Zeta's* junk rig.

After two years of work everything was ready. My stepmother, the classicist and travel writer Anne Mustoe, christened her with an ancient Greek invocation to Poseidon. We thought that to conduct the full Greek launch ceremony, involving the sacrifice of a bull, would not meet with universal approval in rural Suffolk. The boat took the water at Pin Mill on the River Orwell on 27th September 1998. She emerged from her transformation as *Harrier of Down*.

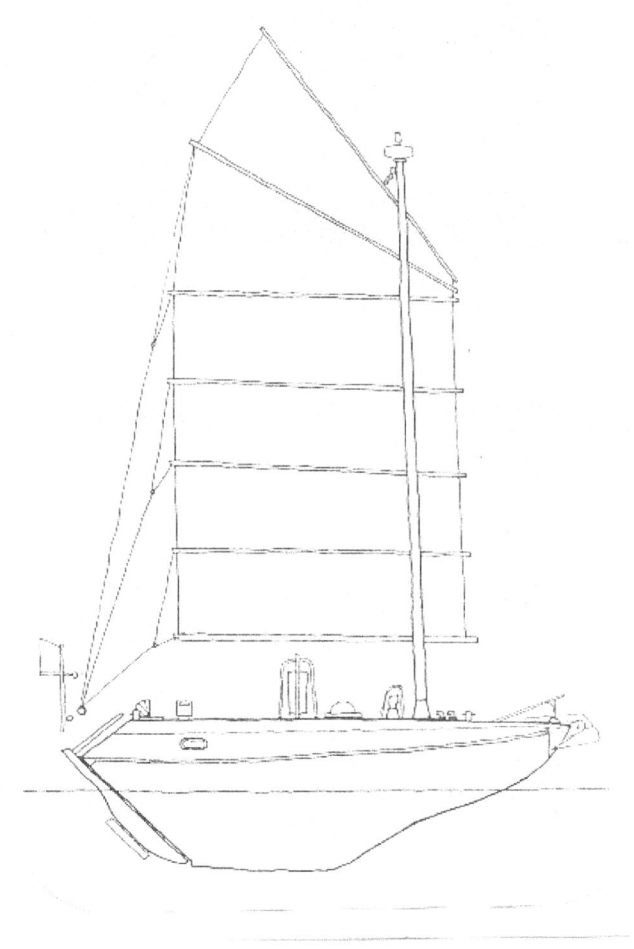

Zeta transformed into *Harrier of Down*

The author on *Harrier of Down*.
Note the raised turtle deck and the aft cabin occupying the part of the hull that is usually devoted to an open cockpit.

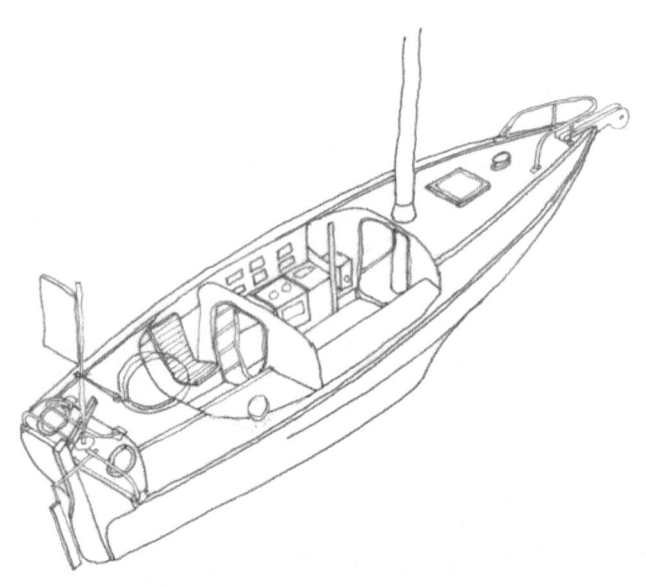

Cut-away drawing of *Harrier's* hull and arrangements

The main cabin forward has a bunk to starboard and the galley and cabin heater to port. The aft cabin is separated from the main cabin by a bulkhead and book shelves, and contains a seat to port and the chart table to starboard. The whole space below deck forward of the mast is devoted to storage.

Her wind-vane steering gear consists of a trim-tab on the rudder which is controlled by a vane. The trim-tab moves the rudder and, in turn, the yacht responds to the rudder.

On account of a mistake in navigation, *Harrier* went aground on the Atlantic coast of the Peninsula Valdés in Patagonia, Argentina, in February 2004. She could not be refloated and the ocean swell broke her up on the beach. The first *Harrier of Down* was a good boat.

Appendix F
Harrier of Down (the second)

In October 2004, seven months after the loss of the first *Harrier* on the Peninsula Valdez, I bought another boat from Juan José, a member of the Yacht Club Argentino in Buenos Aires. *Samba* was built in 1981 to a high standard by the Astillero Marco on the Río de la Plata from a design by Doug Peterson of San Diego, California. Her class, the Peterson 26, measures as a quarter tonner under the International Offshore Rule according to which ocean racing yachts were designed in the 1970s and 1980s. She measures 7.81 metres (25 feet 8 inches) overall, 2.57 metres (8 foot 5 inches) beam and she draws 1.40 metres (4 foot 7 inches) of water.

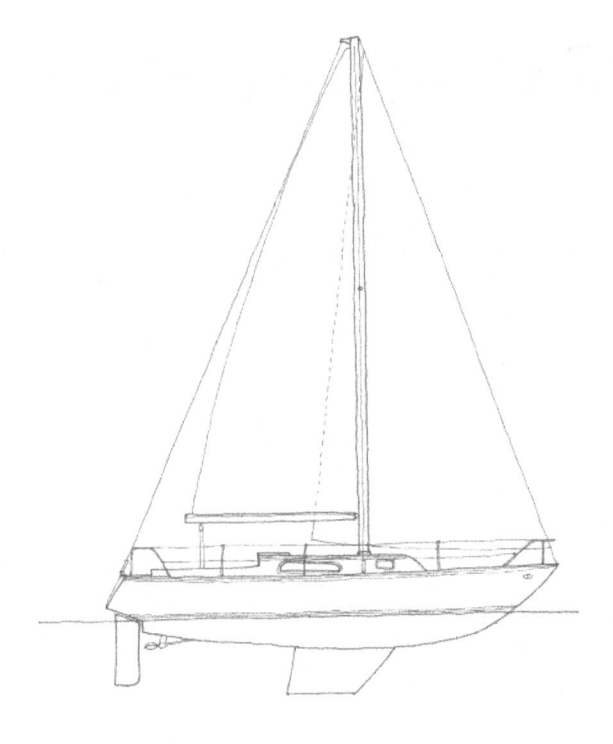

A standard Peterson 26 quarter tonner. Note her racing rig with a tall mast and large genoa, her

Samba had been used as a cruising boat in the delta of the Río de la Plata and during her life she had been little raced. A good deal of work was needed to make her suitable for the more demanding life of an ocean cruiser. The only change that I made to her hull was the installation of a bridgedeck to separate the accommodation from cockpit. Other changes involved in her transformation from *Samba* to *Harrier of Down* can be seen by comparing the drawing above with the next one.

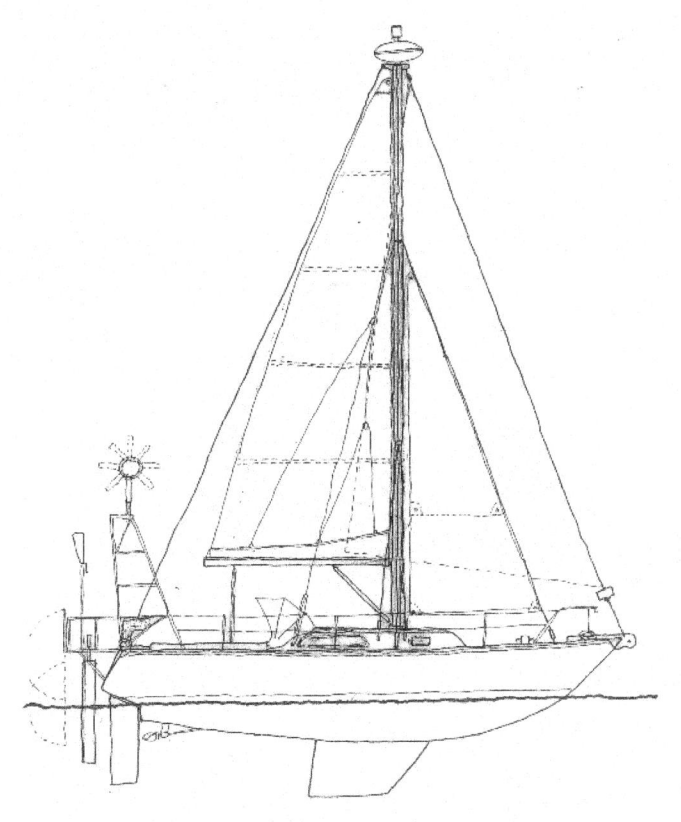

The new *Harrier of Down*. A Peterson 26 modified so as to make her suitable for ocean cruising.

Harrier is furnished with a stainless steel platform aft, which supports a boarding ladder and a wind vane steering gear. Above the aft end of her deck there is a tubular stainless steel gantry which carries a solar panel and a wind generator above head level. She has a really adequate spray dodger over the main hatch. The rugby football shaped object at the masthead is a high performance radar reflector.

A standard Peterson 26 genoa is a powerful racing sail but requires a great deal of effort to handle it properly. A genoa has no place aboard a short-handed ocean cruising yacht. *Harrier* is now rigged for cruising as a cutter, with a high-cut yankee jib and a self-setting staysail, together with a cut-down mainsail, all set on a shorter mast. The boom is higher above deck level than on the standard Peterson 26 layout, so as to give more air to the navigator's head.

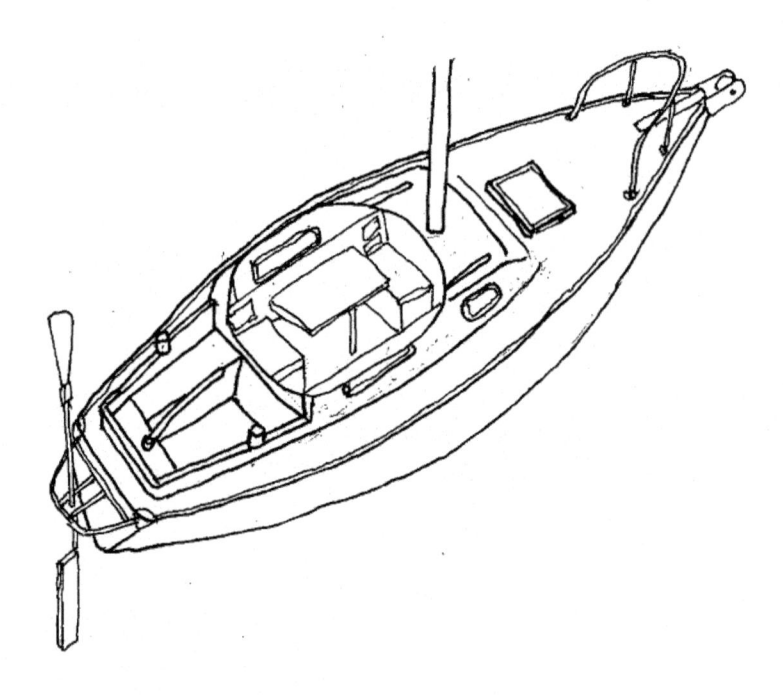

A cut-away view of the second *Harrier of Down*

Sailing a yacht like *Harrier* requires only a modest amount of physical effort, but laying down her anchor and raising it again can be hard work. *Harrier* carries a two heavy anchors, an anchor windlass, 60 metres of 8 millimetre chain and she has two large diameter chain rollers on her bow from which her anchors are deployed.

Harrier of Down the second under way

The modifications to create the new ***Harrier*** took three times as long to carry out as I had planned and they cost me twice as much money. Some things never change.

Appendix G
Table of Distances and Times

Distances measured by Google Earth.
Distances are as navigated from mooring to mooring. They are not distances in a straight line.

	Distances in nautical miles	Time in days
Plymouth to Santa Cruz de Tenerife	1480	21
Santa Cruz de Tenerife to Praia de Santiago	1077	11
Praia de Santiago to Salvador, Brazil	2086	29
Salvador to Vitória	579	17
Vitória to La Paloma, Uruguay	1196	28
La Paloma to Buceo	116	3
Buceo to Buenos Aires, Argentina	124	1
Buenos Aries to Colonia	27	1
Colonia to Buceo	96	2
Buceo to Bahía Blanca	501	7
Bahía Blanca to Viedma	197	3
Viedma to Peninsula Valdés	102	2
Buenos Aries to Colonia	27	1
Colonia to Buceo	96	2
Buceo to Mar del Plata	266	8

Mar del Plata to Puerto Deseado	760	21
Puerto Deseado to Puerto San Julian	154	3
Puerto San Julian to Puerto Santa Cruz	109	3
Puerto Santa Cruz to Bahía Thetis	314	7
Bahía Thetis to Bahía Buon Suceso	11	1
Bahía Buon Suceso to Harberton (with stops)	90	6
Harberton to Ushuaia	37	1
Ushuaia to Puerto Williams, Chile	26	1
Puerto Williams to Faro Fairway (with stops)	268	34
Faro Fairway to Puerto Eden (with stops)	349	20
Puerto Eden to Castro (with stops)	416	42
Castro to Ancud (with stops)	117	4
Ancud to Valdivia	162	3
Valdivia to Talcahuano	250	5
Talachuano to Higuerillas	255	5
Higuerillas to La Herradura	197	3
La Herradura to Caldera	203	3
Caldera to Iquique	431	6
Iquique to Callao	692	3
Callao to Atuona	4347	46

Atuona to Papeete	907	14
Papeete to Moorea	18	1
Moorea to Opua	2619	43
Opua to Sydney	1250	27
Sydney to Hobart	678	13
Hobart to Sydney (with stops)	944	25
Sydney to Brisbane (with stops	457	32
Brisbane to Horn Island (with stops)	1363	46
Horn Island to Darwin	756	16
Darwin to Cocos Keeling	2026	22
Cocos Keeling to Mauritius	2361	31
Mauritius to East London	1820	27
East London to Simon's Town (with stops)	572	11
Simon's Town to Cape Town	66	1
Cape Town to Saint Helena	1700	20
Saint Helena to Ascension Island``	703	8
Ascension Island to Salvador	1500	14
Salvador to Jacaré	506	7
Jacaré to Kourou	1518	20
Kourou to Horta	2606	47
Horta to Angra	72	1

Angra to Falmouth	1198	23
Falmouth to Plymouth	42	1
Total	43740	801

Appendix H
Ship and Boat Rigs

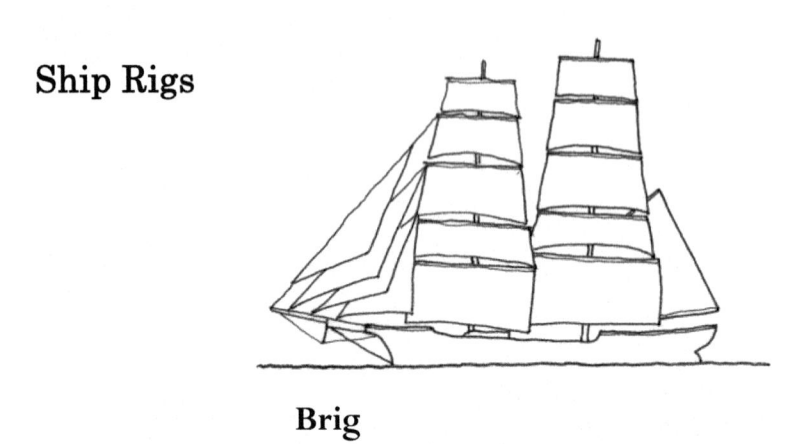

Ship Rigs

Brig

Barque

Full rigged ship

Boat Rigs

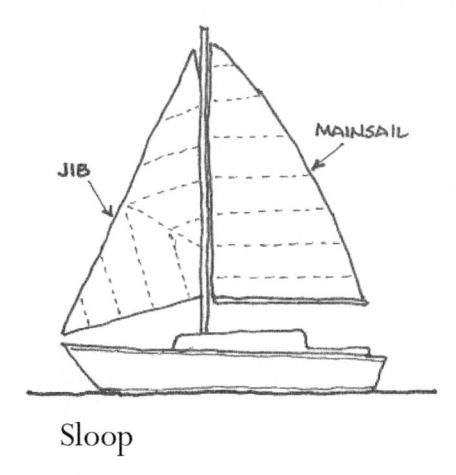

Sloop

The most popular yacht rig, consisting of one mast supporting a mainsail and a single foresail. The drawing shows a genoa jib which overlaps the mainsail. A genoa is a powerful sail, particularly when making to windward. However, it is laborious to handle and it is most suitable for a yacht intended for racing.

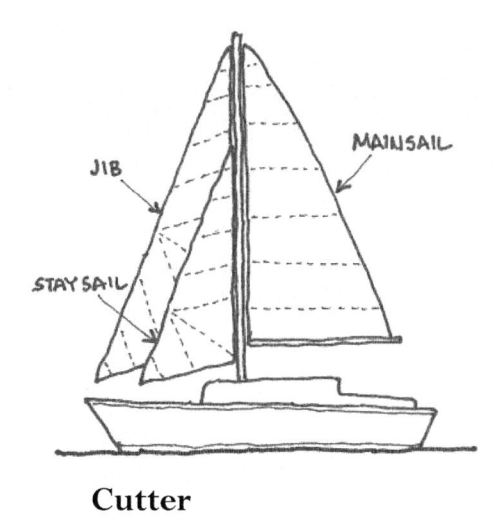

Cutter

A small yacht rigged for cruising is most easily handled when rigged as a cutter. A single mast supports a mainsail and two fails forward. The drawing shows a cutter with an inner staysail and a high-cut yankee jib.

Junk Rig

The type of sail used on traditional Chinese ships has been adopted in recent years for cruising yachts. A junk sail is set on an unstayed mast. The sail is hung from a yard and is extended by full length battens. The end of every batten is controlled by a line, a parrel forward and a sheet aft. Junk sails are less aerodynamically efficient than a sloop or a cutter, but they are very easy to handle and they are less highly stressed than modern Western rigs.

Appendix I
Parts of a Sail

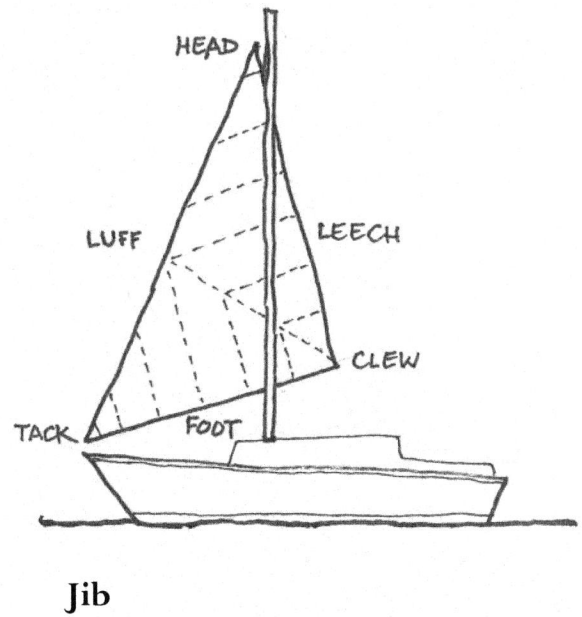

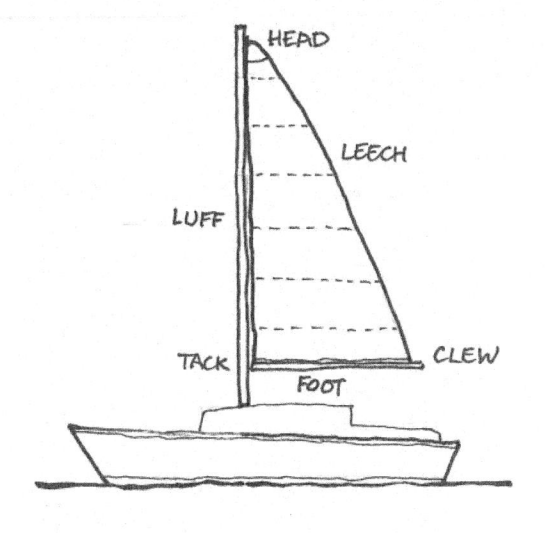

Jib

Mainsail

Appendix J
Beaufort Wind Scale

The Beaufort wind scale was invented by Francis Beaufort, the Hydrographer of the Navy, in 1806 as a method of estimating wind speed without the use of instruments. It was in use at the time of the *Beagle's* voyages and it continues to be used today.

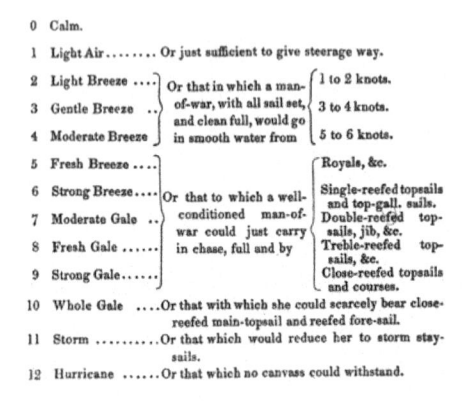

```
 0  Calm.
 1  Light Air........Or just sufficient to give steerage way.
 2  Light Breeze ....⎫                        ⎧ 1 to 2 knots.
 3  Gentle Breeze  ..⎬ Or that in which a man-⎨ 3 to 4 knots.
                     ⎪ of-war, with all sail set,
                     ⎪ and clean full, would go
 4  Moderate Breeze ⎭ in smooth water from    ⎩ 5 to 6 knots.
 5  Fresh Breeze ....⎫                        ⎧ Royals, &c.
 6  Strong Breeze....⎬ Or that to which a well-⎨ Single-reefed topsails
                                                 and top-gall. sails.
 7  Moderate Gale .. ⎪ conditioned  man-of-    ⎪ Double-reefed top-
                     ⎪ war could just carry    ⎨ sails, jib, &c.
 8  Fresh Gale ......⎪ in chase, full and by   ⎪ Treble-reefed top-
                                                 sails, &c.
 9  Strong Gale......⎭                        ⎩ Close-reefed topsails
                                                 and courses.
10  Whole Gale ....Or that with which she could scarcely bear close-
                   reefed main-topsail and reefed fore-sail.
11  Storm ..........Or that which would reduce her to storm stay-
                    sails.
12  Hurricane ......Or that which no canvas could withstand.
```

Wind Scale as Devised by Beaufort in 1806

Force	Speed in knots	Conditions
0	<1	Calm Sea like a mirror
1	1-3	Light Air Ripples only
2	4-6	Light Breeze Small wavlets (0.2m), crests have a glassy appearance
3	7-10	Gentle Breeze Large wavelets (0.6m), crests begin to break
4	11-16	Moderate Breeze Small waves (1m), some white horses
5	17-21	Fresh Breeze Moderate waves (1.8m), many white horses
6	22-27	Strong Breeze Large waves (3m), probably some spray
7	28-33	Near Gale Mounting seas (4m), foam blown in streaks downwind
8	34-40	Gale Moderately high waves (5.5m), crests break into spindrift
9	41-47	Strong Gale High waves (7m), dense foam, visibility affected
10	48-55	Storm Very high waves (9m), heavy sea roll, surface generally white
11	56-63	Violent Storm Exceptionally high waves (11m), visibility poor
12	64+	Hurricane. 14m waves, air filled with foam and spray, visibility bad

Modern Beaufort Wind Scale.

Appendix K
Glossary of Sailing and Yachting Terms

Many words in common use ashore have a different meaning when used aboard a ship.

Aft, Abaft	Relative terms, indicating towards the back end, or stern, of a vessel.
After	A positional term, indicating nearer to a vessel's stern.
Beam	1. The maximum width of a vessel's hull. 2. A horizontal structural member supporting a deck or piece of equipment
Bend	A synonym for knot.
Block	What is called a pulley ashore is known afloat as a ' block'.
Boom	A spar to which the foot of a sail is attached.
Bow	The front end ('sharp end') of a vessel.
Bowsprit	A spar projecting from the bow of a vessel on which t triangular foresails are usually set.
Canvas	A collective term for a vessel's sails. She may be said to be sailing under 'full Canvas' or under 'short can vas' according to the strength of the wind.
Carvel	A wooden hull on which each plank abuts its neigh bour flush is said to be 'carvel built'.
Clinker	A wooden hull on which each plank overlaps its neighbour is said to be 'clinker built'.
Clew	The aft lower corner of a sail.

Cockpit	A part of the deck of a yacht, usually in the form of a shallow well, from which she is steered.
Companion	A staircase or ladder providing communication between a vessel's decks.
Cruising	A yacht engaged in sailing at ease or exploring, as opposed to racing, is said to be cruising.
Cutter abaft	A fore-and-aft sail plan consisting of a mainsail the mast and two foresails, a jib and a staysail, set forward.
Davit	A small crane used to hoist a vessel's boats and stow them clear of the water.
Dinghy	A small open boat used to service a larger vessel. Dinghy design classes are popular racing boats.
Draft	The measurement from water level downwards to the bottom of a vessel's keel.
Ensign	*person* A junior officer. *signal* A flag, usually flown at a vessel's stern, denoting her nationality.
EPIRB	Emergency Position Indicating Radio Beacon
Fetch	A distance over the surface of the water.
Foot	The lower edge of a sail.
Fore	A shortened term in common use to signify 'forward'.
Forefoot	The lower forward end of a vessel's keel.
Fore-and-Aft	A term used to denote a sail which can be set close to the centre line of a vessel's hull. The sails of nearly all yachts are fore-and-aft.

Forward		A relative term indicating towards the front end, or bow, of a vessel

Freeboard		The vertical distance between a vessel's main deck and the surface of the water in which she is floating.

Galley		What is known ashore as a kitchen is referred to afloat as a galley.

Genoa		A type of low-cut jib which overlaps the mainsail. It is a powerful sail when going to windward and is frequently seen aboard racing yachts.

Gooseneck		A universal joint connecting a boom to a mast.

GPS		An acronym standing for Global Positioning by Satellite. A set of between 24 and 32 radio satellites is maintained in geostationary orbit by the American military. A GPS receiver on the earth can calculate its position accurately to within a few metres from the satellite signals. The system is supplied to the world free by the American taxpayer.

Gunwale		The external angle formed by the perimeter of a vessels deck and the side of her hull. Pronounced 'gunnel'.

Halyard		A rope or wire cable used to haul a sail up a mast.

Head		The top corner of a sail.

Heads		What is called the lavatory ashore is known afloat as the 'heads'.

Helm		*noun* The steering apparatus of a vessel. It usually takes the form of a wheel or a tiller controlling the movement of a rudder.
		verb To steer a vessel.

HMS	Royal Navy warships are referred to as Her (or His) Majesty's Ship, or HMS. An auxiliary naval ship such as a tanker, supply ship or workshop ship is known as an RNA, or Royal Naval Auxiliary.
Jib	A triangular fore-and-aft sail set at the forward part of a vessel's sail plan.
Junk Rig	The type of fore-and-aft rig set by traditional Chinese sailing vessels. A junk sail is hung from a yard and is controlled by several battens which are sheeted at both ends. A westernised version of the traditional junk design is used on some modern cruising yachts.
Kedge	A small anchor used to moor a vessel temporarily.
Keel	A plate-like extension below a vessel's hull, designed to give her a grip on the water. The keel of a sailing boat will usually carry a weight intended to provide her, pendulum fashion, with lateral stability.
Knot	1. A configuration used to tie two or more pieces of rope together or a rope to another object. 2. In modern usage a knot is a measure of speed, one knot signifying a speed of one nautical mile per hour. One knot equals approximately 1.15 statute miles per hour. At the time of the voyage of the *Beagle* a knot meant a unit of distance and was used as a synonym for a nautical mile. Hence the use of such phrases in FitzRoy's *Narrative* as "at a rate of eight knots per hour."
Leadline	A calibrated length of light line with a heavy lead weight tied at one end. It is lowered over the side of a vessel in order to measure the depth of the water in which she is floating.

Leech	The after edge of a sail.
Length	1. *Overall* Measured bow to stern at the level of a vessel's main deck. 2. *Waterline* Measured bow to stern at the level of the water in which the vessel is floating.
Luff	*verb* To steer a sailing vessel more directly towards the wind. *noun* The forward edge of a sail.
Mile	1. Statute mile, an artificial unit equal to 5280 feet 2. Nautical mile, a geometric unit equal to one minute of latitude. Due to the fact that the shape of the earth is an oblate spheroid the nautical mile varies in length from 1.843km (6046 feet) at the poles to 1.862km (6108 feet) at the equator. 3. The International Nautical Mile is an average distance defined as 1852 metres. 4. The Imperial definition of the nautical mile, 6080 feet, is obsolete.
Port	1. *noun* A place on a coast offering access and shelter to a vessel. 2. *adjective* The left–hand side of a vessel when facing forward.
Reef	1. *noun* A body of rock or coral situated at or just below the surface of the sea so as to pose a danger to ships. 2. *verb* To reduce the area of sail set in order to take account of the strength of the wind.
RIB	Rigid Inflatable Boat
Rudder	A hinged plate-like extension at or near the aft end of a vessel's hull used to control her direction of motion.
Sheet	Any rope used to control the shape and setting of a sail. Afloat, the word has nothing to do with bed clothes.

Sloop	A fore-and-aft sailplan consisting of a mainsail abaft and a single jib set forward of the mast.
Sound	*noun* A protected body of water connected to the sea. *verb* To measure the depth of the water.
Spar	A pole or beam whose function is to support or to extend the set of a sail. A spar may be a yard, boom gaff or bowsprit.
Square Sail	A square sail is set across the centre line of a vessel's hull. Ocean-going ships in the days of sail were nearly always square rigged.
Starboard	The right-hand side of a vessel when facing forward.
Staysail	A triangular fore-and-aft sail set before a mast but abaft a jib or other sail.
Stern	The back, aft, end of a vessel.
Tiller	A lever-like attachment used to control the horizontal angle of a rudder, and so to steer a vessel.
Warp	*noun.* A rope used to tie a boat to a dock, mooring or to another vessel. *verb.* To move a boat through the water by hauling on one or more warps
Way	The motion of a vessel through the water. When moving she can be said to be 'under way', to be 'making way' or to 'have way on'.
Weigh	A verb used to describe the operation of raising a ship's anchor from the sea bottom.
Tack	*verb* A sailing vessel, which cannot make directly in to the wind, when she is sailing as close to the wind as possible is said to be 'tacking'. *noun* The forward lower corner of a sail.

Transom	The flat after end of a vessel's hull.
Weatherly	A vessel which is well able to cope with strong winds and high seas is said to be weatherly.
Vessel	A general term for any seagoing ship, yacht, boat or craft, It is not usually applied to small dinghies, canoes or to rowing boats.
Yacht	A ship or boat used for pleasure.
Yankee	A type of jib which is popular on cruising yachts It is high cut so as to afford good visibility ahead and to leeward.
Yard	A spar of wood or metal fixed along the top of a sail to hold it in shape and position.

Appendix L
Spanish Terms Used in the Text

Angostura – narrows
Arena - sand
Armada - navy, fleet
Bahía - bay
Barrio - poor urban neighbourhood, a slum
Caleta - cove, spit
Calle - street
Canal – channel
Carretera - highway
Cerro - hill
Cordillera - mountain range
Darsena - dock
Deportivo - sporting
Estancia - farm, ranch
Estrecho - strait
Faro - lighthouse
Fondeadero - anchorage
Frío - cold
Golfo - gulf
Isla - island
Islote - islet
Municipio - borough, municipality
Negro - black
Paso - pass
Plata - silver
Profundo - deep
Puerto – port
Puna – altitude sickness
Punta - point, headland
Racha - strong gust of katabatic wind
Río - river
San - saint
Seno - sound
Trafalgar – 'the furthest edge' (from the Arabic)
Ventisquero - exposed mountainside where snow and ice accumulate, glacier
Volcán - volcano

References

A full description of every citation is provided in the bibliography.

Foreword
www.unknown

Chapter 1. To the Canary Islands
1. Narrative, Volume II, page 42.
2. Diary, page 15.
3. Diary, page 18.
4. Diary, page 17.
5. Diary, page 10.
6. Diary, page 10.
7. Nature, page 547.
8. Narrative, Volume II, page 49.

Chapter 2. Robert FitzRoy, Charles Darwin and Me
1. Sulivan, page 12.
2. Narrative, Volume IV, page 90.
3. Autobiography, page 28.
4. Narrative, Volume II, page 18.
5. Correspondence, Volume I, letter 105.
6. Autobiography, page 72.
7. Correspondence, Volume I, letter 119.

Chapter 3. Atlantic Ocean
1. Essay, Book III, 12.
2. Correspondence, Volume I, letter 177.
3. Narrative, Volume II, page 21.
4. Diary, page 37.
5. Diary, page 21.
6. Diary, page 22.

Chapter 4. Salvador
1. Narrative, Volume II, page 60.
2. Correspondence, Volume I, letter 171.
3. Diary, page 46.

Chapter 5. Winter Journey
1. Slocum, chapter VI.

Chapter 6. Río de la Plata
1. Narrative, Volume II, page 26.
2. Narrative, Volume II, page 94.
3. Narrative, Volume II, page 20.
4. Correspondence, Volume I, letter 218.
5. Diary, page 203
6. Correspondence, Volume I, letter 188.

Chapter 7. The Pampas
1. Diary, page 97.
2. Narrative, Volume II, page 111.
3. Narrative, Volume II, page 26.
4. Narrative, Volume II, page 113.
5. Narrative, Volume II, page 107.
6. Correspondence, Volume I, letter 321.
7. Voyage, chapter III.
8. Hudson, chapter I.
9. Diary, page 163.
10. Narrative, Volume II, page 112.
11. DAR, Letter 4th April, 1833, Add MS 8853/43.
12. Diary, page 169.
13. Diary, page 180.
14. Diary, page 169.
15. Diary, page 171.
16. Diary, page 184.

Chapter 9. Argentina
1. Diary, page 209.
2. Narrative, Volume II, page 318.
3. Diary, page 209.
4. Narrative, Volume II, page 12.
5. Narrative, Volume II, page 13.
6. Diary, page 122.
7. Lathrop, page 25.
8. Narrative, Volume II, page 119.
9. Autobiography, page 126.
10. Narrative, Volume II, page 123.
11. Narrative, Volume II, page 125

12. Tilman, page 47.

Chapter 10. In the South
1. Narrative, Volume II, page 202.
2. Narrative, Volume II, page 127.
3. Narrative, Volume II, page 217.
4. Voyage 1836, page 204.
5. Diary, page 244.
6. Diary, page 244.
7. Diary, page 227.
8. Slocum, chapter X.
9. Burke, part II, section XXII

Chapter 11. Chile and Peru
1. Diary, page 245.
2. Diary, page 280.
3. Diary, page 271.
4. Diary, page 286.
5. Narrative, page 400.
6. Diary, page 292.
7. Diary, page 296.
8. Narrative, page 361.
9. Autobiography, page 75.
10 Diary, page 308.
11. Diary, page 316.
12. Narrative, page 426.
13. Diary, page 327.
14. Narrative, page 426.
15. Diary, page 343.
16. Diary, page 343.
17. Narrative, Volume II, page 482.
18. Diary, page 349.
19. Diary, page 350.

Chapter 12. Pacific Ocean
1. Diary, page 356
2. Gauguin, page 60
3. Diary, page 371
4. Diary, page 379
5. Diary, page 380

6. Diary, page 384

Chapter 13. Australia
1. Stockdale, chapter VI.
2. European Magazine, page 462.
3. Diary, page 396.
4. Diary, page 409.
5. Diary, page 409.
6. Diary, page 410.
7. Correspondence, Volume II, letter 1370.
8. Diary, page 418.
9. Slocum, chapter XV.
10. Diary, page 415.

Chapter 14. South about Africa
1. Narrative, Volume II, page 638.
2. Correspondence, Volume I, letter 298.
3. Correspondence, Volume I, letter 299.
4. Diary, page 422.
5. Diary, page 424.
6. Narrative, Volume II, page 658.
7. Autobiography, page 85.
8. South African Christian Recorder, September 1836, page 238.
9. Diary, page 427.
10. Diary, page 427.
11. Diary, page 432.
12. Diary, page 432.
13. Diary, page 432.
14. Narrative, Volume IV, page 345.
15. Narrative, Volume IV, page 327.

Chapter 15. Homeward Bound
1. Slocum, chapter III.
2. Diary, page 437
3. Diary, pager 440.
4. Diary, page 441.
5. Diary, page 439.
6. Ornithological Notes, page 262.

Chapter 16. After the Voyage
1. Correspondence, Volume I, letter 310.

2. Correspondence, Volume I, letter 312.
3. Colonial Papers. Letter by Robert FitzRoy to the Secretary of State, November 10, 1845.
4. Lifeboat, page 711.
5. Correspondence, Volume I, letter 509.
6. Correspondence, Volume I, letter 555.
7. Autobiography, page 119.
8 Autobiography, page 120.
9. Correspondence, Volume I, letter 2285.
10. Correspondence, Volume I, letter 2294.
11. Linnean, May 24th 1859, page viii.
12. Correspondence, Volume I, letter 2337.
13. Correspondence, Volume I, letter 2520.
14. Autobiography, page 76.
15. Autobiography, page 96
16. Hutchinson, page 184.
17. Gazette, April 1882, Issue 5351
18. Correspondence, Volume I, letter 158.

Appendix C. HMS Beagle
1. Thomson, page 32.
2. James, page 409.

I have tried to obtain permission to quote a reference from any copyright holder. However, if I have missed an organisation or person that holds copyright please accept my apologies and write to me. I will ensure that your copyright is acknowledged in the next printing.

Picture Credits

I am indebted to many of the following people and organizations, as listed below, for assistance, copyright permission and graphical files. A full description of citations is provided in the bibliography.

Front Cover (*The author*)

Chapter 1. To the Canary Islands
Drake's Island (*The author*)
Harrier in Barn Pool (*The author*)
HMS Beagle (*Ann Boulter, Paglesham, Essex*)
Map (*The author*)
Puerto Disportivo, Radazul (*The author*)
Mount Teide (*Provenance unknown*)

Chapter 2. Robert FitzRoy, Charles Darwin and Me
Robert FitzRoy (*Provenance unknown*)
Barbara Villiers (*Sir Peter Lely, National Portrait Gallery, London*) ref 6725
Charles Darwin (*George Richmond, Wikimedia Commons*)
The Author (*Tsuruko Uchigasaki-Bremer, Brasilia*)

Chapter 3. Atlantic Ocean
Quail Island (*Charles Darwin, DAR 32.1:16a(2)v*)
Map (*The author*)
Darwin's Plankton Net (*The author, after Darwin*)
Darwin's Microscope (*A. J. Southward*)

Chapter 4. Salvador
Brazilian Forest (*Provenance unknown*)
Pelorinho (*The author*)
National Congress (*The author*)
Saviero (*Otavio de Almeida, Salvador, Brazil*)

Chapter 5. Winter Journey
Map (*The author*)

Chapter 6. Rio de la Plata
Map (*The author*)
Obelisk (*The author*)

Chapter 7. The Pampas
Map (*The author*)
Chart (*Provenance unknown*)
Megatherium (*Provenance unknown*)
Carmen de Patagones (*The author*)
General Rosas (*Banco de la Nación Argentina*)

Chapter 8. Shipwreck
Map (*The author*)
Stricken Harrier (*Stephen Johnson Photographs, Puerto Piramides, Argentina*)
Wreckage (*Stephen Johnson Photographs, Puerto Piramides, Argentina*)

Chapter 9. Argentina
Map (*The author*)
Stephen (*Stephen Johnson Photographs, Puerto Piramides, Argentina*)
Mirador Darwin (*Conrad Martens. Mitchell Library, Sydney*)
Guanaco (*Conrad Martens. Mitchell Library, Sydney*)
Giant Patagon (*Hernán Álvarez Forn, Buenos Aires*)
Hauling Boats, (*Provenance unknown*)
The Beagle at Punta Quilla (*Conrad Martens. Mitchell Library, Sydney*)
After the Gale (*Stephen Johnson Photographs, Puerto Piramides, Argentina*)
Fuegian Supernumeraries (*Robert FitzRoy. Narrative volume II, page 324*)
Fuegian Indian (*Narrative volume II, frontispiece*)
The Beagle Sorely Tried (*Gordon Chancellor*)
Harrier at Harberton (*Stephen Johnson Photographs, Puerto Piramides, Argentina*)

Chapter 10. In the South
Map of Tierra del Fuego	(*The author*)
Wooliya	(*Conrad Marin*, M*itchell Library, Sydney*)
Canal Beagle	(*The author*)
Seno Pia	(*The author*)
Caleta Brecknock	(*Sabina Foeth, Chile*)
Map of Chilean Canales	(*The author*)
Chilean Channels	(*Sandra Wulf, Chile*)
Puerto Eden	(*Provenance unknown*)
Harrier at Castro	(*Teresa Riveros, Valdivia, Chile*)

Chapter 11. Chile and Peru
Church at Achao	(*The author*)
Map	(*The author*)
Pedro de Valdivia	(*The author*)
Lautaro	(*The author*)
Rio Valdivia	(*The author*)
Bahia de Valparaiso	(*Conrad Martens, Mitchell Library, Sydney*)
Bahia de Valparaiso in 2007	(*The author*)
Gemini Sul	(*The author*)
Opera House at Iquique	(*The author*)
Oficina Santa Laura	(*The author*)
Inca Terns	(*Roger Stephens*)
Lima Girl	(*Symes Covington. Mitchell Library, Sydney*)
Chirimoya	(*The author*)

Chapter 12. Pacific Ocean
The Beagle in Galapagos	(Gordon Chancellor)
Map of the Pacific	(*RCC Pilotage Foundation Pacific Crossing Guide, Adlard Coles Nautical*)
Blue Planet	(*Google Maps*)
Sailing the Pacific	The author
Gaugin	(*The author*)
Papieete in 1835	(*Conrad Martens. Mitchell Library, Sydney*)
Modern Papieete	(*The author*)
Harrier at Moorea	(*The author*)

Map of New Zealand	(*The author*)
Auckland Skyline	(*The author*)

Chapter 13. Australia

Sydney Cove	(*Conrad Martens, Michell Library, Sydney*)
Modern Sydney	(*Wikimedia Commons*)
Opera House and Bridge	(*The author*)
Map	(*The author*)
Cullen Bay	(*Wikimedia Commons*)
Cocos Keeling	(*Wikimedia Commons*)
Fairy Tern	(*Stephen Johnson Photographs, Puerto Piramides, Argentina*)

Chapter 14. South About Africa

Sailor's Yarns	(*The author*)
Ile Maurice	(*Provenance unknown*)
Dodo	(*Provenance unknown*)
Paul et Virginie	(*Provenance unknown*)
Simon's Town	(*The author*)
Stephen	(*Stephen Johnson Photographs,* Puerto *Piramides, Argentina*)
Cape Town	(*The author*)
Map	(*The author*)
The Wahoo	(*The author*)
Stephen and Sea Monster	(*The author*)
Napoleon's Grave	(*Symes Covington, Mitchell Library, Sydney*)
Site of Napoleon's Grave	(*The author*)
Arrival	(*Stephen Johnson Photographs, Puerto Piramides, Argentina*)

Chapter 15. Homeward Bound

Black Skimmer	(*The author*)
Port Spacial	(*The author*)
Map	(*The author*)
Horta Harbour	(*Anne Hammick Photographs*)
Falmouth in 1826	(*Andrew Campbell Photographs, Falmouth*)
Modern Falmouth	(*Andrew Campbell Photographs, Falmouth*)

Harrier at Barn Pool   (*The author*)

Chapter 16. After the Voyage
Admiral FitzRoy   (*Greenwich Hospital Trust. Artist unknown*)

Charles Darwin   (*Marion Collier (née Huxley). National Portrait Gallery, London*) ref 3144

The Author   (*The author*)
Harrier at Sea   (*The author*)
Earth in Space   (*National Aeronautical and Space Administration, Washington*)

Appendix A
Map   (*Maxine Heath*)

Appendix B
Map   (*Maxine Heath*)

Appendix C
Beagle Rig   (*The author*)
Beagle Section   (*The author, after Thomson*)
Beagle Deck   (*The author, after Thomson*)
Poop Deck   (*Murray Archive, National Library of Scotland, Edinburgh*)

Scale Model of HMS *Beagle*   (*Australian National Maritime Museum, Sydney*)

Appendix D
Whaleboat   (*The author*)
Appendix E
Folkboat   (*Provenance unknown*)
Zeta   (*The author*)
Zeta Transformed   (*The author*)
Harrier   (*Provenance unknown*)
Cut-away drawing   (*The author*)

Appendix F
Standard Peterson 26 (*The author*)
Peterson 26 modified (*The author*)
Cut-away drawing (*The author*)
Harrier (*The author*)

Appendix H
Ship Rigs (*The author*)
Sloop (*The author*)
Cutter (*The author*)
Junk (*The author*)

Appendix I
Jib (*The author*)
Mainsail (*The author*)

Appendix J
Beaufort Scale, 1806 (*Narrative, Volume II, page 40*)
Modern Beaufort Scale (*The author*)

Back Cover (*Ann Boulter, Paglesham, Essex*)

I have tried to obtain copyright permission to use an image from any copyright holder. However, if I have missed an organization or person that holds copyright please accept my apologies and write to me. I will ensure that your copyright is acknowledged in the next printing.

Bibliography

Abbreviations

Autobiography — *The Autobiography of Charles Darwin, 1809-1882, with original omissions restored*
Nora Barlow (editor).
Published by Collins, London, 1958.
    several subsequent editions

Burke — *A Philosophical Enquiry into the Origin of our Ideas of the Sublime and Beautiful*
Edmund Burke.
Published by Robert Dodsley, London, 1757.
    many subsequent editions

Correspondence — *The Correspondence of Charles Darwin*
Volumes 1-9 (1821-61).
F.H. Burkhardt, S. Smith, et al (editors).
Published by the Cambridge University Press, 1983-94.

Colonial Papers — *Colonial Papers*, Volume 4. Reference CO 209/36
The National Archives, Kew.

DAR — *Darwin Archive*
Cambridge University Library.

Diary — *Charles Darwin's Beagle Diary*
Richard Darwin Keynes (editor).
Published by Cambridge University Press, 1988.

Essay — *An Essay Concerning Human Understanding*
John Locke.
Published by Edward May, 1690.
    many subsequent editions

European Magazine	*Visit of Hope to Sydney Cove Near Botany Bay* Erasmus Darwin. The European Magazine, Volume 16. Published by The Philological Society, London, 1789.
Gauguin	*The Intimate Journals of Paul Gauguin.* Translated by Van Wyck Brooks. Published by William Heinemann Ltd, London, 1923.
Gazette	*Pall Mall Gazette* London, 1882.
Hudson	*Idle Days in Patagonia* William (W.H.) Hudson. Published by Chapman & Hall, London, 1893. many subsequent editions.
Hutchinson	*Life of Sir John Lubbock* Horace G Hutchinson. Published by Macmillan & Co Ltd, London, 1914.
James	*A Naval History of Great Britain* N. James. Published by Macmillan, London, 1902.
Lathrop	*The Indians of Tierra del Fuego* Samuel Lathrop. Published by The Museum of the American Indian, New York, 1928.
Lifeboat boat	*The Lifeboat*, Journal of the National Life-Institution, Volume V. Published by Charles Knight, London, 1865

Linnean   Journal of the Proceedings of the Linnean Society. Volume IV. Botany.
Published by Longman, Green, Longmans and Roberts, London, 1860.

Mitchell Library   State Library of New South Wales. Macquarie Street, Sydney, New South Wales 2000.

Narrative   *Narrative of the Surveying Voyages of his Majesty's Ships Adventure and Beagle between the Years 1826 and 1836 Describing their Examination of the Southern Shores of South America and Beagle's Circumnaviga*
tion   *tion of the Globe*
    Vol I.   Proceedings of the First Expedition 1826-30 under the command of Captain P. Parker King.
    Vol II. Proceedings of the Second Expedition 1831-36 under the command of Captain FitzRoy.
    Vol III. Journal and Remarks 1832-36 by Charles Darwin Esq. M.A.
    Vol IV. Appendices.
Published by Henry Colburn, London, 1839.
    republished with notes by Pickering and Chatto, London, 2011

Nature   *Nature. A Weekly Illustrated Journal of Science.*Volume 88,
Published by Macmillan & Co Ltd. London, 1912.

Origin   *On the Origin of Species by Means of Natural Selection or, The Preservation of Favoured Races in the Struggle for Life*
Charles Darwin.
Published by John Murray, London, 1859.
    many subsequent editions.

Ornithological Notes	*Darwin's Ornithological Notes* Nora Barlow (editor). Bulletin of the British Museum (Natural History),Historical Series 2, 1963.
Recorder	South African Christian Recorder. Published monthly between 1831 and 1837, Cape Town.
Slocum	*Sailing Alone Around the World* Joshua Slocum. Published by The Century Company, New York, 1900. many subsequent editions
Stockdale	*The Voyage of Governor Phillip to Botany Bay* Compiled and published by John Stockdale, London, 1789.
Sulivan	*Life and Letters of the late Admiral Sir Bartholomew Sulivan, 1810 - 1890* Henry Sulivan (editor). Published by John Murray, London, 1896.
Thomson	*HMS Beagle* Keith Thomson. Published by W.W.Norton & Company Inc, New York, 1995.
Tilman	*Mischief in Patagonia* W.H. (Bill) Tilman. Published by Cambridge University Press, 1957.
Voyage	*Voyage of the Beagle* Charles Darwin. Published by Henry Colburn, London, 1839. many subsequent editions.

Further Reading

A Log of the Proceedings of HM Surveying Sloop Beagle. Robert FitzRoy Esq., Captain
Kept by Charles Forsyth Midshipman, unpublished.
Beginning Oct 22 1833 and ending on 17th Nov 1836. First entry 22 October 1833 in Montevideo, last entry in Callao on 27th August 1835.

The log also contains *A Log of the Proceedings of HMS Constitution, tender to HM Sloop Beagle under the orders of Capt Robt FitzRoy. From the 31st of May to the 29th October on our passage to rejoin HM Sloop Beagle with the crew of HM late tender Constitution.* First entry 20th August 1835, last entry May 30th 1836

This book, which has not been published, is in the collection of:
Museo Naval de la Nacion (of the Armada Argentina)
Paseo Victoria 602
Tigre 1648
Buenos Aires
Argentina
tel: (011) 4749 0608
e-mail: museonaval@hotmail.com
contact: Capitan Horacio Molina Pico
Note. The book was bought by Agregado Naval Argentino, reported in the Daily Telegraph on 25 May 1948. Purchase by Captain Oddera. Museum Inventory 3037.

Zoology of the Voyage of HMS Beagle under the Command of Captain Robert FitzRoy RN during the years 1832-36
  Vol 1. Fossil Mamalia, edited by Richard Owen.
  Vol 2. Mamalia, edited by George Waterhouse.
  Vol 3. Birds, edited by John Gould.
  Vol 4. Fish and Reptiles, edited by Leonard Jenyns & Thomas Bell.
Edited and superintended by Charles Darwin Esq., naturalist to the expedition.
Published by Elder & Co, London, 1840.
        Facsimile edition by C.I.L. Ltd, 1994

Charles Darwin   Vol 1, *Voyaging*
                     Vol 2, *The Power of Place*
Janet Browne.
Published by Princeton University Press, 1995 and 2002.

Charles Darwin and the Voyage of the Beagle
Nora Barlow.
Published by Cambridge University Press, 1933.

FitzRoy of the Beagle
H.E.L. Melersh.
Published by Rupert Hart-Davis, London, 1968.

FitzRoy
John and Mary Gribbin.
Published by Headline Book Publishing, London, 2003.

The Royal FitzRoys
Bernard Falk.
Published by Hutchinson, London, 1950.

The Journal of Symes Covington
Ed. Vern Weitzel.
www.asap.unimelb.edu.au

Drawings by Symes Covington
Michell Library, Sydney, ref PXD41

The Beagle Record
Richard Darwin Keynes (editor).
Published by Cambridge University Press, 1989.

HMS Beagle
Keith Thomson
Published by W W Norton & Co Inc, New York, 1995.

Anatomy of the Ship HMS Beagle. Survey Ship Extraordinary
K.H. Marquardt.
Published by Conway Marine, London, 1997.

Personal Narrative of Travels to the Equinoctial Regions of the New Continent
Alexander von Humboldt.
various German publishers, 1814 – 1825.
A flowery translation by Helena Williams was published by Longman, Hurst, Rees, Orme & Brown,   London, 1818 - 1829.

Voyage of Discovery in the Arctic and Antarctic Seas and Round the World
Robert McCormick
Published by Simpson, Low, Marston, Searle and Rivington
London, 1884

Principles of Geology
Charles Lyell
    Volume I, 1830.
    Volume II, 1832.
    Volume III, 1833.
Published by John Murray, London.

Fossils, Finches and Fuegians
Richard Darwin Keynes.
Published by Cambridge University Press, 2001.

Darwin's Finches
David Lack.
Published by Cambridge University Press, 1947.

Darwin's Ghosts. In Search of the First Evolutionists
Rebecca Stott.
Published by Bloomsbury Publishing PLC, London, 2012.

Uttermost Part of the Earth
Lucas Bridges.
Published by Hodder & Stoughton, London, 1948.

Papillon
Henri Charrière.
Published by Editions Robert Laffont, Paris, 1969.
    English translation by Patrick O'Brian, Flamingo, London, 1969.

JM Rosas (Argentine Dictator)
John Lynch.
Published by Oxford University Press, 1981.

In Patagonia
Bruce Chatwin.
Published by Jonathan Cape, London, 1977.
    reprinted by Pan Books, 1979

In the Wake of Darwin's Beagle
Alan Villiers.
National Geographic, October 1969.

The Origin
Irving Stone.
Published by Doubleday, Garden City, New York, 1981.
    A fictionalised text familiar to American readers.

The Folkboat Story
Dieter Loibner.
Published by Adlard Coles, London, 2002.

Southern Cross to Pole Star
A F Tschiffely.
Published by N. Heinemann, London, 1932.

Chasing Venus. The Race to Measure the Heavens
Andrea Wulf.
Published by Windmill Books, London, 2013.

Daniel Deronda
George Elliot.
Published by William Blackwood, Edinburgh & London, 1876.
    many subsequent editions

History, Essays, First Series
Ralph Waldo Emerson.
Published by James Monroe, Boston, 1841.
    many subsequent editions

Comus
John Milton.
Published by Humphrey Robinson, 1637.
    many subsequent editions
New edited translation by James Watson was published by Penguin Books, London, 1995.

The Seafarer
Ezra Pound.
Published by Swift & Co., London, 1912.
    many subsequent editions

The Great Silver River
Sir Horace Rumbold.
Published by John Murray, London, 1882.

Heart of Darkness
Joseph Conrad.
Published by William Blackwood, Edinburgh & London, 1902.
    many subsequent editions

Patagonia
Sophie Blacksell (editor).
Published by Footprint Handbooks, Bath, 2005.

Land of Tempest
Eric Shipton.
Published by Hodder and Stoughton, London, 1963.

Tierra del Fuego. The Fatal Lodestone
Eric Shipton
Published byCharles Knight & Co Ltd, London, 1973

Don Juan
Lord Byron.
Published by John Murray, London, 1819.
    many subsequent editions

Essays of Michel de Montaigne
Published by S. Millange, Bordeaux, 1580.
    English translation by M.A. Screech, published by Penguin Books, London, 1993.

The Princess
Alfred Tennyson.
Published by Edward Moxon, London, 1847.
   many subsequent editions

Sailing Through Life
John Scott Hughes.
Published by Methuen, London, 1947.

Moby Dick
Herman Melville.
Published by Harper & Brothers, New York, 1851
   many subsequent editions

Ulysses
James Joyce
Published by Sylvia Beach, Paris, 1922
   many subsequent editions

A A la Recherche du Temps Perdu
Marcel Proust
Published by various publishers, Paris, 1913-1927
   English translation edited by Christopher Prendergast,
                        Penguin Books, 2003

Phenomenologu of Spirit
Georg Hegel
Published by Joseph Garbhardt, Bamberg, 1807.
   many English translations

Essay Concerning Humane Understanding
John Locke
Published by The Basset, London, 1690.
   many subsequent editions.

Acknowledgements

I am obliged to many people for advice and help while writing this book. These include, among others, Dr Gordon Chancellor, Christopher Darwin, Carlos Diehl, Dr Nigel Erskine, Horacio Ezcurra, Marcos Gallacher, John Harding, Stuart Harris, Maxine Heath, Ros Hogbin, Dr Karen James, Stephen Johnson, Maddy Kerslake, Ivan le Gall, Dr Anne-Flore Laloe, David Paisner, Adam Perkins, Eve Southward and Ben Welham.

I wish to express my thanks and admiration to the Syndics of the Cambridge University Press for the great resource of the *Correspondence of Charles Darwin* and I am indebted to them for quotations from *Charles Darwin's Beagle Diary* edited by the late Richard Darwin Keynes.

I am indebted to the Syndics of the Cambridge University Library for quotations taken from unpublished material held in the Darwin Archive. I am obliged to the National Archives for an excerpt taken from their unpublished holdings of Robert FitzRoy's correspondence.

The assistance and resources of many institutions and organizations have been invaluable. The staff of the Cambridge University Library, the British Library and the Mitchell Library in Sydney have been unvaryingly helpful. A single author cannot hope to proceed far without access to the world-wide resources that are now available on the Internet.

Index

Page references in italics refer to illustrations.

9/11 attacks 21, 22

Achao church, Isla Chiloé 108, 109
Adelaide, Australia 149
Adelaide, Queen 81
Adriana (landlady) 69
Adventure, HMS 12, 71
Adventure (schooner) 71, 72, 97, 109, 116
Alacaloof Indians 82
America see North America; South America; United States of America
Ampton Hall, Suffolk 11
Anaa (earlier Aura), Tahiti 137
Ancud (San Carlos), Isla Chiloé 98, 109
Andes 58, 62, 76, 109, 117–18, 123, 156
Angostura Inglésa 103–4
Angra, Azores 181, 182, 183
Ante Puerto Norte 47
Antón (yachtsman) 53, 60
Arafura Sea 153
Aratu Iate Clube 33–4, 36, 37, 175–6
Araucanian Indians 57–8, 106, 110, 111, 114, 121
Archipelago de los Chonos 104–5, 117
Archipielago de Colón (Galápagos Islands) 120, 128–31, 130, 172, 188–9
architecture, artificial intelligence and 35, 36
Argentina 5, 12, 70–87, 118–19
    see also Buenos Aires; Cabo Corrientes; Carmen de Patagones; Pampas, the; Patagonia; Pedro Luro; Prefectura Naval Argentina; Punta Alta; Punta Norte; Río Negro; Ruta Provincial 76!; Santa Fe; Tres Picos; Viedma; Yacht Club Argentino
Armada Argentina 74, 85
Armada de Chile 91, 93, 99, 102, 105
Arnold, Thomas 57

Arquipelago dos Açores (Azores) 176, 179–80, 181–3
Arrogant, HMS 187
Arthur (island) 105
artificial intelligence 35–6
Arutua 135
Ascension Island 172, 173
   see also Isla Ascension
Ashby's Boatyard, New Zealand 140
Asociacion Fueguina de Actividades Subacuaticas y Nautica (Club AFASyN) 87, 88–90
Astillero Marco 210
Atacama Desert 123
Atlantic Ocean 7, 19–28, 40, 41, 62, 128, 168
Atuona, Îles Marquises 134–5
Auckland, New Zealand 141, 141, 148, 186
Aura (later Anaa), Tahiti 137
Australia 24, 131, 140, 142–55
   see also Cocos Keeling Islands; New South Wales; Sydney
Azores (Arquipelago dos Açores) 176, 179–80, 181–3

Bacon, Francis 195
Bahía Anna Pink 104
Bahía Blanca 43, 49, 50–4, 55, 59, 60, 61
Bahía Buen Suceso 80, 82, 83, 85, 95
Bahía Callao 124
Bahía Concepción 114–15, 121
Bahía Conchali 119
Bahía Coral 109, 114
Bahía de Iquique 123
Bahía de Valparaiso 115, 116
Bahía de Vitória 38
Bahía La Herradura 119–20
Bahía Marina 174, 175
Bahía Saint Martin 84
Bahía San Blas 56
Bahía Sloggett 85
Bahía Thetis 79
Baia de Todos os Santos 28, 31–2, 37, 173, 174
   see also Salvador de Bahia

Baie de Cook 138, 138
Baie de Matavai 136, 137
Banco de San Antonio, Bahia de Todos os Santos 28
Banco del Norte, Bahía Blanca 51
Bantu Expansion 167
Barn Pool 1, 2, 3, 184, 184
barques 218
Barrier Reef Channel 152
Bass Strait 149
Bathurst, Australia 147
Bay of Biscay 3–4, 5
Bay of Islands, New Zealand 140, 142, 186
Beagle Channel, Tierra del Fuego 13
Beagle Gulf, Australia 152
Beagle, HMS 7, 201–3, 201, 202, 203, 204
    first voyage 12–13, 24, 80–1, 103–4
    FitzRoy commander of 13, 80, 81, 117, 201
    length 22, 97, 176, 201
    survey work, Angostura Inglésa 103–4
    third voyage 152
Beagle, HMS, second voyage 4, 14, 34, 201
    anchors 50
    Ascension to Brazil 172–3
    Australia 120, 144, 147, 150, 151
    Azores 181, 182
    Bahía Blanca 51–2, 53–4, 55
    Bahía Buen Suceso 82, 83, 95
    Bahía Concepción 115
    Bahía Conchali 119
    Bahía de Iquique 123
    Bahía La Herradura 120
    Baia de Todos os Santos 173, 174
    Buenos Aires 42, 46, 50
    Cabo de Hornos (Cape Horn) 83–4, 84
    Cabo Santa Maria 41
    Callao 125, 128
    Cape Verdes 22, 176, 181
    Chile 43
    chronometer testing 6, 128, 174, 185

Cocos Islands 156
Copiapó 119
crew 24, 39, 43, 54, 56, 91, 105, 116
departure 1–2, 81
Equator 25, 26
Falkland Islands 56, 71, 75, 95
Fernando da Noronha 28
Fuegian Indians 81–2, 91
Galápagos Islands 128–9, 130
Îles Tuamotu 135
Isla Chiloé 98, 107, 109, 117
Isla Navarino 91
Maldonado 56
map 199, 236
Montevideo 41, 42–3, 59
New Zealand 138, 140, 144, 186
paid off at end of 185
Paso Goree 94, 95
preparations 15, 20, 81, 201–3
Puerto Coral 110
Puerto de Iquique 122
Puerto Deseado 72, 74, 77
Puerto San Julián 74, 75
Punta Arenas 109
Punta Quilla 77, 77
Recife to Cape Verdes 176, 180–1
return to England 185
Rio de Janeiro 39, 41
Río de la Plata 41, 42–3, 50, 55, 56, 71, 82, 95
Río Negro 56–7
Río Santa Cruz 75
St Helena 166, 170
St Paul Rock 25
Salvador de Bahia 28, 31
Seno Ponsonby 98
Simon's Town 165, 166, 168
South Indian Ocean 159
Tahiti 136–8
Tasmania 147, 148

    Tenerife 8
    Tierra del Fuego 43, 56, 71, 75, 82, 87, 97–8
    Valdivia 110, 111
    Valparaiso 115, 116, 116, 117, 121
    Woollya 92, 93, 94, 95, 98
Beagle, HMS, survey work 6, 12, 13, 81, 128
    Admiralty instructions 42
    Azores 181
    Bahía Blanca 43, 51–2, 55
    Buenos Aires 50
    Cape Verdes 22
    Chilean coast 117, 119, 121
    Chonos archipelago 105, 117
    Cocos Islands 156
    Falkland Islands 71
    Galápagos Islands 128–9
    Golfo de Penas 117
    hindered by sale of Adventure 116
    Isla Chiloé 109, 117
    Peru 125
    Puerto Deseado 74
    Río Deseado 72
    schooners Paz and Liebre in 43, 51, 55, 57
    Tasmania 148
    Tierra del Fuego 13, 71
    whaleboats 204
Beaufort, Francis 15, 17, 187, 222
Beaufort Wind Scale 222
Bell, Thomas 191
Benijos, Tenerife 9
Benjamin (island) 105
Bergquist, Eric 206
Bermagui, Australia 150
Blonde, HMS 121, 122, 125
Blue Mountains, Australia 151
Boat Memory (Fuegian Indian) 81
boat and ship rigs 218–20, 218–20
    see also junk rig; saveiros
bolas 54–5, 75

Bolivia 122
Bonaparte, Napoleon, grave 170–1, 171
Bonpland, Aimé 8
Botany Bay 144
Brasilia 30–1, 37, 40
    see also Universidade de Brasilia
Brazil 29–36, 29, 37–40, 175–6
    Beagle's passage to 28, 172–3
    Darwin in 29, 34–5, 39
    Harrier of Down [I] 28, 31, 33, 34, 36, 37, 39
    Harrier of Down [II]'s passage to 168, 173, 175
    see also Farol da Barra; Fernando da Noronha; Rio de Janeiro; Salvador de Bahia; Vitória
Brazo Nordeste, Canal Beagle 93, 93
Brazo Sudeste, Canal Beagle 95
Bridges, Lucas 86–7
Bridges, Thomas 86, 87, 98
brigs 218
Brisbane, Australia 152
Buceo, Uruguay 46, 48, 70, 71
Buenos Aires 46–8, 50, 55, 60, 61, 118–19, 175
    after wreck of Harrier of Down [I] 66, 68–9
    Beagle's second voyage 42, 46, 50
    Darwin at 48, 57, 58–9, 60
    Yacht Club Argentino 47, 69, 70, 71, 210
Buffalo River Yacht Club 164
Bundaberg, Australia 152
Burke, Edmund 102
Butler, Dr 15
Bynoe, Benjamin 24

Cabo Corrientes 50
Cabo de Hornos (Cape Horn) 71, 74, 83–4
Cabo Desolatión 80
Cabo Longchase 95
Cabo Raper 104
Cabo San Diego 80
Cabo San Pío 85
Cabo San Vicente 79

Cabo Santa Maria 41
Cabo Trafalgar 5
Cabo Tres Montes 104
Cairns, Australia 152
Caleta Bolina 102
Caleta Brecknock 96–7, 96
Caleta Hale 104
Caleta Hoskyn 104
Caleta Ichuac 105
Caleta Luis 97, 98
Caleta Melliones 92
Caleta Olla 93
Caleta Rachas 100
Caleta Río Frío 102
Caleta Saudade 104
Callao, Peru 121, 124–5, 128, 130
Calle Maipú, Ushuaia 89
Calle San Martin, Ushuaia 89
Cambridge University 15, 17, 186, 188, 190
Cammeray Marina 146, 151
Campo Grande, Salvador de Bahia 32–3, 175
Canal Acualisnan 98–9
Canal Beagle 85, 90, 93, 93, 95
Canal Cockburn 96, 97, 98
Canal Concepción 102
Canal FitzRoy 13
Canal Haava 135
Canal Morelada 105
Canal Murray 93
Canal O'Brien 95
Canal Perez Norte 105
Canal Perez Sur 105
Canal Sarmiento 101
Canal Scorpio 105
Canal Smyth 101
Canal Wide 101
Canary Islands (Islas Canarias) 7, 23
Cape Agulhas 164
Cape Brett 140

Cape Colony 167
Cape of Good Hope 164, 168
Cape Hangklip 164
Cape Horn 71, 74, 83–4
Cape Hotham 152
Cape Leeuwin 149
Cape San Antonio 42
Cape Town 166, 168, 168
Cape Verde islands 8, 22, 23–4, 41, 156, 176, 181
Carlos (Buenos Aires acquaintance) 47–8, 70
Carlos (Uruguayan agronomist) 44
Carmelo, Uruguay 43
Carmen de Patagones, Argentina 51, 55, 56, 57, 58, 59, 60, 62
Carnaval, Salvador de Bahia 32–3
Carrasco, Captain 125
Carretera Panamericana 119
Cartegena, Juan de 75
Castlereagh, Lord 14, 81, 188
Castro, Isla Chiloé 105–6, 106, 108
catastrophism 22
Cawsand Bay 3
Cayenne, French Guiana 176
Cerro de la Ventana 60
Cerro de los Claveles 44–5
Cerro Pachón 120
Cerro Pintado 123
Chacabuco 104
Chafers, Edward 72, 73, 74, 105
Challenger, HMS 119, 121
Chambers, Robert 190
Charles Darwin Research Station, Isla Santa Cruz 130
Charles II, King 11
Charles Island (Isla Floreana) 129
Charrière, Henri, Papillon 177
chart-making see Beagle, HMS, survey work
Chatham Island (Isla San Cristóbal) 128
chilamoya (custard apple) 126, 126

Chile 5, 43, 58, 107–24, 182
  see also Armada de Chile; Isla Ascension; Puerto Eden;
Puerto Williams; Santiago
Chilean Andes see Andes
Chilean Channels 99, 104–5
Chiloé see Isla Chiloé
Chiquita 141
Chonos archipelago 104–5, 117
Christ's College, Cambridge 15
chronometers 6, 128, 174, 185
Chuy, Uruguay 40
Cimentière Calvaire, Îles Marquises 134
Club AFASyN 87, 88–90
Club de Yates 112
Club de Yates y Botes 123
Club Marina el Manzano 115
Club Náutico Bahía Blanca 52–3
Club Náutico Capitan Oneto 71–2
Club Nautico el Delfin 75
Club Náutico la Ribera 62
Club Náutico Sudeste 69
Clunies-Ross, John 155, 156
Cocos Keeling Islands 147, 155–8, 159, 164
Colinsplaat (Dutch yacht) 38
Colonia del Sacramento, Uruguay 43–4, 70
computers 35–6
Concepción, Chile 115, 117, 121
Concón, Chile 116
Cook, James 136
Cooktown, Australia 152
Copiapó 119, 121, 122
Coquimbo 98, 119
Coral Sea 152
coral structure 156
Cordillera Andes see Andes
Cordillera Darwin 94, 94
Cornwall see Falmouth
Costa, Lucio 30
Covington, Symes 59, 149, 150–1, 180, 182

Cullen Bay, Australia 153, 153
Cutfinger Cove 91
cutters 219, 219
Cyclops radar reflector 37

Dangerous Archipelago, the see Îles Tuamotu
Darwin (Australia) 151–2, 153, 153
Darwin, Anne 188
Darwin, Caroline 48, 54, 159
Darwin, Charles 14–17, 16, 17, 151, 188–95, 194
    autobiography 83, 194
    Covington and 150–1, 180
    Down House 20, 188, 189
    FitzRoy and 17, 57, 117, 185–6, 187, 194
    FitzRoy's correspondence after return home 185, 186, 189
    Humboldt and 9, 156
    Locke and 19
    Lyell and 5, 23, 118, 190, 191, 195
    marriage 20, 150
    microscope 27
    obelisk 44, 45
    On the Origin of Species by Means of Natural Selection 2, 129, 182, 191–2, 193, 195
    religion 129, 166–7, 189, 192
    Structure and distribution of coral reefs 156
    Voyage of the Beagle 2, 55, 188
    Zoology of the Voyage of HMS Beagle 188
    see also Charles Darwin Research Station
Darwin, Charles, Beagle voyage 9, 24, 80, 182, 194
    Andes 117–18, 156
    Australia 144, 145, 147, 150
    Azores 181–2
    Bahía Concepción 115
    bolas throwing 55
    Brazil 29, 34–5, 39
    Buenos Aires 48, 57, 58–9, 60
    Carmen de Patagones, Argentina 56, 57, 59
    Cerro de la Ventana 60
    Cocos Islands 156, 158

Copiapó 119, 121, 122
Coquimbo 119
departure 1–2
Equator crossing 26
FitzRoy and 4–5, 17, 53, 54, 57, 117, 119, 166–7
food 21
Fuegian Indians 82
Galápagos 129
geological theories 63–4
hammock 4
Isla Chiloé 107, 109, 117
Lima 125
Lyell and 5, 23, 118
Martens and 43
Mendoza 118
Montevideo 42, 59
New Zealand 140
nickname 54
Patagonia 56, 58–9
plankton net 26–7, 27
preparations 15–17
Puerto Deseado 77
Puerto Deseado-5 72, 73
Puerto Williams 91
Punta Alta 53–4
Quail Island sketch 23
return to England 180, 185
Río Santa Cruz 76
Rosas and 58
St Helena 170, 171, 172
St Paul Rock 25
Saint-Pierre's Paul et Virginie 163
Santa Fe 57, 59
Santiago, Cape Verdes 22, 156
Santiago, Chile 117, 119
sea sickness 4, 26, 181, 196
Seno Pía 94
Seno Ponsonby 98
Simon's Bay, South Africa 165

Tahiti 137
　　　Tasmania 148–9, 159
　　　Tenerife 8, 19
　　　Tierra del Fuego 82, 83, 98
　　　Uruguay 43
　　　Valdivia 110, 112
　　　Valparaiso 117, 119
　　　Vicensio 118
　　　Woollya 91, 94
Darwin, Charles (CD's son) 191
Darwin, Charles (CD's uncle) 14
Darwin, Chris 151
Darwin, Emma 150, 188, 194–5
Darwin, Erasmus (CD's grandfather) 14, 144, 151, 190
Darwin, Erasmus (CD's uncle) 14
Darwin, Robert Waring 14, 16–17
Darwin, William 188
Darwin's Finches 129, 188–9
D'Entrecasteaux Channel 149
Derwent (river), Tasmania 148
Devil's Island see Îles du Salut
Devonport 13, 15, 20, 81, 201
Dias, Bartolomeo 168
Direction Island 155
dodo 161–2, 162
Doldrums, the 24–5, 154
Doughty, Thomas 75
Down House, Kent 20, 188, 189
Drake, Francis 75
Drake's Island, Plymouth Sound 1, 2

Earle, Augustus 43
East Australian current 142, 146
East London, South Africa 164
Easter Island (Isla Pascua) 109
Ecuador 129, 130
Eden, Australia 150
　　see also Puerto Eden
Edinburgh University 15

El Portillo, Tenerife 9, 10
Emery Point, Port Darwin, Australia 153
Endeavour, HMS 136
Equator, the 25–6
Estrecho de le Maire 77
Estrecho de Magellanes (Strait of Magellan) 12, 71, 78, 96, 98, 99, 139
European Space Agency 178

Faial, Azores 179–80
Falkland Islands 56, 71, 75, 76, 95, 172, 182
Falmouth 182, 183, 185
False Bay, South Africa 164
False Bay Yacht Club 165, 167
Faro Fairway 101, 102
Faro San Pedro 104
Farol da Barra, Brazil 173, 173
Fern Tree, Tasmania 149
Fernando da Noronha, Brazil 28
fishing 40–1, 169, 169
FitzRoy, Lord Charles 12
FitzRoy, Henry, 1st Duke of Grafton 11–12, 11
FitzRoy, Robert 11–14, 13, 17, 24, 186–8, 187
    Beagle's commander 14, 80, 81, 117, 201
    Darwin and 17, 57, 117, 185–6, 187, 194
    Darwin's correspondence after return home 185, 186, 189
    depression 14, 15, 117, 187–8
    Fuegian Indians and 80–1, 82, 91, 92, 95
    Narrative 1, 34, 122, 129, 144, 186
    religion 166–7, 186, 189, 192
FitzRoy, Robert, Beagle's second voyage
    Admiralty's instructions to 42, 52
    Adventure (schooner) 71, 116
    Ascension to Brazil 172–3
    Australia 144
    Azores 181
    Bahía Blanca survey 43, 51–2
    Bahía Conchali 119
    Bahía La Herradura 120

    Cabo de Hornos (Cape Horn) 83–4
    Challenger helped by 119, 121–2
    Cocos Islands 156
    crew 24
    Darwin and 4–5, 17, 53, 54, 57, 117, 119, 166–7
    departure 1
    food 21
    Gálapagos 129
    Harris, James 51
    Harris and Roberts paid for survey work 57
    Isla Chiloé 107
    lunar distances measurement 128
    Martens and 43
    mistaken for smuggler 119
    Montevideo 42
    opinion of chronometers 174
    opinion of Stebbings 174
    Paz and Liebre (survey vessels) hired by 43, 51
    Peru 125
    preparations 15, 20, 81, 201–3
    Puerto Deseado, assessment of damage to ship 74
    Puerto Williams 91
    Recife to Santiago 181
    return to England 185
    ride to Río Leubu 115, 121
    Río Santa Cruz 76
    St Paul Rock 25
    Saint-Pierre's Paul et Virginie 163
    Santa Cruz de Tenerife 8
    Seno Pía 94–5
    Tahiti 137–8
    Tierra del Fuego 98
    Valdivia 110, 111, 114
    Valparaiso 116–17
    Woollya 91, 92, 94, 95
FitzRoy, Lord William 12
Fleuve Kourou, French Guiana 176–7, 178, 179
Fleuve Mahury, French Guiana 176
Folkboats 19–20, 63, 205–6, 205

Folksong boats 19–20, 63, 206
    see also Harrier of Down [I]
food on voyages 20–1
Forsyth (island) 105
fossils 53–4, 118
Fotro San Pedro, Baia de Todos os Santos 174
Fox, William Darwin 163
Fraser Island, Australia 152
French Guiana 176–9
French Polynesia 134, 136
Fuegia Basket (Fuegian Indian) 80, 80, 84, 92, 95, 98
Fuegian Indians 80–2, 80, 83, 84–5, 91, 92, 95, 98, 99
full-rigged ships 218
Fuller (FitzRoy's steward) 185

Galápagos Islands (Archipielago de Colón) 120, 128–31, 130, 172, 188–9
Gallagher, Marcos 71
Gama, Vasco da 168
Ganges, HMS 13
Gauguin, Paul 134
    Aha Oe Feii 134
Gaulle, General de 178
Gemini Sul 120, 121
Geoff (boatyard operator) 153
geological theories 22–3, 63–4, 118, 156
    see also Lyell, Charles
Georgetown, Ascension Island 172
Gladstone, Australia 152
Glyptodon fossil 53
Golfo Corcovado 104, 105
Golfo de Ancud 111
Golfo de Penas 104, 117
Golfo Nuevo 63, 66
Golfo San José 63
Gonzales, Mariano 117, 119, 122
Gould, John 188
Graeme (yachtsman) 141
Gray, Asa 191, 192

Great Australian Bight 140, 150
Great Barrier Reef 152
Green, Charles 136
Greenwich 185
guanaco 73, 74
Guiana Space Centre 178
Gulf of Carpentaria, Australia 152

Harberton estancia 85–7, 86
Harrier of Down [I] 17, 19–20, 40, 63, 205–9, 208
    Bahía Blanca 50, 53, 55
    Barn Pool 3
    Bay of Biscay 5
    Brazil 28, 31, 33, 34, 36, 37, 39
    Buenos Aires 46–7, 50
    departure 3
    Equator crossing 26
    length 22
    map of voyage 237
    mast damage and repair 37–9, 46, 47
    provisions for voyage 20–1
    Río Negro 56, 62
    Tenerife 10, 19
    Uruguay 37, 39, 41, 43, 45–6, 48–9
    wrecked 64–8, 67, 68, 72, 209
    Zeta transformed to 206–7, 207
Harrier of Down [II] 69, 147, 176, 197, 210–13, 211, 212, 213
    Australia 142, 146, 149–50, 151, 153
    Baie de Cook, Moorea 138
    Barn Pool 184
    Brazil 168, 173, 175–6
    Caleta Brecknock 96, 96
    Castro 106
    Direction Island 155
    Harberton 86
    Îles Marquises 133–4
    La Herradura 120, 122
    maintenance 112, 119, 140, 151, 153, 163–4, 176
    map of voyage 237

    Mauritius 159
    New Zealand 140
    Pacific Ocean crossing 132–5, 133, 139
    problems 88, 163–4
    problems with engine 88, 95–6, 101–3, 150, 163–4, 168, 180
    problems with wind vane steering gear 71, 164
    Puerto Caldera 122
    Puerto Deseado 72
    Puerto San Julián 74
    Puerto Tamar 100
    rammed by smugglers' vessel 154–5
    Río de la Plata 70, 88, 210, 211
    Río Santa Cruz 75–6
    sea anchor 139
    Seno Pía 95
    Tierra del Fuego 78, 85, 87, 88–9, 90, 92, 95–6
    Valdivia 112
Harris, James 51, 57
Hasler, Blondie 20, 63
Haush Indians 82
Hawaii 120
Hazel Branch (steamer) 101
Hegel, Georg 124
Hellyer, Edward 56
Henri (mechanic) 97
Henslow, John 15, 54, 188, 190
Herald Island, New Zealand 141
Herodotus 168
Hiva Oa, Îles Marquises 133–4, 135
Hobart, Tasmania 147, 148–9, 159
Hooker, Joseph 190, 191
horse latitudes 21, 179
Horta marina, Azores 180
Hudson, William 55–6
Huet, Karine 105
Humberstone, Chile 123–4
Humboldt, Alexander von 8–9, 118, 156
Humboldt ocean current 124, 132

Humid Pampas 61
Huxley, Thomas 191, 192, 193

Iate Clube do Espiritu Santo 38, 39
Île d'Ouessant 3
Îles du Salut (Salvation Islands/Devil's Island) 177
Îles Marquises 133–4, 136
Îles Tuamotu 105, 133, 135
Ilha Bom Jesus 32
Ilha dos Frades (Isle of Monks) 32
Ilhas Cabo Verde (Cape Verde islands) 8, 22, 23–4, 41, 156, 176, 181
Ilhas Salvagens 8
Inca terns 124, 125
Indian Ocean 40, 147, 151, 153, 159
Indians 54–5, 58, 75, 82, 95
    see also Araucanian Indians; Fuegian Indians; Haush Indians; Ona Indians; Yamana Indians
Indonesia 153, 190
Inlet Waikari, New Zealand 140
Inman, Rev. George 12
Iquique see Puerto de Iquique
Isla Angle 102
Isla Ascension, Chile 105
    see also Ascension Island
Isla Basket 80
Isla Brecknock 95
Isla Chiloé 95, 98, 106, 106, 107–9, 117
Isla Clarence 97, 98
Isla de Flores 46
Isla de Lobos 45
Isla de los Estados 77, 80
Isla del Diablo 93, 98
Isla Desolación 99
Isla Floreana (Charles Island) 129
Isla Gordon 95
Isla Guerrero 104
Isla Hermite 84
Isla Jechica 105

Isla Leadline 95
Isla Lemuy 105
Isla Lennox 84, 91
Isla London 80
Isla Mancera 109, 114
Isla Mocha 114–15
Isla Navarino 84, 91, 92
Isla Nueva 91
Isla Orlebar 104
Isla Pascua (Easter Island) 109
Isla Picton 85, 91
Isla Quiriquina 115
Isla Ribero 105
Isla Royas 105
Isla San Cristóbal (Chatham Island) 128
Isla San Lorenzo 124
Isla Santa Cruz 130
Isla São Miguel 181
Isla Saumarez 102
Isla Tamar 101
Isla Wellington 103
Isla Williams 105
Islander (yawl) 157
Islas Canarias (Canary Islands) 7, 23
Islotes Adelaide 101
Itaparica, Brazil 32

Jacaré, Brazil 176
James Island, Galápagos 130
James (island, Chonos archipelago) 105
James, Karen 43–5, 60
Jamestown, St Helena 170, 172
Jay (friend) 90
Jean (yachtswoman) 146
Jemmy Button (Fuegian Indian) 80, 80, 81, 82, 92, 95, 98
Jenkin, Fleeming 192
Jester (Folkboat) 20, 63
jib sail parts 221
Johnson, Alexa 167, 172, 175

Johnson, Charles 24
Johnson, Eliot 167, 172, 175
Johnson, Stephen 72, 72, 87, 167, 175
    Bahía Buen Suceso 85
    Brazil 173, 175
    first gale at sea 78
    fishing success 169, 169, 170
    help after Harrier of Down [I] wrecked 67
    Puerto San Julián 75
    St Helena 172
    South Africa 167
    views on Falkland Islands 76
José (Aratu Iate Clube member) 33, 34
José, Juan 210
junk rig 19, 37, 63, 206, 207, 220, 220

Keeling Cocos 156–7
    see also Cocos Keeling Islands
Kelvin, Lord 192, 195
Kent (island) 105
Kerikeri, New Zealand 140
Kermadec Islands 139
King George's Sound, Australia 149
King, Philip Gidley 24, 202–3
King, Philip Parker 12, 13, 51
Koisan (bushmen) 167
Kororarika (later Russell), New Zealand 140
Kourou, French Guiana 177–9
Kubitschek, Jucelino 31

La Herradura 119, 120, 122
La Irma estancia, Patagonia 65, 68
La Laguna 8
La Orotava 8, 9
La Paloma, Uruguay 41, 43, 45
La Punta, Callao 124
Lago Argentino 77
Lamarck, Jean-Baptiste 190
Lautaro (Araucanian Indian) 110, 111

Liebre (survey vessel) 43, 51, 55, 56, 57, 105
Lima, Peru 121, 125–6
   girl in 1835 127
Lincoln, Abraham 14
Linnaeus, Carl 14
Linnean Society 191
Liverpool, Lord 14
Locke, John 19, 195
London 148, 186
Londonderry, Lord 81, 186
Longwood House, St Helena 170, 171
Lord Howe Island 142, 146
Lunar Society 151
Lyell, Charles 5, 23, 118, 190, 191, 195

McClintock, Robert 24
Macruchenia fossil 53
Madagascar 159, 163
Madeira 8
Magallanes, Fernando de 74–5
   see also Magellan Strait
Magdalene College, Cambridge 17
Magellan Strait 12, 71, 78, 96, 98, 99, 139
   see also Magallanes, Fernando de
Magellanes (ferry) 103
mainsail parts 221
Maldonado, Uruguay 40, 56, 71
Malthus, Thomas 189
Mar del Plata 50, 71
Marcos (yachtsman) 55, 56
Maria (rescuer) 65–7, 68
Maria (teacher) 113–14
Marshall, Noel 87
Martens, Conrad 43, 73, 77, 80
Mason, Commander/Commodore 121, 125, 137
Mastodon fossil 53
Matanza, Tenerife 8
Matthews, Richard 80, 91, 92, 95
Mauna Kea volcano 120

Mauritius 147, 159–63, 161
May, Jonathan 77, 105
Megatherium americanum fossil 53, 54
Melinka, Chile 105
Mellersh, Arthur 24, 51
Mellersh (island) 105
Melville Island, Australia 152
Mendel, Gregor 192
Mendoza, Argentina 118
Mercedes, Uruguay 43, 44, 60
Midhurst (island) 105
Mirador Darwin 72–3, 73
Mischief 87
Mitchell Library, Sydney 43
Mont Orohena, Tahiti 136
Monte Brasil, Azores 181
Monte Hermoso, Patagonia 51
Montevideo, Uruguay
    Beagle's second voyage 41, 42–3, 59
    Mustoe's voyage 46, 48–9, 60, 70
    Slocum's voyage 40
    Tilman's voyage 87
Moorea 136, 138, 138
Morro Mestre Álvares, Brazil 38
Mossel Bay, South Africa 164
Mount, the, Shrewsbury 14, 185
Mount Edgecombe 1, 2
Mount Teide see Pico del Teide (Mount Teide)
Mount Victoria, Australia 151
Mount Wellington, Tasmania 148–9
Murphy, Devla 61
Murray, Matthew 80, 95, 174
Museo Histórico Nacional, Buenos Aires 47
Museo Municipal de Ciencias Naturales Carlos Darwin, Punta Alta 53

Mustoe, Anne 61, 69, 143, 184, 207
Mustoe, James 17, 143

Mustoe, Julian 18, 78, 121, 160, 173, 196, 208
    background 2, 17, 97
    Beagle project 2, 17–18, 47, 59
    eyesight 85, 90, 118–19
    horses and 43, 59–60, 181
    navigation 6
    provisions for voyage 20–1

Natalia, South Africa 167
National Congress of the Federal Republic of Brasil 31
navigation 5–6
Navimag ferry 103
Nelson, Lord 4
Neruda, Pablo 114
Neutral Bay, Australia 143
New Guinea 131, 153
New South Wales 24, 140, 150, 151, 152
    see also Port Jackson; Sydney
New York 21, 22, 31, 148
New Zealand 131, 139–42, 147, 166
    Auckland 141, 141, 148, 186
    Bay of Islands 140, 142, 186
    Beagle's second voyage 138, 140, 144, 186
    FitzRoy as Governor General of 186
Newport, Rhode Island 40
Newton, Isaac 195
Niceto (Yacht Club Argentino member) 47
Nick (friend) 90
Niemeyer, Oscar 31
Niven, David 53
Noel (yachtsman) 146–7
North America 131
    see also United States of America
North Island, New Zealand 140–1, 142
north-east trade winds 7, 19, 24, 37, 39, 176, 179, 181
Northanger (ketch) 88–9

Oasis (yacht) 103
obelisk to Darwin 44, 45

O'Brien, Mary 186
Ocean Passages for the World 24, 130, 149
Olivia Day, Marcos 72, 74
Ona Indians 82, 86
Optimist sailing dinghies 48
Opua, New Zealand 140, 142
Orange Free State, South Africa 167
Otavio (Aratu Iate Clube member) 33, 34, 175–6
Otway, Sir Robert 12, 13
Owen, Fanny 39

Pacific Ocean 40, 98, 104, 105, 120, 126, 128–43, 131
    see also War of the Pacific
Pahia, New Zealand 140
Pambula, Australia 150, 151
Pampas, the 50–61
pamperos 46, 70
Panama Canal 157
Papeete, Tahiti 135–6, 135, 136
Paraguaçu (river) 32
Paso Cerro estancia 73
Paso Gonzalez 96, 97
Paso Goree 84, 85, 91, 94, 95
Paso Piloto Pardo 102
Paso Portillo 118
Paso Roda 100
Paso Tamar 100
Paso Uspallata 118
Passe de Papeete 135
Patagón (giant) 75, 75
Patagonia 49, 50–4, 55–8, 60, 62, 74, 75–8, 167
    see also Bahía Blanca; Carmen de Patagones; La Irma estancia; Península Valdés; Tierra del Fuego
Paul et Virginie 162–3, 163
Paz (survey vessel) 43, 51, 55, 56, 57, 105
Pedro Luro, Argentina 60
Pelorinho, Salvador 30
Península de Taitao 104
Península Mitre 79

Península Tumbes 115
Península Valdés 63–4, 65, 209
Pernambuco 176
Peru 121, 122, 124–6, 128, 130
Peter (yachtsman) 103
Peterson 26 boats 210, 210, 212
Peterson, Doug 69, 210
Phillip, Arthur 144
Pica, Chile 123
Pico del Teide (Mount Teide), Tenerife 7, 8–10, 10, 19
Pigeon, Harry 157
Pin Mill, Essex 206, 207
Pizarro (frigate) 9
Pizarro, Francisco 110
plankton net 26–7, 27
Plaza de Mayo, Buenos Aires 47
Plaza Independencia, Montevideo 42
Plymouth 81, 185
    see also Devonport
Plymouth Sound 1, 2, 3
    see also Barn Pool
Pointe Venus, Tahiti 136
Polynesia 134
Pomare, Queen of Tahiti 137–8
Port Darwin, Australia 153
Port Jackson, Australia 142, 143, 144, 146–7, 151
Port Louis, Mauritius 159, 160, 163
Port Refuge, Cocos Islands 155, 156
Port Spatial de l'Europe, French Guiana 178–9, 178
Porto Praia 21, 22, 23, 24
Porto Santo 8
Portsmouth 12, 185
Portuguese trade winds 5, 7, 8
Praia see Porto Praia
Praia da Vitoria, Azores 181
Prefectura Naval Argentina 66–8
Proust, Marcel 133, 134
provisions for voyage 20–1
Puerto Angusto 99

Puerto Atracadro 95
Puerto Aysén 104
Puerto Belgrano 51, 52
Puerto Caldera 122
Puerto Coral 110
Puerto de Iquique 122, 123, 123, 124
Puerto de Talcuhano 115, 121, 122
Puerto Deseado 62, 72, 74, 77
Puerto Desportivo 70
Puerto Desportivo Radazul 7, 8, 10, 21
Puerto Eden 102–3, 103, 163
Puerto Español 85
Puerto Hambre 12
Puerto Ingeniero White 53
Puerto Madryn 61, 67
Puerto Montt 103
Puerto Natales 103
Puerto Pirámdes 63, 66, 72
Puerto Profundo 101
Puerto San Julián 62, 74, 75
Puerto Tamar 99–100
Puerto Townsend 80
Puerto Williams 90–1, 92
Punta Alta 52, 53–4
Punta Arenas 96, 109
Punta del Este 39, 40, 45
Punta Gallows 75
Punta Norte 63
Punta Quilla 77, 77

Quail Island 23, 23
Queensland, Australia 24, 152
    see also Brisbane
Quito, Ecuador 130

Rada de Monte Hermoso, Bahía Blanca 51
Radazul see Puerto Desportivo Radazul
Rangiroa, Îles Tuamotu 135
Recife 176, 180

Reina, Pedro Sancho de 75
Rice-Trevor, Frances, Lady 57
Río Bío Bío 111, 115, 121
Río Chubut 76
Río Colorado 52, 59, 60
Río Copiapó 122
Rio de Janeiro 30, 31, 32, 39, 41
Río de la Plata 2–49
    Beagle's second voyage 41, 42–3, 50, 55, 56, 71, 82, 95
    Harrier of Down [I] 37, 40, 41, 46–7
    Harrier of Down [II] 70, 88, 210, 211
Río Deseado 72
Río Leubu 115, 121
Río Negro 43, 44, 51, 55, 56–7, 58, 62, 105
Río Paraiba 176
Río Paraná 59, 61
Río Santa Cruz 62, 75–7
Río Valdivia 110, 112, 113
Rivier Tuauru 136–7
Roberto (lighthouse keeper) 101
Roberts, Mr. (pilot) 51–2, 57
Robinson (Beagle crew member) 91
Roca Beagle 74
Rosas, General Juan Manuel de 58, 58, 59, 60
Rowlett, George 24, 98
Rowlett (island) 105
Royal Botanic Gardens 190
Royal Cape Yacht Club 168
Royal Cruising Club 87
Royal Dockyard, Woolwich 185, 186, 201
Royal Geological Society 190
Royal Naval College, Portsmouth 12
Royal Naval Dockyard, Devonport 81, 201
Royal Naval Hospital, Plymouth 81
Royal Observatory, Greenwich 185
Russell, New Zealand 140
Ruta Provincial 76, Argentina 59

Sadko (cutter) 87
sail parts 221
St Francis Bay, South Africa 164
St George's Bay 42
St Helena 166, 168, 170–2
St Paul Rock 25
Saint-Pierre, Bernardine de, Paul et Virginie 162–3
Salvador de Bahia, Brazil 24, 28, 29–36, 37, 41, 173, 173, 175
    Pelorinho 30
    see also Baia de Todos os Santos
Samba (later Harrier of Down [II]) 210–13
San Carlos (Ancud), Isla Chiloé 98, 109
San Cornelio estancia 71
San José church, Isla Chiloé 108
San Julián see Puerto San Julián
Santa Cruz
    Patagonia 75–6, 77
    see also Isla Santa Cruz
Santa Cruz de Tenerife 7, 8–9
Santa Fe, Argentina 57, 59, 60, 61
Santa Laura oficina 124, 124
Santiago, Chile 61, 117, 118, 119
Santiago island, Cape Verdes 22, 156, 181
Santo Antonio shoal, Brazil 173
São Jorge, Azores 183
São Paulo, Brazil 175
saveiros (sailing boats) 32, 32
sea sickness 4, 26, 181, 196
Sedgewick, Adam 15
Seno Ballenero 95
Seno Christmas 84, 98
Seno Darwin 95
Seno Ladrones 95
Seno Otway 12, 13
Seno Pía 93–4, 94, 95
Seno Ponsonby 92, 93, 98
Seno Skyring 12–13
Seymour, Michael 121
Shanty (yacht) 103

ship and boat rigs 218–20, 218–20
    see also junk rig; saveiros
Shrewsbury 15, 44, 185
Sierra de la Ventana 59
Simon's Town/Simon's Bay, South Africa 164–5, 165, 166, 168
Simpson (island) 105
Skyring, William 12–13
slavery 34–5, 58
Slocum, Joshua 40, 99, 149, 152, 156–7, 179
sloops 219, 219
smugglers 119, 154–5
Somalia 159
South Africa 153, 159, 164–8
South America 5, 12–13, 132
    see also Argentina; Brazil; Chile; Ecuador; Peru; Uruguay
South Atlantic Ocean 26, 41, 62, 128, 168
South Indian Ocean 147, 151, 153, 159
South Keeling, Cocos Islands 155, 155, 156, 157
South Pacific Ocean 105, 128, 132, 135
south-east trade winds 25, 132, 169, 170, 173
Souza, Tomé de 29
Spray (Slocum's yacht) 40, 99, 149, 152, 156, 179
Stanley, Lord 186
Stark, Freya 61
Stebbing/Stebbings, George 6, 174
Stevens, Brian 176
Stewart, Frances Anne 14
Stewart, Robert see Castlereagh, Lord
Stokes (island) 105
Stokes, John 24, 128
Stokes, John Lort 51
Stokes, Pringle 12, 80
Storm Bay, Tasmania 148
Sulivan, Bartholomew 24
Sullivan's Cove, Tasmania 148
Sundeck Cave, Australia 152
Sunden, Tord 205
supernumeraries 43, 80
Sydney, Australia 43, 120, 142, 143, 144, 146–7, 146, 152

Sydney Cove 144, 145

Table Bay, South Africa 168
Table Mountain, South Africa 168
Tahiti 125, 128, 130, 135–8, 135, 136, 139, 166
Talcahuano see Puerto de Talcuhano
Tasman Sea 140, 142, 143, 146
Tasmania 147, 148–9, 150, 159
Tenaun church, Isla Chiloé 108
Tenerife 7, 8–10, 10, 19
Terceira, Azores 181
Teresa (museum curator) 53
Ternate, Indonesia 190
Thetis, HMS 12
Thomson, William (later Lord Kelvin) 192, 195
Three Kings Islands, New Zealand 142
Thursday Island, Australia 152
Tierra del Fuego 62, 77–81, 82–90, 167
    Beagle's first voyage 12, 13, 80–1
    Beagle's second voyage 43, 56, 71, 75, 82, 87, 97–8
    Darwin and 82, 83, 98
    Harrier of Down [II] 78, 85, 87, 88–9, 92, 95–6
    Slocum's voyage 40
    see also Fuegian Indians; Ushuaia
Tilman, Bill 71, 87
Timor 153
Timor Sea 153–4, 159
Tonga 139, 142
Torres Strait, Australia 151
Townsville, Australia 152
Toxodon fossil 53
trade winds 5, 7, 8, 19
    see also north-east trade winds; south-east trade winds
Trafalgar, Battle of 5, 11
Transvaal, South Africa 167
Tres Picos, Argentina 59
Trouville, Uruguay 70
Truro (merchant vessel) 137
Tuamotu see Îles Tuamotu

Tuauru (river) 136–7

uniformitarianism 23, 118
United States of America
    independence 30
    see also New York; Newport
Universidade de Brasilia 31, 35, 36, 43
Urangan, Australia 152
Uruguay 37, 39, 41, 42–9, 70–1
    see also Maldonado; Mercedes; Montevideo; Río de la Plata
Ushant see Île d'Ouessant
Ushuaia 87, 88–90, 96, 97
Utzon, Bjorn 145

Vaihere (schooner) 96–7, 96
Valdivia 104, 110–14
Valdivia, Pedro de 110, 111
Valle Intersierra 59
Valley of the Willows, St Helena 170
Valparaiso 105, 116–17, 118, 119, 120, 121
Van Diemen Gulf, Australia 152
Velas, Azores 183
Ventisquero Romanche 93, 94
Vernon Islands, Australia 152
Vespucci, Amerigo 28, 29
Vicensio 118
Victoria (rescuer) 65–7, 68
Victoria, Tenerife 8
Viedma, Argentina 55, 56, 61, 62
Villa Darwin, Uruguay 44
Villiers, Barbara 11, 11
Viña del Mar 116
Vitória, Brazil 38, 39, 40, 41
Vogelberg, Anthony 121, 122

Waitemate Harbour, Auckland, New Zealand 141
Wallace, Alfred Russel 190, 191
War of the Pacific 122
Wedgwood, Emma 150, 188, 194–5

Wedgwood family 14
Wedgwood, Josiah 16
Westminster Abbey 195
whaleboats 76, 91, 94–5, 109, 204, 204
    Beagle's loss of 57, 80–1, 95
whales 4, 64, 90
Wickham, John 24, 51, 117, 121
William IV, King 81
Williams, Corporal 56, 105
Woollya 91, 92–3, 92, 94, 95, 98
Woolwich Dockyard 185, 186, 201
World Trade Center, 9/11 attack on 21, 22

Yacht Club Argentino 47, 69, 70, 71, 210
Yacht Club da Bahia 28
Yacht Club Higuerillas 115–16, 119
Yacht Club Micalvi 91
Yacht Club Peruano 124
Yacht Club Sudeste 55
Yacht Club Uruguayo 46, 48, 70
Yamana Indians 82, 86, 92, 95, 98
York Minster (Fuegian Indian) 80, 81, 82, 84, 92, 95, 98

Zeta 206–7, 206
    see also Harrier of Down [I]
Zoonomia (Erasmus Darwin's poem) 14

Index compiled by Linda Sutherland
www.tarristi.co.uk